AGS
PUBLISHING

English for the World of Work

by
Carolyn W. Knox

AGS Publishing
Circle Pines, Minnesota 55014-1796
1-800-328-2560

About the Author

Carolyn W. Knox received her undergraduate degree from Towson State University and her master's degree from Loyola College. She completed course work at American University, Temple University, and Johns Hopkins University. Mrs. Knox served 27 years in the Baltimore City Public Schools as a secondary English teacher, demonstration teacher, and English department head. She was also a supervisor of English and elementary language arts, head of English textbook adoption, and director of English and language arts curriculum production. In addition to learning packages, workbooks, and textbooks, Mrs. Knox wrote critiques and other materials as a consultant for several leading educational publishers.

Photo credits for this textbook can be found on page 306.

The publisher wishes to thank the following educators for their helpful comments during the review process for *English for the World of Work*. Their assistance has been invaluable.

Judith Baldwin, Teacher, City of Angels, San Fernando, California; **Diane Box,** Teacher, City of Angels, San Fernando, California; **Patricia C. Brinson,** Special Education Teacher, Treutlen High School, Soperton, Georgia; **Joyce Cramer,** Supervisor, Omaha Public Schools, Omaha, Nebraska; **Melanie Deck,** Teacher, Carlton Comprehensive High School, Prince Albert, Saskatchewan, Canada; **Linda J. Dickson,** Assistant Director, South Metro PsychoEd Program, Ash Street Center, Forest Park, Georgia; **Geraldine Dumas,** Consultant, Bibb County Schools, Macon, Georgia; **Melanie Eick,** Disabilities Specialist, Oklahoma Department of Vocational Technical Education, Stillwater, Oklahoma; **Gordon W. Garrison, Jr.,** Special Education Teacher, Mt. Anthony Union High School, Bennington, Vermont; **Cathy Guzzo,** Special Education/Transition Coordinator, Penn Hills Senior High School, Pittsburgh, Pennsylvania; **Patsy P. Land,** Special Education Teacher, Oak Ridge High School, Oak Ridge, Tennessee; **Gilda Meyers,** Special Education Specialist, E. D. Walker Special Education Center, Dallas, Texas; **Marjorie Nichta,** Teacher, Clark High School, San Antonio, Texas; **Karen L. Piscopo,** Acting Assistant Principal, Frankford High School, Philadelphia, Pennsylvania; **Gladys Uri,** Teacher, Foothills Adult Center, El Cajon, California; **Judith Wallace,** Educable Mentally Handicapped Teacher, Bloomingdale High School, Valrico, Florida

Publisher's Project Staff

Director, Product Development: Karen Dahlen; Associate Director, Product Development: Teri Mathews; Assistant Editor, Karen Anderson; Development Assistant: Bev Johnson; Graphic Designers: Tony Perleberg and Diane McCarty; Design Manager: Nancy Condon; Purchasing Agent: Mary Kaye Kuzma; Marketing Manager/Curriculum: Brian Holl

Editorial and production services provided by The Mazer Corporation

Printed in the United States of America

ISBN 0-7854-3074-1

Product Number 93640

A 0 9 8 7 6 5 4 3 2

Contents

Part 2: On the Job

How to Use This Book: A Study Guide

Welcome to *English for the World of Work*. Everyone needs to know how to find, get, and keep a job. There are skills you can learn to make getting a job and keeping a job easier.

In this book, you will learn how to write a résumé, make telephone calls, and interview to get a job. You will also learn how to follow directions, understand written information concerning your job, and learn other skills to help you keep your job.

As you read this book, notice how each lesson is organized. Information is presented and then followed by examples and activities. Read the information. Then practice what you have read. If you have trouble with a lesson, try reading it again.

It is important that you understand how to use this book before you start to read it. It is also important to know how to be successful in this course. The first section of the book can help you to achieve these things.

How to Study

These tips can help you study more effectively:

◆ Plan a regular time to study.

◆ Choose a quiet desk or table where you will not be distracted. Find a spot that has good lighting.

◆ Gather all the books, pencils, paper, and other equipment you will need to complete your assignments.

◆ Decide on a goal. For example: "I will finish reading and taking notes on Chapter 1, Lesson 1, by 8:00."

◆ Take a five- to ten-minute break every hour to keep alert.

◆ If you start to feel sleepy, take a break and get some fresh air.

11 Communicating with the Public

All jobs today require some form of communication. Employees may have to greet customers, answer the telephone, send e-mail messages, or answer customer letters. What you say and how you say it often will determine how successful you will be at your job.

In Chapter 11, you will become familiar with several work situations that require good communication skills. You will see how knowing what to say and what to write can help you handle yourself with confidence.

Goals for Learning

◆ To understand the correct way to answer a telephone call

◆ To learn how to take helpful telephone messages and transfer calls

◆ To learn to send e-mail messages

◆ To recognize the elements of a good business letter to customers and to be able to write one

187

Before Beginning Each Chapter

◆ Read the chapter title and study the photograph. What does the photo tell you about the chapter title?

◆ Read the opening paragraphs.

◆ Study the Goals for Learning. The Chapter Review and tests will ask questions related to these goals.

◆ Look at the Chapter Review. The questions cover the most important information in the chapter.

Note these Features

Writing Tip
Quick tips to help improve writing skills

Note
Hints or reminders that point out important information

Writing Tip

If your handwriting is difficult to read, print the messages you take. This will help make the messages clear to the reader.

Look for this box for helpful tips!

Application

Applies skills
or concepts
from the chapter
to everyday life
or to the workplace

Vocabulary Builder
Vocabulary practice

Spelling Builder
Spelling practice

Where To Find It
Information about various
reference materials
such as dictionaries,
encyclopedias,
and more

Writing On Your Own
Writing practice

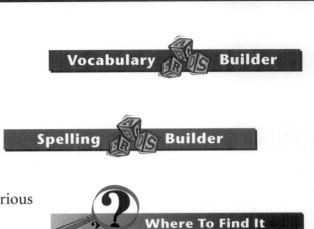

Before Beginning Each Lesson

Read the lesson title
and restate it in the form
of a question.

For example, write:
How do you transfer calls?

Look over the entire lesson,
noting the following:

◆ bold words
◆ text organization
◆ activities
◆ notes in the margins
◆ photos

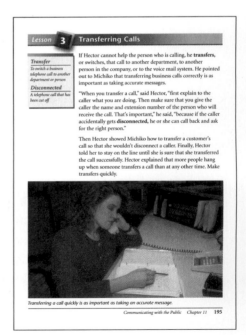

Lesson **3** Transferring Calls

Transfer
To switch a business
telephone call to another
department or person

Disconnected
A telephone call that has
been cut off

If Hector cannot help the person who is calling, he **transfers,** or switches, that call to another department, to another person in the company, or to the voice mail system. He pointed out to Michiko that transferring business calls correctly is as important as taking accurate messages.

"When you transfer a call," said Hector, "first explain to the caller what you are doing. Then make sure that you give the caller the name and extension number of the person who will receive the call. That's important," he said, "because if the caller accidentally gets **disconnected,** he or she can call back and ask for the right person."

Then Hector showed Michiko how to transfer a customer's call so that she wouldn't disconnect a caller. Finally, Hector told her to stay on the line until she is sure that she transferred the call successfully. Hector explained that more people hang up when someone transfers a call than at any other time. Make transfers quickly.

Transferring a call quickly is as important as taking an accurate message.

Communicating with the Public   Chapter 11   **195**

As You Read the Lesson

◆ Read the major headings.

◆ Read the subheads and paragraphs that follow.

◆ Before moving on to the next lesson, see if you understand the concepts you read. If you do not, reread the lesson. If you are still unsure, ask for help.

◆ Practice what you have learned by doing the activities in each lesson.

Using the Bold Words

Bold type
Words seen for the first time will appear in bold type

Glossary
Words listed in this column are also found in the glossary

Knowing the meaning of all the boxed words in the left column will help you understand what you read.

These words appear in **bold type** the first time they appear in the text and are often defined in the paragraph.

> If the company has a **voice mail** system, ask the caller whether he or she wants to leave a message.

All of the words in the left column are also defined in the **glossary**.

> **Voice mail**—(vois māl) An electronic system that records telephone messages that are played back later by the person receiving the phone calls (p. 191)

Word Study Tips

◆ Start a vocabulary file with index cards to use for review.

◆ Write one word on the front of each card. Write the chapter number, lesson number, and definition on the back.

◆ You can use these cards as flash cards by yourself or with a study partner to test your knowledge.

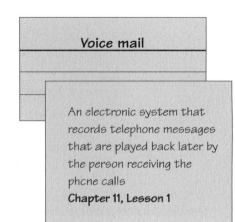

> **Voice mail**
>
> An electronic system that records telephone messages that are played back later by the person receiving the phone calls
> **Chapter 11, Lesson 1**

Using the Reviews

◆ Answer the activity questions in the lessons.

◆ In the Chapter Reviews, answer the questions about vocabulary under Part A. Study the words and definitions. Say them aloud to help you remember them.

◆ Answer the questions under the other parts of the Chapter Reviews.

◆ Review the Test-Taking Tips.

Preparing for Tests

◆ Complete the activities in each lesson. Make up similar activity questions to practice what you have learned. You may want to do this with a classmate and share your questions.

◆ Review your answers to lesson activities and Chapter Reviews.

◆ Test yourself on vocabulary words and key ideas.

◆ Use graphic organizers as study tools.

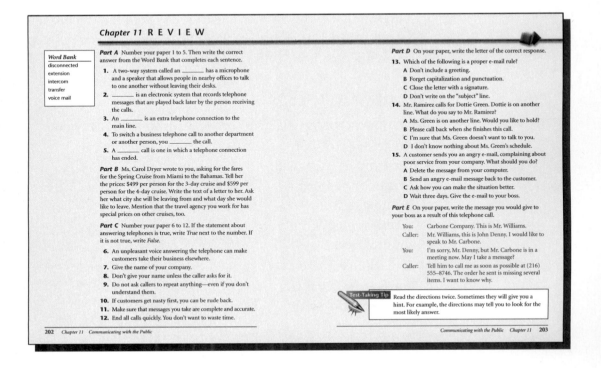

Using Graphic Organizers

A graphic organizer is a visual representation of information. It can help you see how ideas are related to each other. A graphic organizer can help you study for a test or organize information before you write. Here are some examples.

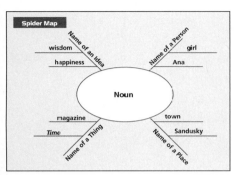

Spider Map

The Spider Map shown here can be used to connect related ideas to a central idea or concept. Write the main or central idea or concept in the circle in the center. Identify related ideas and write them on the lines that angle out from the circle. Write examples that support the ideas on the horizontal lines that are attached to the angled lines.

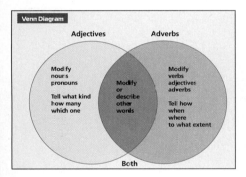

Venn Diagram

The Venn diagram shown here can be used to compare and contrast two things. For example, this diagram compares and contrasts adjectives and adverbs. List the characteristics for adjectives in the left circle. List the characteristics for adverbs in the right circle. In the intersection of the two circles, list the characteristics that both have.

1

Looking for Job Openings

Throughout your life you probably will have to look for several jobs. Before you graduate, you may have to look for part-time jobs after school, and after you graduate, you will have to look for a full-time job. There are some skills that you can learn that will make finding these jobs a little easier.

In Chapter 1, you will find important information that will help you find a job.

Goals for Learning

◆ To learn how to read help-wanted ads in the newspaper

◆ To be able to determine whether you qualify for a particular job

◆ To be able to decide whether a particular job is suitable for you

◆ To understand the different services offered at employment agencies, at job placement offices, and on the Internet

Patrick Adams needed a full-time job. The jobs he had before were part-time jobs that he found by reading signs in store windows. Now he wanted to use the computer skills he had learned in high school to find a full-time job. His friends told him to read the **classified ads** in the newspaper and to go to job placement centers. When Patrick looked at the **help-wanted ads** in the newspaper, he wished he understood them better.

Help-wanted ads sometimes can be confusing if they include unfamiliar terms and **abbreviations.** In his local newspaper, Patrick saw this help-wanted ad. Are there any words in this ad that you do not understand?

Classified ads

Advertisements (also known as want ads) that appear in the newspaper in different groups; for example, ads for cars are listed together, ads for pets are in another section, and job openings are in another

Help-wanted ads

Advertisements for employment or job openings

Abbreviations

The shortened forms of written words; for example, req. for required

| DATA ENTRY CLERK | Fast-growing pipe, valve & fitting distributor loc on W side. Ability to use wd. proc. prog. a must. Call Ms. Goodman, Mon. or Tues. 8–10 a.m., 740-555-4857. |

Although Patrick understood that the ad was for a data entry clerk for a distributor of pipes, valves, and fittings, he was unsure what the abbreviations *loc* and *W side* meant. He decided to ask his friend Tony for some help.

"Tony, would you read this ad for a data entry clerk for me?" he asked. "It may be a job I can do, but I'm not sure."

"Sure, Patrick," answered Tony. "The ad says that a business located on the west side of town wants to hire a data entry clerk. You must be able to use word processing programs."

"Do you think that the company would count part-time experience?" asked Patrick.

"Why not call Ms. Goodman and ask her? You can call Monday or Tuesday between 8 o'clock and 10 o'clock in the morning."

Tony was able to make sense out of the ad because he understood the terms and abbreviations in it. You will need to be able to do the same thing when you are looking for a job.

Activity A Number your paper 1 to 5. Then read these five ads and write the meaning of each underlined word.

1. COOK exp'd cook w/refs. needed for busy restaurant nr. college. Practical exp. making soups and din. items. 937-555-4542.

2. SALES
Nat'l co, high comm. New product. No exp. nec. Mon.
215-555-8695.

3. MAINTENANCE ASS'T. Must have at least 3 yrs. exp. in htg. and AC. All phases of maintenance nec. 937-555-4891.

4. Servers Lunch & dinner, days & eves. FT/PT. Apply in person at Red Rose Café. 4740 Main St., or call 215-555-0101.

5. DELIVERY/SET-UP We are looking for people to deliver and set up household goods. Must have good driving rec. Apply in person: 2187 Easton St. EOE.

Activity B Number your paper 1 to 10. Then match each abbreviated phrase in the first column with its meaning in the second column.

Words	Meanings
1. exp'd.	A no experience necessary
2. w/refs.	B call 612-555-8695 on Monday
3. appt.	C assistant
4. ass't.	D experienced
5. temp.	E temporary
6. $7/hr.	F seven dollars per hour
7. nec.	G evenings and weekends
8. no exp. nec.	H necessary
9. Mon. 612-555-8695	I appointment
10. eves. + wknds.	J with references

There are other terms and abbreviations that you need to know before you can fully understand some help-wanted ads. Study this list carefully.

admin.	administrative	lic.	license
aft.	afternoon, after	mfg.	manufacturing
agcy.	agency	min.	minimum
avail.	available	pd.	paid
beg.	beginning	pos.	position
bene.	benefits	pref.	preferred
comp.	computer, compensation, comprehensive	proc.	processing
des.	desired	prog.	program
ed.	education	PT	part time
eves.	evenings	req.	required
exc.	excellent	sal.	salary
FT	full time	trng.	training
grad.	graduate	20K	$20,000
incl.	including/included	wd.	word
ins.	insurance	yrs.	years

Activity C Number your paper 1 to 3. Then rewrite these ads by changing the abbreviations to full words.

1. DRIVER Lic. req. Must work aft. & eves. Sal. and tips. Ins. and other bene. provided.
713-555-0853

2. P/T CLERK
Mfg. co. Will provide trng. Beg. min. wage. Exp. pref. Hrs. 2–6 aft. 513-555-3745

3. SECRETARY Pos. avail. for h.s. grad with exp. Sal. 20K incl. pd. vacation and ed. bene. Must wk. F/T and some eves.
614-555-7588

Alphabetical order

Arranged in the order of the letters of the alphabet (A, B, C, etc.)

How Help-Wanted Ads Are Arranged

Along with understanding the terms and abbreviations used in the help-wanted ads, you need to know how most newspapers organize these ads. As you learned earlier in this lesson, the classified ads part of the newspaper contains the help-wanted ads. The job listings in that section are in **alphabetical order;** for example, *artist* would come before *clerk,* and *janitor* would come before *server.*

CLASSIFIED ADVERTISING
Employment

HELP WANTED 905	HELP WANTED 905	MISCELL
ADMINISTRATIVE SECY This top-co. needs polished sect'l talents! Good skills and math aptitude. 713-555-0773.	**CHEF-PASTRY** 4 yrs. exp. req., knowledge of European pastry pref. Send résumé to Box CS 47822.	**COUCH AND** good cond.
AIR COND & HEAT PUMP MECHANIC Fully exp. only. Call Frosty Refrig. Mondays, 713-555-2024.	**CLERICAL** If you love to type, my firm needs your skills. Excellent salary & benefits. Call Lisa 713-555-5804.	**DOG HOUSE** first home fo
AUTO SALESPERSON Sell and make big money on cars and trucks. Salary plus comm. Benefits. 713-555-1320.	**COMPUTER OPERATOR** Must have know. comp. lang. and be able to use var. comp. software progs. Call 9–5 at 713-555-TYPE.	**GAME SYSTE** controllers, z cleaning kit.
		PAPASAN co $150/obo. K range, $75. a
BOOKKEEPER Comp. exp. nec. Dependable. 713-555-1118.	**DATA ENTRY CLERK** General data entry, 5 days, vic. Smallwood St. 713-555-5806.	**REFRIGERATO** excellent wor

Look for the help-wanted ads in the classified ads section of your newspaper. You will find ads for such jobs as dental assistants, mechanics, nurses, secretaries, and computer operators. Also notice that these ads appear in alphabetical order.

Jobs listed in the help-wanted ads appear in alphabetical order. Jobs that start with *A* appear first, jobs that start with *B* appear next, and so on.

A B C D E F G H I J K L M N O P Q R S T U V W X Y Z

Activity D Rewrite these words in alphabetical order.

tailor	bookkeeper	cook	librarian
driller	farmer	mechanic	programmer
engineer	server	auditor	janitor
guard	woodworker	orderly	

When several jobs start with the same letter, look at the second letter. For example, if *bookkeeper* and *barber* are two jobs in the ads, *barber* appears first because the second letter is *a*. *Bookkeeper* follows *barber* because the second letter is *o*. If the first two letters are the same, you have to look at the third letter, and so on.

Activity E Rewrite these words in alphabetical order.

mechanic	janitor	salesperson	machinist
secretary	carpenter	hair stylist	plumber
biller	chef	pet groomer	buyer

If several job titles have more than one word and the first words are the same, look at the second word. For example, if one ad is for an *auto mechanic* and another is for an *auto attendant, auto attendant* appears first because the second word begins with *a*.

When alphabetizing, remember that if the second letters are the same, look at the third letter, and so on. However, when first words are the same, look at the second word.

Activity F Rewrite these words and phrases in alphabetical order.

sales

engineer, industrial

secretarial lab aide

computer specialist

dry cleaner

secretary

engineer, civil

auto salesperson

computer programmer

auto mechanic

engineer, electrical

secretarial assistant

Being able to alphabetize is an important skill. Not only will it help you locate information in the classified ads, but you will find many other uses for it. For example, the names in a **telephone directory** and the businesses described in the **Yellow Pages** appear in alphabetical order. The listings in store directories, **reference books** such as dictionaries and encyclopedias, book catalogs in libraries, rows of seats in an auditorium, compact discs in music stores, and street directories appear in alphabetical order.

Activity G Rewrite these job titles from the help-wanted section of a newspaper in alphabetical order.

engineer, electrical

salesperson

guard

receptionist

claims supervisor

retail salesperson

electrician

dietitian

research assistant

data entry clerk

clerk

animal handler

engineer, chemical

engineer, manufacturing

You are now familiar with the abbreviations used in help-wanted ads, and you know that the ads appear in alphabetical order in the newspaper. Now practice reading and understanding these ads. Think about Patrick Adams again. Although he has had some word processing experience, not every ad for a data entry clerk will be a job that he can do or even one that he would want to do.

To use the help-wanted ads wisely, apply only for jobs for which you are qualified. For example, Patrick Adams has experience as a sales clerk in a computer store. He also has word processing skills. However, he is not very good in math, and he has not learned to do spreadsheets on a computer. As a result, when he looks at ads, he should not bother with the ones that say the applicant must be good in math or the ones that say the person needs to do spreadsheets on a computer.

How will you know if you are qualified for a particular job? The answers to the following questions will help you decide whether or not you should apply.

- Do I have the education required?
- Can I work the hours and days listed?
- Do I have the skills needed?
- Am I able to operate the equipment needed for this job?
- Can I use the tools needed to do this job?

Activity A Number your paper 1 to 5. Read these ads, and then answer the questions that follow them.

A CLERK Gen. off. duties and proofrdg. Must have good grammar and word processing skills. Apply in person 9–4 p.m. 20 E. Main St.

C **CLERK** No exp. nec. Will train. 40-hr wk. Mon–Fri 8 to 4. Many bene. inc. health ins. Call Mr. Merton 940-555-1921.

B CLERK Comp. exp. req., math aptitude a must. Typ. req. Send letter of application by fax to Jeanna Santiago at 212-555-1632.

1. Which job requires good word processing skills?

2. Which job should you apply for by fax?

3. Which job requires an ability to proofread?

4. Which ad describes a benefit the employee will receive?

5. Which job does not require experience or special skills?

Vocabulary Builder

Synonyms

A **synonym** is a word with the same or nearly the same meaning as another word.

Example begin   start
education schooling
needed   necessary

Choose the synonym for the first word and use the synonym in a sentence. Write the sentences on your paper.

1. accept	A receive	B send	C give
2. ornament	A destroy	B nicely	C decoration
3. blend	A mix	B fly	C accent
4. angry	A happy	B upset	C sad
5. beneath	A beside	B bottom	C under

Is This Job Right for Me?

When you apply for a job, you need to think about the pleasure or satisfaction that working at that job could bring day after day. You should also consider whether this is the kind of job that you would like to do. Then ask yourself these questions. The answers will help you decide whether a particular job is right for you.

- Is this the kind of job that I will enjoy doing?
- Will I make enough money to meet my needs and to make me feel good about the work I do?
- Can I get to this place easily so that I am never late?

Find the help-wanted ads in your newspaper. After you read some of the ads, use the questions on page 8 to help you decide whether or not you are qualified for the jobs. Then use the questions above to decide whether any of the jobs are suitable for you. Of course, you may not be able to answer all these questions because employers do not always list the **salary** or **wage,** complete **benefits** such as vacations or insurance, chances for advancement, and other such information.

Activity B After you read this help-wanted ad, read about the three people described below. Then decide which person could do the job best. Be ready to discuss the reasons for your decision.

> **ASST. CARPENTER'S HELPER** No exp. nec. Must have knowlege of tools and talent for this kind of work. Perm. pos. Opp. for advancement to good worker. Must have driver's lic. Apply in person. Ace Company, 115 Orange Street.

1. Leroy enjoys working with his hands. He knows how to use most tools and fixes all the small appliances in his home. He has a license to drive a car, and he lives on a bus line that goes right by the Ace Company. It would take him about 30 minutes to get there. He can work any hours.

2. Myra went to a vocational school and studied carpentry. She is skilled with most of the tools that a carpenter uses. She has a car and can drive to the Ace Company in about 35 minutes. If she has to take the bus, it will take an hour. She can work any hours.

3. Carlos needs a job. He can use simple tools. He really likes meeting people and working with them. He has a car and a license. He can get to the Ace Company in about 15 minutes. He is not sure that he will like this job, but he needs to earn some money.

Patrick Adams thought about going to an **employment agency** or to a **job placement office.** These places help people find jobs. Most employment agencies charge a fee after a company hires you. The fee can be as much as 10 percent of your first year's pay. Sometimes the person looking for the job pays the fee, and sometimes the employer pays the fee. Before you sign with an employment agency, make sure you find out who pays the fee and what the fee is. You may find that it is worth paying a fee to get a job. However, if you cannot afford the fee, do not use an agency that charges you one.

The best way to find an employment agency is to look in the Yellow Pages of your telephone directory. Many agencies specialize in only certain kinds of jobs. Many of the ads will also state whether the employee or the employer pays the fee.

Employment agency

A company that is in business to help people find jobs

Job placement office

A city or state office where a person can get help finding a job

Activity A Number your paper 1 to 5. Read this ad, and then answer the following questions.

1. Could this agency help you find a job as an automobile mechanic?
2. Patrick Adams knows word processing. Would this agency be able to help him find a job?
3. Would Patrick have to pay the agency's fee?
4. What is the name of this agency? Where is it located?
5. What telephone number should Patrick call to get more information?

Job Placement Offices

Most states and many large cities have job placement offices that can help you find a job without paying a fee. At these offices you can fill out an application and talk with a **counselor.** The counselor will give you advice and work with you to help you find a job.

The United States government also has an Office of Personnel Management through which you can apply for jobs within the federal government. The blue section of a telephone directory lists the telephone numbers of these kinds of job placement offices.

Patrick went to his state's job placement office. He found that he could get lots of help there for no charge. Most city and state job placement offices offer some of the following services.

The office has a list of job openings with local employers. Trained counselors meet with people interested in a particular job and then send each of them to a **job interview.** At the interview, an employer can decide whether the person would be good to hire.

Apprenticeship programs are available for a person who wants a job in a trade, which is a job using a special skill. In these programs people are trained while they work on the job. They gain practical experience under the direction of skilled workers.

People can get information about jobs available all over the country, not just in their city or state.

If people are not sure what they can do or what they want to do, job counselors may give them tests to see what they do best and to learn more about their abilities and interests.

When Patrick first talked to a counselor, he was a little uncomfortable answering so many personal questions. However, he knew that the counselor had to ask such questions because his answers would enable the counselor to match his skills with a job that suited him.

Many job placement offices may ask you to fill out an application. Chapter 4 of this book will help you do a good job filling out an application for a job.

Finding a Job on the Internet

The newspaper classified section and job placement offices are not the only places to look for job openings. The **Internet** also has help-wanted sites. These sites are free, but you do have to enter the kind of job you are looking for and the state in which you would like to work. Some Web sites are

www.ajb.dni.us   *www.opm.gov*

Many companies now post job openings on their Web sites. If you know which company you would like to work for, go to its Web site to look for job openings. Most business Web sites give a description of the job and the name of the person to contact for more information.

Many companies post job openings on the Internet.

Although looking for a job on the Internet is fast and simple, there are drawbacks. The job sites often list thousands of jobs from all over the country. Be specific about what kind of job you want, what skills you have, and where you would like to work. You may want to reply to a job described on the Internet, but be careful about the kind of information you offer about yourself. It may be better to call someone at the company to set up an interview.

Where To Find It

Index

An index is a good place to start when you are looking for information. School books, encyclopedias, almanacs, and newspapers all have indexes to make it easy for you to find information.

Most newspapers include an index on the front page. Section titles and page numbers tell you where to find information. You might find an index that looks like this:

The Springvale Daily News

Business 1C
Classified Ads 1D
Deaths 2A
Editorials 8A
Sports 1B
Weather 6B

Classified ads often have their own index. Ads may be divided into several sections such as *General, Computer/Information Services, Drivers, Engineers, Medical/Dental, Office/Clerical, Restaurant,* and *Sales*. Within each section, the paper lists help-wanted ads alphabetically by the first letter of the job.

1. Go to your school library, and find a newspaper's classified index. Then write down which section of the help-wanted ads would include the following jobs: *restaurant server, supermarket clerk, truck driver, mechanic, secretary,* and *registered nurse.*

2. List three types of jobs that interest you. Using the classified index, write down which section lists each job. Then find a help-wanted ad for each job and copy it onto your paper.

Activity B Number your paper 1 to 10. Then write short answers to these questions.

1. Where would you go to apply for work with the U.S. government?

2. Do you have to pay a fee at a city or a state job placement office?

3. Where can you find the telephone numbers of government placement offices?

4. Why do counselors interview people who want jobs?

5. What is an apprenticeship program?

6. Why might you want information about jobs available in other cities and states?

7. Why would a counselor give you a test?

8. Why does an employer interview a person who wants a job?

9. Why would you use a computer to find a job?

10. Name one drawback to looking for a job on the Internet.

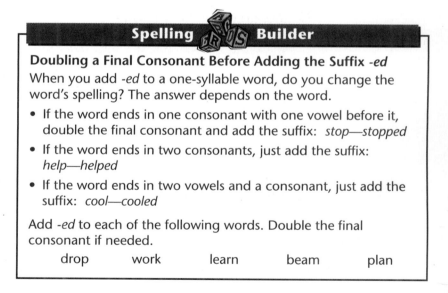

Spelling Builder

Doubling a Final Consonant Before Adding the Suffix -ed
When you add -ed to a one-syllable word, do you change the word's spelling? The answer depends on the word.

- If the word ends in one consonant with one vowel before it, double the final consonant and add the suffix: *stop—stopped*
- If the word ends in two consonants, just add the suffix: *help—helped*
- If the word ends in two vowels and a consonant, just add the suffix: *cool—cooled*

Add -ed to each of the following words. Double the final consonant if needed.

    drop   work   learn   beam   plan

Planting the Idea for a Job

Tami likes working with plants and working outdoors. She has had a garden since she was 12, and last year she volunteered to plant the city gardens. When she stopped at Greene Gene's Nursery to buy a plant for her grandmother, she saw her friend Antonia working in the greenhouse.

"Antonia, when did you start working here?"

Antonia said, "I started two weeks ago. When summer comes, I will be taking care of an entire section and operating the cash register."

"Did your volunteer work in the school greenhouse help you get this job?" asked Tami.

"I think that helped," said Antonia. "Mrs. Estevez said that my science grades were good, and she told me about the job."

"Do you like working here?" Tami asked.

"Mr. Greene has been very nice," Antonia said. "He understands that I am still going to school. The other people I work with are very friendly, too."

"Do you know whether they need any more help?" asked Tami.

"They plan to hire three more people for the summer," Antonia said. "If you are interested, I could talk to Mr. Greene."

For Discussion

1. What information does Tami already know about the job?

2. What other information could Tami learn from Antonia?

3. How can friends help you find a job?

Chapter 1 R E V I E W

Part A On a sheet of paper, write the correct word or words from the Word Bank to complete each sentence.

1. Items arranged in order of the letters of the alphabet are in _____ .

2. A _____ is a fixed amount of money paid on a regular basis for work done.

3. A _____ is a city or a state office in which a person can get help in finding a job.

4. _____ are services such as vacations a company pays for.

5. A meeting during which an employer asks questions of the person applying for work is a _____ .

6. An _____ is a company that helps people find jobs.

7. An _____ is a work-training program.

8. The _____ is the section of a telephone book that lists businesses in alphabetical order by kind of business.

9. _____ , such as a dictionary or an atlas, contain useful information.

10. _____ are advertisements (also known as want ads) that are listed in the newspaper in different groups.

11. A person at an employment agency or job placement office who helps another person find a job is a _____ .

12. _____ are advertisements for job openings.

13. A _____ is money paid for hourly work.

14. _____ are the shortened forms of words.

15. A _____ contains names, addresses, and phone numbers.

Part B Review your understanding of ad abbreviations. Rewrite these two ads, replacing the abbreviations with complete words.

16.
DRIVER Coll. stu. w/car. P/T, Tues. and Thurs. Must have good driving record. Ref. req. No exp. nec. Pos. avail. immed. Send letter of app. and refs. by fax to 817-555-7650.

17.
SALES
Exp'd. w/refs. High comm. Must be h.s. grad. F/T, eves. Good sal. Bene. incl. ins. Apply in pers. - 8900 Business Blvd.

Part C Number your paper 18 to 20. Read the ad at the left, then choose the letter of the correct answer.

ADMINISTRATIVE ASSISTANT
Should have exc. keybrding skills & at least some exp. w/word processing prog. Grammar & math skills are req. — plus knowledge of comp. spreadsheets. Exc. sal., bene. Call Sue at 312-555-0653 between 10 A.M. & noon, Mon & Tues.

18. What does the abbreviation *exc.* mean in this ad?

    A experienced   **C** exclusive

    B excellent   **D** excess

19. In what school subject would you expect a person applying for this job to have good grades?

    A American history   **C** geometry

    B Earth science   **D** English

20. Where would this ad be in the help-wanted section of a newspaper?

    A before an ad for *administrator*

    B after an ad for a *clerk*

    C after an ad for an *assistant buyer*

    D before an ad for an *actor*

Part D Number your paper 21 to 25. Write short answers to these questions.

21. What are three places to find information about jobs that are available?

22. What services do city and state job placement offices provide? List at least three services.

23. What questions should you ask yourself to determine whether you should apply for a particular job? List at least five questions.

24. What things should you know about an employment agency before you go there for help in finding a job?

25. Name two ways to use the Internet to find a job.

Test-Taking Tip Sometimes it is easier to learn new vocabulary words if you make them a part of your speaking and writing in other subject areas.

FOR LOCAL POSTMARK

" FOR TODAYS POSTMARK "
MAIL MUST BE DEPOSITED
PRIOR TO 6:30 P.M.

MONDAY – FRIDAY

5:00PM ON SATURDAY

NONE ON SUNDAY

2

Applying for a Job

L ong before an employer meets you in person, he or she may begin to judge you by the way you write a letter. If a letter you send does not look good and is not well written, you may never get a chance to ask about the job—even if you qualify for it.

In Chapter 2, you will learn not only the correct form for a business letter but also what information to put in it.

Goals for Learning

◆ To understand the seven parts of a business letter and how to punctuate letters correctly

◆ To be able to use either the full block style or the modified block style for a business letter

◆ To know what information to include in a letter of application

◆ To be able to address a business envelope correctly

◆ To be able to use the two-letter post office abbreviations for states in your letters and on your envelopes

Letter of application

A letter that a person sends to ask for a job

Return address

The street address, city, state, and ZIP code of the person writing the letter

ZIP code

The postal delivery area number that is written after the name of a state in an address; in Canada, it is called the Postal Code and is written after the name of the province

When Aldo Carducci applied by letter for three jobs and was not interviewed for any of them, he was concerned. He went to his teacher at night school and asked her what he should do. After Ms. Levy looked at copies of Aldo's letters, she had an idea why he had not been asked to interview for any of the jobs. She said to him, "Your letter may be the reason you did not get an interview. A good **letter of application** can greatly improve your chances of getting a job. A good letter follows a certain form and includes just the right information."

"How can I learn to write a letter that will get me a job?" Aldo asked.

"Come to class a half an hour early for the next few weeks, and I will give you some extra help," promised Ms. Levy.

Aldo needed a good job, so he went early to Ms. Levy's class every evening for three weeks. First, Aldo learned the parts of a business letter. Although business letters may differ some in form, they all have seven basic parts:

1. Return address

2. Date

3. Inside address

4. Salutation or greeting

5. Body

6. Complimentary close

7. Signature

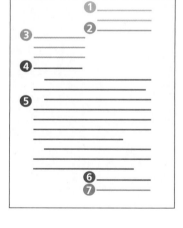

1. The **return address** begins with your house number and street name or your apartment number and street address. On the next line, directly below, come the city and state in which you live, plus your **ZIP code.** This number identifies the postal delivery areas in the United States.

2. Below your address, include the **date** on which you write the letter. The return address and date should look like the following example. Notice that a comma goes between the city and the state but not between the state and the ZIP code. A comma goes between the day and the year.

1230 Girard Drive
Houston, TX 77013
November 24, 2003

3. The **inside address** includes the complete name and address of the person and/or the company receiving the letter—as in the following example. Again, notice that a comma goes between the city and the state but not between the state and the ZIP code.

Ms. Julia Evans
Division of Personnel
Landers Advertising Agency
1600 West South Street
Louisville, KY 40201

4. The **salutation** is a way of greeting the person to whom you are writing. In a business letter, the salutation should be formal—as in the following example. Notice that a colon follows the salutation.

Dear Ms. Evans:

5. The **body** of the letter tells why you are writing. Read the following example of a letter written in answer to a help-wanted ad.

I am applying for the cashier's job advertised in *The Evening Chronicle*. I am a recent graduate of Samuel Jones High School. While I was in school, I helped run the school store. I have more than two years of experience in using a cash register.

In addition, I am good in math, and I know how to operate several machines. I also like meeting people.

I would very much like to come in for an interview. Please call me at (312) 555-3211.

6. The **complimentary close** is a way of ending the letter politely. In a business letter, the complimentary close should be formal—like the following example. Notice that a comma follows the complimentary close.

   Sincerely yours,

7. The **signature** tells the person receiving the letter who you are. Your signature should be neat and easy to read. In a business letter, it is common to include a handwritten signature above a printed full name—as in this example.

   Aldo Carducci

   Aldo Carducci

Vocabulary Builder

Homonyms

Have you ever confused two words? These words may be homonyms. Homonyms are words that sound alike but have different meanings and different spellings.

When you write, it is important to use the correct word. Imagine writing "I where my jeans to class" instead of "I wear my jeans to class." The English language has many homonyms:

Example   ate—eight   hole—whole

Use a dictionary to find the meanings of the following homonyms. Then use each word correctly in a sentence.

1. four/for	6. weak/week
2. peak/peek	7. buy/by
3. paws/pause	8. red/read
4. peace/piece	9. led/lead
5. grate/great	10. loan/lone

Address your letter to a specific person. If you do not know the person's name, use a general greeting such as *Good Morning* or *Dear Sir or Madam.*

After Aldo had studied the parts of a business letter, Ms. Levy gave him a test on the seven parts of a business letter.

Activity A Number your paper 1 to 7. Then match the parts of a letter in the first column with the correct description in the second column.

Terms	Descriptions
1. return address	**A** handwritten name; tells the reader who you are
2. signature	**B** is a way of greeting the person to whom you are writing
3. salutation	**C** has your address and the city and state where you live
4. date	**D** tells why you are writing
5. complimentary close	**E** includes the name and address of the person to whom you are writing
6. inside address	**F** tells when you wrote the letter
7. body	**G** is a polite way of closing your letter

Aldo is careful to include the seven parts in his letter.

Full block style

A form of business writing in which all the parts of a letter appear against the left margin; no paragraphs are indented

Ms. Levy told Aldo that most business letters use either the **full block style** or a variation of the block style. She gave him this diagram of the full block style so that he could see where the parts of the letter appear on a page.

| Return Address and Date |
| Inside Address |
| Salutation |
| Body |
| Complimentary Close |
| Signature |

Next, Ms. Levy showed Aldo a sample letter in full block style. Compare this letter with the diagram above.

4326 Arden Avenue
Houston, TX 77013
September 30, 2005

Ms. Esther Fine
Mighty Fine Company
4511 Leeds Road
Houston, TX 77015

Dear Ms. Fine:

I am writing in answer to your ad for a file clerk that appeared in yesterday's *Daily Report*.

I have worked at Bell, Inc., for three years as a file clerk and have always received very high ratings on my job performance. However, because Bell, Inc., is closing, I am looking for another position.

I would like to come in for an interview. Please call me at 832-555-3255 to set up an appointment.

Yours very truly,

Lillian S. Levy

Lillian S. Levy

Aldo noticed that all seven parts of the letter lined up against the left **margin.** He also noticed that one blank line appeared between paragraphs.

Activity A Number your paper 1 to 7. Then write the correct name of the letter part next to each number.

5617 Kelly Street
Madison, WI 53701 ❶
June 5, 2003 ❷

Personnel Director
Clean Soap Company ❸
2 East 33rd Street
Madison, WI 53702

Dear Personnel Director: ❹

I am writing to apply for the job of packer that was advertised at the Wisconsin Employment Placement Center.

I have had no experiences as a packer, but I learn quickly. I had a good attendance record at Green Waters High where I just graduated. I was never late in four years of high school. ❺

If you would be interested in interviewing me, I can be reached at 608-555-0008.

Very truly yours, ❻

Fred Soames
❼
Fred Soames

Activity B Write your own full block style letter in answer to this ad.

MAILROOM CLERK Good rdg. skills. F/T Mon. thru Fri., 6 A.M. to 2:30 P.M. Apply by mail, Griner, Inc., 44 Court Square, (your city).

Modified block style

In this form of business letter, the person sending the letter lines up the return address, date, complimentary close, and signature near the center of the page; paragraphs are indented

After Aldo had learned the full block style, Ms. Levy said, "Aldo, the **modified block style** is another form you should learn."

She then gave Aldo this diagram of the modified block style of the business letter for him to study.

Aldo remembered that he had a letter in his notebook. He showed it to Ms. Levy and said, "Is this letter written in modified block style?"

Ms. Levy looked at the letter and said, "Yes, Aldo, this letter is a good example of the modified block style."

This is what Aldo's letter looked like.

47 Winslow Drive
Cedar Rapids, IA 52401
December 12, 2003

Mr. Aldo Carducci
1230 Girard Drive
Houston, TX 77013

Dear Mr. Carducci:

    Thank you for ordering our special digital watch. This item has been so popular that it will be three weeks before we can send the watch you ordered.

    We hope this delay will not cause you any inconvenience. We know you will be glad you waited!

Sincerely,

Isabel Diaz

Isabel Diaz
Mail Order Division

Aldo noticed that several parts of the modified block style letter were **indented** and did not line up against the left margin. He also noticed that the return address, date, complimentary close, and signature lined up with one another. He saw that the writer had carefully spaced the letter with one blank line between the parts of the letter and between paragraphs.

Writing Tip

If you refer to a newspaper in your letter, remember to underline or italicize its title: for example, The Evening News or *The Williston Post.*

Activity C On your paper, answer this ad in a letter that follows the modified block style.

SCHOOL CROSSING GUARD No exp. nec. Will train. Must be able to wk. Mon –Fri. from 7:45 A.M. to 9:15 A.M. and from 2:30 P.M. to 3:30 P.M. Apply by letter to: Dept. of Transportation, 115 Main Street, (your city).

Activity D On your paper, list the seven parts of a business letter in the order in which they should appear.

- inside address
- body
- return address
- signature
- date
- salutation
- complimentary close

You have just studied two styles of business letters: full block and modified block. The following review activities will help you understand the differences between these two forms.

Activity E Number your paper 1 to 10. Then answer these questions about the full block style of a letter.

1. If you were writing a letter using full block style, where would you put your street address?
2. Where would you put your city, state, and ZIP code?
3. Where would you put the date?
4. Where would you put the name of the person to whom you are writing?
5. Should you indent each paragraph?
6. How many blank lines would you leave between paragraphs?
7. How many blank lines would you leave between the inside address and the salutation?
8. Where would you put the complimentary close?
9. Where would you put your signature?
10. Many people who use computers write their letters in the full block style because they say that it is easier and that they make fewer mistakes. Why do you think they feel this way?

Activity F Number your paper 1 to 5. Answer these questions about the modified block style of a letter.

1. If you were using the modified block style, where would you put your city, state, and ZIP code?
2. Where would you put the date?
3. Where would you put the name of the person to whom you are writing?
4. Should you indent each paragraph?
5. How many blank lines would you leave between paragraphs?

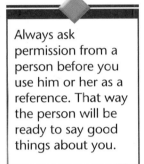

References

People who can tell what you are like and what kind of a worker you would be

Always ask permission from a person before you use him or her as a reference. That way the person will be ready to say good things about you.

"I've learned a lot about business letters," Aldo said to Ms. Levy. "You've been a big help to me."

"Thanks, but you still have more to learn about business letters," said Ms. Levy. "After you know the correct form for a letter of application, you need to learn what goes into the body of a letter of application. It must contain the right information."

"What is the right information?" asked Aldo.

"The right information is everything that the employer will need to know. Before you begin writing, plan what you will say. Then write your letter," Ms. Levy said.

"But how will I know whether I have written a good letter?" asked Aldo.

Ms. Levy said, "Here are five questions to ask yourself after you have written your letter of application. If you can answer *Yes* to all these questions, you have written a good letter."

1. Have I named the job title and told exactly how I found out about the job?

2. Have I listed the skills I have that would help me do the job?

3. Have I given **references** if they are asked for? References are names of people you know who can tell the kind of person you are, the things you do well, and how you get along with others. Good references include friends, teachers, clergy, and past employers.

4. Have I given the company my telephone number to contact me?

5. Have I told the person at the company what times I am available at this phone number?

"Check your finished letter for correct spelling, punctuation, and capitalization," Ms. Levy said. "An employer will look for these things!"

Activity A Number your paper 1 to 5. Imagine that you have written the body of this letter of application. After you read the letter, ask the five questions listed on page 31. If you can answer *Yes* to the question, write *Yes* next to the number. Otherwise, write *No.*

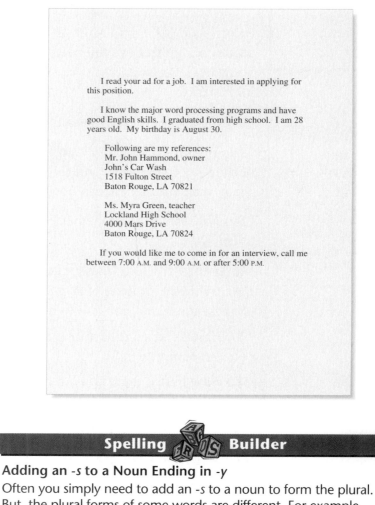

I read your ad for a job. I am interested in applying for this position.

I know the major word processing programs and have good English skills. I graduated from high school. I am 28 years old. My birthday is August 30.

Following are my references:
Mr. John Hammond, owner
John's Car Wash
1518 Fulton Street
Baton Rouge, LA 70821

Ms. Myra Green, teacher
Lockland High School
4000 Mars Drive
Baton Rouge, LA 70824

If you would like me to come in for an interview, call me between 7:00 A.M. and 9:00 A.M. or after 5:00 P.M.

Spelling Builder

Adding an -s to a Noun Ending in -y
Often you simply need to add an -s to a noun to form the plural. But, the plural forms of some words are different. For example, some words ending in -y have special rules.

Use these rules:

For a noun ending in a -y preceded by a consonant, add -es after changing y to i: *company, companies.*

For a noun ending in a -y preceded by a vowel, just add -s: *toy, toys.* Form the plural of the following nouns.

tray   victory   salary   secretary   highway

Know What to Leave Out

"It is just as important to know what to leave out of a letter of application as it is to know what to put in," Ms. Levy explained. "Employers do not want to read letters full of information that has nothing to do with the job they are offering." In the body of the letter on page 32, two pieces of information should have been left out: the writer's age and birthday.

Aldo asked, "How do I know what to leave out?"

"Provide only the information asked for in the ad or in the job summary at the agency or placement office," Ms. Levy replied. "If a person at the company wants to know more about you, he or she will call you for an interview."

Activity B Number your paper 1 to 10. Then decide which of the following facts you should include in a letter answering this ad. Write *Yes* or *No* for each answer.

PRINTER'S ASST.
H.S. grad w/exp. Have good attend. rec. Apply by letter to Good Printing Co., 487 Oak Lane, (your city).

1. Word processing skills
2. Whether you have a driver's license
3. Whether you graduated from high school
4. Your high school grades
5. Two references
6. Your good history grades
7. The award you got for perfect attendance
8. Your part-time job as a printer's helper
9. The distance between your house and the company
10. Your telephone number

Activity C Number your paper 1 to 5. Then decide which of the following facts you should include in a letter answering this ad. Write *Yes* or *No* for each answer.

> **BOOKKEEPER** Some exp. pref. Must be good in math. Driv. lic. helpful. Apply by letter. Morgan Bros., 27 Lee Ave., (your city).

1. Your good math grades
2. Your poor grades in physical education
3. Your experience in helping your father keep his books
4. The time it will take you to get to work
5. Your new car

Activity D On your paper, list the information that you would include if you wrote a letter of application for each of these jobs.

1. You are writing to apply for the job of carpenter. The company wants a person with experience and a good attendance record. The employer wants someone who has served as an apprentice carpenter and knows how to use all the tools. You think you can handle this job. What information would you include in your letter of application?

2. You are writing to apply for the job of nurse's assistant in a hospital. The ad states that the hospital wants someone who has worked in a hospital and who has experience in working with patients. The employer also wants someone who can work odd hours. You think you would like this job. What information would you include in your letter of application?

"The best way to become a good letter writer is to practice," advised Ms. Levy.

"Writing letters is hard work," Aldo said with a sigh.

"That's true," said Ms. Levy, "but the more letters you write, the easier it will be. You will begin to see which kinds of sentences sound good and which kinds do not. You will begin to remember what should be included in each letter. When you get a good job, all that hard work will have been worth it!"

Ms. Levy is right. The letter you send to someone is a part of you. The person judges you from the way the letter looks and sounds. If you want to make a good impression, work hard and practice your skills. Then when someone looks at your letter, that person will think, "This is someone I would like to hire."

Activity E Read this help-wanted ad. Then write the body of the letter that you would write to apply for this job.

> **SALES TRAINEE** for ins. co. No exp. nec. Should have good math and English skills. Answer by letter including 2 refs. to McGill Company, 904 Glenn Drive, (your city).

Activity F Read this next help-wanted ad. Write a complete letter answering the ad. Use full block or modified block style. Be sure to include the seven parts of a business letter.

> **SHIPPING CLERK** for nat'l. co. Must be h.s. grad. No exp. nec. Should have good org. skills. Apply by let. to Tamara Kirk, K. L. Auto Parts, 3281 Fernwood Road, (your city).

There is one more thing you need to know—the proper way to address an envelope.

This is the sample envelope Ms. Levy showed Aldo.

Ms. Ella Black
112 South Central Street
Cheyenne, WY 82001

Brown, Ellis, and Company
8832 Louden Avenue
Pittsburgh, PA 15219

The return address on an envelope is important. If the post office cannot deliver your letter for some reason, you will receive it back if it has a return address.

Notice that the return address, which is in the upper left corner of the envelope, includes the name of the person who sent the letter. On the second line is the street address, and directly below that are the city, state, and ZIP code—all on the same line.

Notice also that the name and address of the person and/or the company receiving the letter is several lines below the return address and considerably to the right. This arrangement gives the envelope a balanced look. The stamp, of course, goes in the upper right corner.

Remember to include the ZIP code on every letter you send. Leaving it out may delay the delivery of your letter. If you don't know a ZIP code, you can look it up in a ZIP code book at a post office, in the library, or on the Internet.

Activity A On your paper, draw an envelope measuring $9\frac{1}{2}$ inches wide and 4 inches high. Then use this information to address the envelope.

Joseph Hall is sending this letter. Mr. Hall lives at 6715 Hartsfield Road in Baltimore, MD. His ZIP code is 21218. He is sending the letter to Hans Olsen. Mr. Olsen lives at 13 North Lanier Place in Trenton, NJ. His ZIP code is 08608.

Post office abbreviations

Two-letter state and province abbreviations that do not include periods

An abbreviation is a shortened form of a word. In writing a letter, you will need to use the abbreviations *Mr.* or *Ms.* in front of a person's last name. When you write to a woman, use the abbreviation *Ms.* unless she has a professional title such as *Capt., Dr.,* or *Rev.* However, Aldo learned that those are not the only abbreviations on a letter.

Ms. Levy handed him a list of state abbreviations and said, "Use these two-letter **post office abbreviations** both on the envelope and on the inside addresses of a letter. These short abbreviations help keep the city, state, and ZIP code all on one line. Notice that both letters in each post office abbreviation are capital letters and no periods are used."

The two-letter postal abbreviations for the states aren't always formed in the same way. It is difficult to remember all of the abbreviations. Use the list on the next page to help you.

Where To Find It

ZIP Codes

The telephone book not only contains addresses and phone numbers of the people and businesses in a city or town, it also features a national map of area codes and a list of ZIP codes for your area. ZIP codes may also be found on the Internet.

You can find the ZIP code list in the telephone book. The list is arranged alphabetically by city. A portion of the list may look like this.

Union	49130	Uniontown	49129
Union City	49094	Unionville	48767
Union Lake	48387	Utica	*

The asterisk (*) tells you that this city is divided into sections, each of which has its own ZIP code. You need to check with your local post office or with a more detailed ZIP code book to find ZIP codes for this city.

Activity A Copy this list of state abbreviations that Ms. Levy gave to Aldo. Then keep your copy where you can always find it.

Alabama	AL	Montana	MT
Alaska	AK	Nebraska	NE
Arizona	AZ	Nevada	NV
Arkansas	AR	New Hampshire	NH
California	CA	New Jersey	NJ
Colorado	CO	New Mexico	NM
Connecticut	CT	New York	NY
Delaware	DE	North Carolina	NC
District of Columbia	DC	North Dakota	ND
Florida	FL	Ohio	OH
Georgia	GA	Oklahoma	OK
Hawaii	HI	Oregon	OR
Idaho	ID	Pennsylvania	PA
Illinois	IL	Rhode Island	RI
Indiana	IN	South Carolina	SC
Iowa	IA	South Dakota	SD
Kansas	KS	Tennessee	TN
Kentucky	KY	Texas	TX
Louisiana	LA	Utah	UT
Maine	ME	Vermont	VT
Maryland	MD	Virginia	VA
Massachusetts	MA	Washington	WA
Michigan	MI	West Virginia	WV
Minnesota	MN	Wisconsin	WI
Mississippi	MS	Wyoming	WY
Missouri	MO		

Activity B Draw a $9\frac{1}{2} \times 4$ inch envelope. Then address the envelope with this information.

Maria Gonzalez is sending this letter. Ms. Gonzalez lives at 202 Adams Street in Detroit, Michigan. Her ZIP code is 48238. She is sending the letter to Rose Chang. Ms. Chang lives at 45 South Elm Place in Houston, Texas. Her ZIP code is 77015.

This Does Not Compute

Hector bought a computer for his business. Six months later the computer stopped working.

Hector called the store where he bought the computer and talked to a sales clerk. Hector said, "My new computer has stopped working. What should I do?"

After Hector described the problem, the clerk said, "It could be the hardware, which the manufacturer handles. You need to write to the company."

"What do I say in my letter?" Hector asked.

"Include the model number and the serial number. Tell where and when you bought it and what is wrong," said the clerk. "Also, give the company an idea of what you expect. State clearly whether you want the manufacturer to repair the computer, replace it, or refund your money."

"Thank you. That's good to know. Where do I send the letter?" asked Hector.

The clerk gave him the address.

Hector needed his computer repaired soon, so he wrote his letter immediately. He offered to return the computer to the manufacturer but asked the company to pay shipping costs. He stated that he wanted the company to repair his computer or replace it.

For Discussion

1. What kind of letter will Hector write?

2. What information should he include?

3. Why is this information important?

4. What other information should Hector include?

5. Hector needs to include the seven parts of a business letter. What are they?

Chapter 2 REVIEW

Word Bank

full block style

indented

letter of application

margin

modified block style

post office abbreviations

references

ZIP code

Part A On a sheet of paper, write the correct word or words from the Word Bank to complete each sentence.

1. The writer does not indent paragraphs in a _____ letter.
2. A letter used in asking for a job is a _____ .
3. The postal delivery area written after the name of a state in an address is the _____ .
4. People who can tell what you are like and what kind of a worker you would be are _____ .
5. The outside edge of a page on which there is no writing or printing is the _____ .
6. _____ means "set in from the left margin of the page."
7. _____ are two-letter state abbreviations that do not include periods.
8. In a _____ letter, paragraphs are indented.

Part B Number your paper 9 to 11. Write the letter of the correct answer.

9. In the full block style letter, everything in the letter lines up at the _____ .

   A right margin   C left margin

   B center of the page   D bottom of the page

10. Which of the following should you leave out of a letter of application?

    A your address   C your skills

    B your telephone number D your age

11. Always include a _____ on an envelope.

    A margin   C return address

    B signature   D date

Part C Number your paper 12 to 18. Rewrite this list of the seven parts of a business letter to show the order in which they should appear in a letter. Then tell the number of the lines of each part of the letter below.

- body
- date
- signature
- return address
- complimentary close
- inside address
- salutation

1)	2517 Bartley Street
2)	Chicago, Ill. 60609
3)	September 12, 2004
4)	Dr. Phillip Moore
5)	12 Arrington Circle
6)	Miami, FL
7)	Dear Mr. Moore
8)	I saw your ad in the *Chicago Flash* for a
9)	receptionist. I will be moving to Miami next
10)	month. I am interested in applying for the job.
11)	I have worked as a receptionist for a doctor
12)	here in Chicago for four years. I like meeting
13)	and working with people
14)	If you would like an interview, please call
15)	me when I get to Miami.
16)	Love
17)	
18)	Cynthia

Part D Number your paper 19 to 30. Read the full block style letter above that contains mistakes and leaves out important information. Write the numbers of the lines that need to be improved, and then explain each mistake. Remember, missing or incorrect punctuation is a mistake. Then, make an envelope for the letter and address it.

Test-Taking Tip When studying for a test, use the titles and subtitles in the chapter to help you recall the information.

Preparing a Résumé

3

To get a job that you really want, you have to make yourself stand out from all the other people applying for the same job. One way to do that is to include a résumé along with a job application. A résumé highlights important information about you in an easy-to-read form. Your application with a résumé is more likely to get attention than someone else's application without a résumé.

In Chapter 3, you will learn what information you should include on a résumé and how to organize that information.

Goals for Learning

◆ To understand the advantages of a résumé

◆ To know what information to include on a résumé

◆ To know how to organize the information on a résumé

◆ To learn the differences between a résumé for a recent high school graduate and an experienced worker

◆ To write your own résumé and be able to make it perfect

Résumé

A summary of a person's skills, achievements, training, and jobs

Calvin Williams went to see an employment counselor at his state's job placement office. He had not been able to get the type of job he wanted even though he had been trying since he got out of high school three months before.

When Ms. Drake interviewed Calvin, she recognized his many good qualities. He had a good school record and had a part-time job. His references were excellent. Calvin also was pleasant and polite, and he seemed to know how to apply for a job both in person and by letter. After Ms. Drake asked more questions, she thought she knew what Calvin was missing.

"Perhaps," she said, "employers haven't gotten a good idea of your ability from your letter. You might consider developing a **résumé** to include with your letters."

"How could a résumé help me?" asked Calvin.

"You can tell only so many facts in a letter of application," Ms. Drake answered, "but a résumé gives an employer a clearer picture of you and your qualifications. It gives you a chance to tell an employer important additional information in an easy-to-read style."

"I learned to write a résumé in high school," Calvin said. "If I go back and look over my notes, I think I could write a good description of my skills." Then he asked Ms. Drake, "After I write my résumé, will you look it over?"

"Of course, I will," she said with a smile. "As soon as you finish writing your résumé, call and make an appointment to see me."

Business machines

Office equipment including a telephone, a computer, a calculator, a fax machine, and a copier

Writing Tip

First brainstorm a list of things to include in your résumé. Then set the list aside. Over the next few days you may think of other things. Add these to your list as you think of them.

Among his notes at home, Calvin found a list of reasons for submitting a résumé with a letter of application. Here is that list.

1. A résumé gives you a chance to present yourself in a positive manner.

2. You can give more information about yourself in a résumé than you can include in a letter or on most applications.

3. A good résumé will show an employer how well you organize information.

4. A résumé tells the employer that you really care about getting the job because you have taken the time and trouble to write a résumé.

The four points on this list made sense to Calvin. He remembered thinking after job interviews, "I wish I had been asked about my attendance record at school or my math grades." He also wanted to tell more about himself than he could on job applications.

Activity A Follow these tips to begin creating your résumé.

Put your mind to work. What information should you include on your résumé? Think of some of the important things about yourself that you would like an employer to know. Have you had any jobs? Did you do well in certain subjects in school? Have you won any awards? Are there some **business machines** that you know how to operate? For example, do you know how to operate a computer, a fax machine, or a copier? Whom would you list as references?

On a sheet of paper, write down everything you can think of that you would like to include on your résumé. Then keep this list in your notebook to use later in this chapter.

Extracurricular

Activities in school other than course work, including sports, band, chorus, and clubs

As Calvin looked over his notes, he remembered that a résumé has several important parts that include specific information. This is what he had written in his notes.

A résumé should include the following parts:

- Personal information
- Career goals
- Education
- Employment experience
- **Extracurricular** and community activities
- Awards and honors
- References

Personal information appears first on a résumé. The arrangement or order of what follows the personal information depends on your age, your experience, and the job for which you are applying. Generally, the most important information appears near the beginning. List your most recent job or education first, followed by the next most recent.

Although a résumé does not include it, your age plays a role in what you have done and what your skills are. Extracurricular activities are also important for recent graduates to include. However, if you have been out of school for a while, you probably should not list extracurricular activities. Instead, list the community groups you belong to or activities in which you take part.

If you are a recent graduate, you probably will have little or no work experience. Put this section near the middle of your résumé. On the other hand, people who have had several jobs should put the employment section near the top of their résumé to show that they have experience and qualify for a new job.

Activity A Number your paper 1 to 10. Then write the correct answer from the box that completes each statement. Use each answer only once.

references	goals	awards
order	community	graduated
information	age	applying
experience		

The seven parts of a résumé include the following: personal **1.** _____ , career **2.** _____ , education, employment experience, extracurricular and community activities, **3.** _____ and honors, and **4.** _____ .

Don't use a definite **5.** _____ when writing a résumé. The arrangement should be decided by your **6.** _____ , your **7.** _____ , and the job for which you are **8.** _____ .

Extracurricular activities would be important for someone who has just **9.** _____ from high school. For people who have been out of high school for a while, it would be better to list **10.** _____ activities.

> Make your résumé look professional. Use white or off-white paper with a matching envelope. Avoid fonts that are fancy or hard to read. Use a laser printer to print your résumé.

Coaching at the community center is one of Calvin's volunteer activities.

Personal information

Your name, address, telephone number, and e-mail address

E-mail

Electronic mail, or messages sent between computers

Career goal

What you hope to become or to achieve in your job

Experience

A job you have had or a skill you developed

Personal Information

Personal information is your name, address, telephone number, and **e-mail** address. Your e-mail, or electronic mail, address lets someone reach you on your computer. Be sure to include your ZIP code with your address and your area code with your telephone number. This section should always come first on your résumé.

Career Goals

Although you should word your **career goal** to fit the specific job you want, you should make it broad enough to fit more than one job. For example, if you are looking for a job as a plumbing trainee or apprentice, your career goal might be "to become a master plumber." Even though it may take many years to reach your goal, stating it lets an employer know that you have future plans.

Education

This is an important section for recent graduates. Include special courses you took, especially those that relate to the job for which you are applying. Mention areas or courses in which you got good grades.

Employment Experience

Work **experience** includes all of your full-time and part-time jobs. This section should also include any volunteer jobs or jobs you did without being paid. This would include baby-sitting, snow shoveling, lawn mowing, or other similar jobs done for neighbors or friends. Volunteer jobs show that you are responsible, dependable, and willing to work.

On a résumé, job experience includes the dates you were employed, company name and address, your duties, manager, and the reason you left the job.

Other Activities

Recent high school graduates should include any extracurricular activities—things you took part in beyond the regular school courses. Sports, the school newspaper, the band, and student government are extracurricular activities. All applicants should also include any community groups or activities in which they take part—such as offices held, specific duties performed, and awards or honors earned. Employers often believe that people who are active in clubs and organizations will be hardworking and dependable on the job.

References

Include at least three references on your résumé. Relatives are not good choices for references. Employers think that relatives will say nice things about you just because you are related to them. Instead, references should be former employers, coaches, club sponsors, teachers, neighbors, and other adults who know you. Anyone you choose as a reference should be able to tell what you are like, how well you do things, and how well you get along with others. You should get permission from your references before listing their names on your résumé. Keep in mind that by law, previous employers can discuss only job-related issues when giving a reference.

Where To Find It

The Yellow Pages

If you wanted to take part in a community club, where could you find information about it? One source for information is the local telephone book, which usually lists clubs and groups in the Yellow Pages.

To find information in the Yellow Pages, first look in the index. Headings include associations, clubs, and community groups. The index will list page numbers for each type of club or group.

Using the Yellow Pages index, find an example of a group from three of the following types. List each group's name and telephone number on your paper.

a business association	a community club	a youth group
a sports group	a service group	

Activity B On a sheet of paper, draw a chart like the following one. Then read the list of information about Calvin Williams. Write the number of each item in the column of the chart in which it belongs.

Personal Information	Goals	Education	Experience	Extracurricular/ Community Activities

1. Wants to be a licensed automobile mechanic

2. Sang in a school chorus

3. Graduated from high school

4. Worked part-time in a gas station

5. Lives at 511 North Marine Street

6. Took an advanced course in auto mechanics at a night school

7. Played on a community basketball team

8. Helped neighbors fix their cars

9. Would like to own an auto repair shop

10. Took auto mechanics courses in high school

11. Lives in Walla Walla, WA 98511

12. Was treasurer of the high school shop club

13. Was a high school student government representative

14. Worked on weekends at AA Appliance Repair Shop

15. Telephone number is (509) 555-7760

Keep your résumé in a computer file. Then you can easily make changes when necessary. Also, you will have your résumé ready when a job opportunity comes up quickly.

Calvin Williams gathered the information he needed for his résumé by listing personal information plus facts about his career goals, education, experience, extracurricular and community activities, and references. Then he was ready to write the first version, or **rough draft,** of his résumé.

On the next page is a copy of the rough draft of Calvin's résumé. As you read it, find the main parts of the résumé. Also notice the information that he included in each part. Be prepared to answer questions about his résumé after you have studied it.

Vocabulary Builder

Synonyms for the Word *Job*

If you are looking for a job, you may find other words for *job* listed in the help-wanted ads. If you know the meanings of the words, you will see more opportunities in your job search.

In a dictionary, look up the following words that mean *job.* Then use each word in a sentence and write the sentences on your paper. Your sentences should show that you understand the words' meanings.

1. career
2. profession
3. employment
4. business
5. occupation

Calvin J. Williams
511 North Marine Street
Walla Walla, Washington 98511
(509) 555-7760
cjw@personsaddress.net

CAREER GOALS
- To be a licensed automobile mechanic
- To own an auto repair shop

EDUCATION
- Graduated from Northwest High School, June 2003
- Studied auto mechanics
- Received best grades in math, science, and auto mechanics (Bs)
- Completed advanced course in auto mechanics at Adult Night Center, August, 2003

EXTRACURRICULAR ACTIVITES
- Treasurer of Shop Club
- Student government representative
- Member of the school chorus

EXPERIENCE
- Worked part time at Steiner's Service Station for two years
- Worked on Saturdays during senior year at AA Appliance Repair Shop
- Helped neighbors with car repairs

REFERENCES

Mr. Jacob Steiner, owner
Steiner's Service Station
11 Pacific Highway
Walla Walla, WA 89503
(509) 555-1742

Mr. William Turner,
Teacher, auto mechanics
Northwest High School
62 Elm Street
Walla Walla, WA 98513
(509) 555-6756

Mrs. Jeannette Robinson, neighbor
515 North Marine Street
Walla Walla, WA 98511
(509) 555-9443

Activity A Number your paper 1 to 10. Answer these questions about Calvin Williams's résumé.

1. What education did Calvin list that relates to the job of auto mechanic?

2. Why would an employer be interested in Calvin's extracurricular activities?

3. Which two of Calvin's jobs relate most directly to the job of auto mechanic?

4. Why is Mr. William Turner a good reference if Calvin is applying for a job as an auto mechanic?

5. Mrs. Robinson is one of the neighbors for whom Calvin has done car repairs. Why is she a good person for him to use as a reference?

6. Why do you think an employer would be interested that Calvin went to night school?

7. Why is Mr. Jacob Steiner a good reference?

8. How do Calvin's career goals relate to the job of mechanic's assistant?

9. If you were think of hiring Calvin, which reference would you call first? Why?

10. What questions would you ask Mr. Steiner or Mr. Turner to get information that is not included on the résumé?

A Sample Résumé for an Experienced Person

Among his high school notes, Calvin found a sample résumé for an experienced job applicant. He knew that he could not use that sample, so he loaned it to Norman Flynn, a neighbor who wanted a new job.

Mr. Flynn still had a copy of his old résumé. He wrote it 12 years ago when he graduated from high school. However, he quickly realized that he could not use it any longer for two reasons. First, the information was out of date. He had gained work experience that he wanted to include. Second, Norman also wanted to change the order of his résumé to point out his work experience. His new résumé is on the next page.

Spelling Builder

Words Often Confused

When you are writing your résumé, it is important to use just the right word. If you write that you took a *coarse* in word processing, the person who receives your letter or résumé will see that you are careless. To make sure that you are using the correct word, check the dictionary. You may also find it helpful to make a list of confusing words and their definitions to keep handy when you are writing.

Use the dictionary to find the definitions of each pair of words listed below. Then number your paper 1 to 5. Choose the word that best completes the sentence.

affect/effect   course/coarse   loose/lose   choose/chose

1. How will his promotion (affect, effect) me?
2. This fabric is too (coarse, course) for a shirt.
3. Did the football team (loose, lose) the game?
4. Anita (choose, chose) to wear a black sweater.
5. The Midwest has not felt the (affect, effect) of the hurricane.

Norman H. Flynn
510 North Marine Street
Walla Walla, Washington 98511
(509) 555-2233
nhf@personsaddress.net

CAREER GOAL
- To be head bookkeeper for a large corporation

EXPERIENCE

2002 to present:	Assistant Bookkeeper Elgin's Department Store Walla Walla, WA 98546
1996 to 2002:	Bookkeeper Trainee Link's Hardware Stores Walla Walla, WA 98530
1999 to present:	Income Tax Consultant, part-time position Fill out income tax forms for 20 clients

COMMUNITY ACTIVITIES

2002 to present:	Treasurer, Walla Walla Community Center
2000 to present:	Treasurer and Business Manager, Walla Walla Little League
1999 to present:	Member, South Shores Community Group
1999 to present:	Volunteer, South Shores General Hospital

EDUCATION

1995 to 1997:	Attended Washington University with course in bookkeeping
June 1995:	Graduated from South Shores High

REFERENCES

Mr. Arthur Day, current employer
Elgin's Department Store
3468 Main Street
Walla Walla, WA 98546
(509) 555-6983

Ms. Caroline Baxter, manager
Walla Walla Community Center
7819 Wells Avenue
Walla Walla, WA 98511
(509) 555-4635

Mr. Felix Wist, president
South Shores General Hospital Volunteers
44 Hospital Road
Walla Walla, WA 98545
(509) 555-1297

Writing On Your Own

Imagine that you have a new job that uses the skills you have just learned in a training program. Write a letter to your former employer, telling him or her that you are leaving. Be sure you include the date of the last day you will work and thank the employer for the chance to work there.

Notice the differences between the résumé Calvin Williams wrote and the one Mr. Flynn wrote. For example, Calvin and Mr. Flynn arranged the information on their résumés differently to reflect differences in age and experience. The employment section and the references section are different, too. Mr. Flynn was able to include more specific information in these two parts.

Mr. Flynn listed his work experience second in his résumé because it would be most interesting to an employer. He put community activities next because they relate to accounting, the kind of work he is looking for.

Notice what a good selection of references Mr. Flynn made. First, he listed his current employer. Anyone interested in hiring Mr. Flynn would know that he is open about his present job.

Then Mr. Flynn listed the manager of the community center where he volunteers. Ms. Baxter could tell an employer about Mr. Flynn's character and volunteer work.

Finally, he listed the president of the volunteer group at the hospital. Mr. Wist could tell an employer about Mr. Flynn's volunteer work.

Checklist for Résumés

Calvin found among his papers a list of capitalization, punctuation, and spelling rules that apply to résumés. At the top of the list was this sentence written in bold type: **A Résumé Must Be Perfect!**

Calvin was glad he found the list because it reminded him of the little things that can be very important when an employer looks at a résumé.

This is Calvin's list.

A Résumé Must Be Perfect!

1. When writing an address, put a comma between the city and state. No punctuation goes between the state and the ZIP code. Use the two-letter state abbreviations for all addresses. Do not use a period after these abbreviations.

2. When writing a telephone number, put the area code in parentheses. Put a hyphen after the first three numbers of the telephone number.

3. Use capital letters for the first letter of people's names, and names of streets, cities, states, businesses, schools, and so on.

4. Spell all words correctly. Have someone else check the spelling on your résumé before you make a final copy.

Activity B Number your paper 1 to 5. Correct any résumé items that have errors.

1. Oklahoma City, OK, 73125

2. Mr. John A fisher, Manager

3. 2634 Green Street

4. Mark Twain senior High School

5. 301/555/4736

Activity C On your paper, write the rough draft of your résumé. First, review the sample résumés in this section. Second, begin with the list of information you made in *Activity A*, page 45, and then add any other information. Third, after you write your rough draft, use the following checklist. Finally, use a computer to type a final draft.

Résumé Checklist

1. Have I chosen the best résumé order for my age and my experience?

2. Have I worded my career goal to match the job that I want?

3. Have I listed all of my education—including any outside courses? Have I emphasized the things I did well in during school? Have I mentioned courses that relate to the job I want?

4. If I have work experience have I listed the specific skills and duties related to the job I want?

5. Have I listed extracurricular activities and/or community activities that show my interest in areas related to the job I want?

6. Have I selected the most impressive references from all of the people who know me? Have I spelled their names correctly? Have I included their correct addresses and telephone numbers?

7. Are the headings clear? Do they stand out on the page?

8. Is all my information correct?

9. Is my wording consistent?

10. Have I corrected all spelling errors and typing errors?

11. Have I corrected all errors in capitalization and punctuation? Is my résumé perfect?

12. Have I followed all of the suggestions and the checklists in the chapter?

13. Did I center my name, address, phone number, and e-mail address at the top of the page? Is the rest of my résumé spaced well?

14. Have I been able to keep my résumé on one page—and definitely not more than two pages?

15. Is my final printed or typed copy neat and attractive?

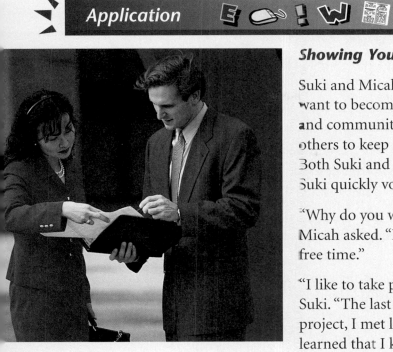

Showing You Care

Suki and Micah both work for the City Bank and want to become assistant managers. Bank officers and community leaders have asked them and others to keep records for a new community park. Both Suki and Micah are accurate bookkeepers. Suki quickly volunteered.

"Why do you want to give up your free time?" Micah asked. "Nobody is going to take up my free time."

"I like to take part in community activities," said Suki. "The last time I worked on a community project, I met lots of interesting people. They learned that I keep accurate records and that I work well with people. When the bank had a job opening, I applied for it. People who had worked with me knew I could do the job. They also knew that I cared about the community."

"I don't do anything more than my job," said Micah. "Nobody is going to take up my free time."

"That's too bad," said Suki. "Ms. James, the manager, told me last Thursday that she will be looking for an assistant manager for the branch on your side of town. She needs someone who can work well with people in the community."

For Discussion

1. Why does Suki want to work on the park project?

2. How does Micah feel about working on community activities?

3. How does the bank feel about employees working on community activities?

4. What benefits do employees get from working on community projects?

5. How would you describe Suki's feelings about others? How would you describe Micah's attitude?

Chapter 3   R E V I E W

Word Bank

career goals

community
activities

education

e-mail

employment
experience

extracurricular
activities

personal
information

references

résumé

volunteer

Part A On a sheet of paper, write the correct word or words from the Word Bank to complete each sentence.

1. The _____ section of your résumé includes all full-time and part-time jobs you have had.

2. _____ are the names, addresses, and phone numbers of people who can describe your ability to do the job.

3. The school from which you graduated would appear under the heading _____.

4. Your name, address, telephone number, and e-mail address are _____.

5. _____ are the school clubs and other high school activities you joined.

6. When you apply for a job, you send a _____, or summary of your qualifications.

7. Electronic mail, or _____, are messages sent between computers.

8. Your _____ are what you hope to be doing in the future.

9. The groups or clubs that you join in your town appear under the heading _____.

10. A _____ is a person who does a job without being paid.

Part B Number your paper 11 to 15. If the statement is true, write *True* next to the number. If it is not true, write *False*.

11. A recent high school graduate should probably list work experience before education.

12. The order of the items in a résumé depends upon the job that the person wants.

13. You may leave your address and phone number out of your résumé.

14. An experienced person should probably list work experiences near the beginning of a résumé.

15. You should use your mother and father as references.

Part C Number your paper 16 to 20. Write the letter of the correct answer on your paper.

16. Which of the following is not an extracurricular activity?
    A school band   C the pep squad
    B student government   D math class

17. Which of the following would be the best reference for a résumé?
    A a former employer   C a friend
    B your uncle   D a boss you don't get along with

18. Which one of the following does not belong under the category *Employment Experience* on a résumé?
    A full-time job   C school work
    B part-time job   D volunteer work

19. Which of the following is a good way to order the employment experience information in your résumé?
    A in order of how much you liked each boss
    B most recent first
    C in alphabetical order
    D in order of increasing salary

20. What do you call the first copy of a piece of writing?
    A a résumé
    B a return address
    C a rough draft
    D a volunteer

Part D On a sheet of paper, rewrite the résumé shown at right, making all necessary corrections.

willaim t rogers
1758 maple streat
philadelphia pennsylvania, 19032
215 555 8493

referances

mr john dilland owner
dilland corner store
788 cherry lane
philadelphia pennsylvania 19024
215/555/4466

eduction

graduated from central high school,
june 2003
took courses in english and math
at pennsylvania state college

Test-Taking Tip If you have trouble with a question on a test, go on to the next question. Come back to any you skipped.

Filling Out a Job Application

Sometimes a company will make a judgment about you long before you step inside its front door. Other times, a company might reject you without meeting you. How well you fill out an application might determine whether a company accepts or rejects you for a job.

In Chapter 4, you will learn how to fill out an application so that it represents you positively.

Goals for Learning

◆ To write a fact sheet that contains information needed on job applications

◆ To understand why fact sheets should be updated from time to time

◆ To understand vocabulary that commonly appears on job applications

◆ To be able to fill out job applications thoroughly and completely

Human resources department

The part of a company (also known as a personnel department) that deals with employees; a human resources department might hire people and keep records about how well they do their jobs

Job application

A form used in making a request to be hired

Supervisor

Someone who is in charge of others; a boss

Yolanda Medina worked as an administrative assistant in the **human resources department** of Caine Supply Company. Every day she saw people come in to apply for jobs, and every day she saw some of their **job applications** thrown into the wastebasket. This puzzled her. She asked her **supervisor,** "Why are so many job applications thrown away?"

Her supervisor explained, "If applications have mistakes in them or if information is missing, we simply do not bother with them. Why should we consider someone with a sloppy, careless application when we can hire someone with a completed application?" She added, "We think that the way a person fills out an application shows what kind of employee he or she might be. A carefully filled out application usually indicates a thoughtful, hard-working person."

A few weeks after this talk with her supervisor, Yolanda's younger brother Carlos graduated from high school. He was already looking for a job. Yolanda told him what her supervisor had said and warned him to do a good job filling out job applications.

After several weeks went by and Carlos still did not have a job, Yolanda asked him why he was having trouble.

"I am really not sure, Yolanda," he said. "I have filled out 20 applications and still no job! I am filling out another application now to turn in this afternoon."

"Before you turn it in, let me take a look at it," said Yolanda. She did not have to look long before she shook her head and said, "I think I know the problem. This application has mistakes in it, you left out information, and you made some sloppy corrections." She put her arm around her brother's shoulders and said, "Remember, employers judge people by their applications. If they don't like what they see, they won't interview you."

"I guess I forgot," replied Carlos. "How about some help?"

Fact Sheet

"First," said Yolanda, "I suggest you prepare a **fact sheet** with all the information you may need to put on an application. Then take the fact sheet with you when you apply for a job. It is especially helpful if you have to fill out an application at the company's human resources department. Even if you fill out an application at home, the fact sheet is useful because all the information you need is in one place!"

"What would I put on a fact sheet?" Carlos asked.

"What information have you needed most often for those other 20 applications?" questioned Yolanda.

"You mean information like my **Social Security number** and the schools I attended?" asked Carlos.

"Exactly," said Yolanda. "Look at my fact sheet."

This is the fact sheet that Yolanda showed her brother.

FACT SHEET

Social Security Number: 777-38-0976

EDUCATION

John Murphy Senior High
1600 McNair Avenue
Topeka, Kansas 66656

Course: Business
Years attended: 4
Graduated: June 2, 2002

Topeka Community College
203 South Plains Road
Topeka, Kansas 66623

Course: Computer Programming
Years attended: 2
Graduated: June 4, 2004
Degree: Associate of Arts

EXPERIENCE

2002 to present:
Caine Supply Company
1543 Travis Street
Topeka, Kansas 66609
(913) 555-1758

Position: Administrative Assistant
Supervisor: Timothy Clark
Reason for leaving: To get job as
computer programmer

REFERENCES

Ms. Amelia Carter
Business Education Teacher
John Murphy Senior High
(See above for address)
(913) 555-0770

Ms. Lillian Newly
Programming Instructor
Topeka Community College
(See above for address)
(913) 555-9063

Mr. Timothy Clark, President
Caine Supply Company
(See above for address)
(913) 555-7718

As Carlos looked over his sister's fact sheet, he could see why she had included the information she did. He remembered that when he was filling out an application one day, he was so nervous that he forgot his Social Security number. Because he had not brought his card with him, he had to leave that space blank. He was unsure, too, how long he had worked at a part-time job during high school. He also guessed at the spelling of several important names.

Later that evening Yolanda gave him a few helpful hints. "If you don't remember how to spell people's names, call and ask them. Most people won't mind. If you are unsure how to spell street or business names, look them up in the telephone book and check the spelling."

Activity A Number your paper 1 to 10. Then write *Yes* for the items that you should include on your fact sheet. Write *No* for the items that you should not include.

1. The full name of the high school you attended

2. Your Social Security number

3. The number of basketball games in which you scored more than five points

4. The name of a teacher who was very nice to you—even though you were never in one of her classes

5. The address and ZIP code of the high school you attended

6. The name and address of your favorite aunt (as a reference)

7. The name of the company where you work

8. The name and address of the math teacher you had last year (as a reference)

9. The name of the principal of your school (as a reference)

10. The reason you want to leave your present job

Writing Tip

Revise your fact sheet when you have new or additional information. If you fill out another application in six months or a year, you will have the new information.

Activity B Write your own fact sheet. Include all of the information that Yolanda included on hers. Then add any other information you might need on a job application. Use the hints that Yolanda gave her brother.

Updating Your Fact Sheet

From time to time you will have to update your fact sheet to include new jobs or additional education. In fact, each time you apply for a job, you should check your fact sheet to make sure that all the information on it is current.

Activity C On a sheet of paper, list the names of six people you could use as references. Write their names, spelling them correctly. Then write their addresses and telephone numbers. Remember not to list your relatives as references.

Spelling Builder

Troublesome Words

Some common words can spell trouble on a job application. Sometimes, companies ask about your *experience* or the education you *received*.

Two other troublesome words on applications are *references* and *salary.* Remember that the word *references* contains only the vowel *e.* The word *salary* contains only the vowel *a.* Do not confuse the word *salary* with *celery,* a vegetable.

Begin writing a list of words that you find difficult to spell and that may appear on job applications. Include these troublesome words: *experience, receive, references,* and *salary.* List the words in alphabetical order so that you can find them easily. Then you will have your list ready when you apply for a job.

As Yolanda looked over her brother's application, she realized that he might not understand some words on it. To help him, she gave him this list of words and their definitions. Understanding the meanings of these words will help you do a better job of filling out a job application.

Make a checklist of things to bring with you when you apply for a job. Include your fact sheet, pens, and maybe a pocket dictionary.

Application Glossary

address   The place where you live, where to reach your references, or the location of your school or employer. An address should include the house number and street name, the city and state, and the ZIP code. Remember that a comma goes between the city and state but not between the state and ZIP code.

college   The name of the college or university you attended. You do not have to have graduated to include it.

company   The place where you work now or the places where you have worked before.

course   The subject in which you majored in school. For example, in high school, you might have taken an academic, a college preparatory, a business, an auto mechanics, or a general course.

degree   An award given if you graduated from a two-year or four-year college. For example, you could earn an Associate Degree of Arts, Bachelor of Arts, or Bachelor of Science degree (abbreviated as A.A., B.A., or B.S.)

experience   Other jobs that you have held. This section of the application may also ask for the dates worked at these jobs, the names and addresses of the companies, your duties and title, the names of your direct supervisor, and the reasons you left these jobs.

position   Job or job title, such as short-order cook or receptionist.

If possible, deliver your application in person. It will help the employer remember you.

references The names, positions, addresses, and sometimes the telephone numbers of people who know you and can talk about the kind of person you are. References usually tell how well you do things and how well you get along with other people. References can include previous employers, friends, teachers, coaches, or clergy. Previous employers can only discuss job-related information when giving a reference.

signature A handwritten (rather than typed or printed) name. Most applications require that you write, not print, your name somewhere near the bottom of the application.

Vocabulary Builder

The Name Game

Job applications may ask for your *surname,* your *maiden name,* or your *title.*

The first blank on an application may ask for your *title.* Unless you are a doctor or are a member of the clergy or armed forces, your choices are *Mr., Miss, Mrs.,* or *Ms.* Men have only one choice, *Mr.* Women have a choice of *Miss, Mrs.,* or *Ms.* The title *Miss* says that you are a single woman. *Mrs.* is a title for a married woman or a woman who has been married. *Ms.* is a title for either a married or a single woman.

The word *surname* may also appear on your application. *Surname* is another word for last name.

If you are a woman, your *maiden name* is your family name before your marriage.

Number your paper 1 to 5, and then write a short answer for the following.

1. your title
2. your principal's surname
3. your teacher's title
4. your best friend's surname
5. your mother's maiden name

Writing On Your Own

Suppose the company for which you last worked fired you because you did not come to work regularly. What reason would you give for leaving your last job? Write a short paragraph explaining what you would say.

Activity A Number your paper 1 to 10. Then match each term in the first column with its definition in the second column.

Term

1. signature
2. address
3. company
4. references
5. college
6. course
7. position
8. degree
9. experience
10. job application

Description

A   the number of the house or building and the name of the street, city, state or province, and ZIP code or postal code

B   the name of the two-year or four-year college you attended

C   the name(s) of the place where you work or have worked

D   the type of subjects you took in school

E   what you get when you graduate from college

F   jobs you have held

G   a form used in making a request to be hired

H   names of people who can say what kind of person you are and what kind of work you do

I   your written name

J   job title

Place of birth

City and state or country where a person was born

"Some phrases on applications," Yolanda explained to her brother, "can be confusing. For example, many applications ask for your **place of birth.** That does not mean the name of the hospital where you were born. It means the city and state where you were born." She added, "People who were born in another country should write the name of that country."

Yolanda handed Carlos a sheet of paper. "Here are other confusing phrases you probably will find on most applications," she said. "It is a good idea to keep this list with your fact sheet. That way you will have it handy when you fill out an application."

Confusing Phrases on a Job Application

"Position applied for"
The job or jobs you want

"List last or present employer first"
Your employment record, starting with the last job you had or the job you currently have. Then list the job before that, and the job before that, and so on, until you have listed your very first job last. That section of an application might look something like this:

2002 to present:	Garrett Supply Company 1530 Williston Road Boston, MA 02109
1999 to 2002:	The Design House 3390 Caudill Avenue Boston, MA 02110
1997 to 1999:	Rodin's Body Works 10 High Street Cambridge, MA 01566

"Reason for leaving"
The reason you left a job. Maybe you learned new skills or changed your goals. Perhaps the company went out of business or laid you off your job.

"May we call your present employer?"
A request to use your present employer as a reference. If you do not want your current supervisor to know that you are looking for another job, answer *No* after this question.

Activity B Number your paper 1 to 5. Then write the section of the application in which each item belongs. Refer to the information on page 71.

1. I want to get into a new line of work.

2. I am moving out of town.

3. server

4. yes

5. 2002 to present: Caton's Diner
309 Bolton Steet
Salt Lake City, UT 84123

2000 to 2002:   Dario's Pizza Palace
209 Royalton Road
Salt Lake City, UT 84101

As Carlos continued to apply for jobs, he found that he still did not understand all of the phrases on a few applications. As he came across unfamiliar words or phrases, he wrote them in a notebook. Then one day, he took his list to his sister. Yolanda used his list to make the guide sheet shown below.

Application Guide

"Kind of work desired"
    Means "What kind of job would you like to have?"

"Have you ever been employed by this company?"
    Means "Did you ever work for this company before?"

"Have you ever been employed by a similar concern?"
    Means "Did you ever work for a company that makes the same
    kind of product or offers the same kind of service as this company?"

> "Is all the information on this application true? If we discover that it is not, that will be considered sufficient cause for dismissal"
> Means "If our company hires you and then finds out you did not tell the truth on your application, we could fire you."
>
> "In case of emergency, notify"
> Means "if you have an accident or get sick, whom should the company call?"
>
> "Final rate of pay"
> Means "before you left that job, how much did you earn?" (refers to a previous job)
>
> "Nature of work done"
> Means "What kind of work did you do on this job?" (refers to a previous job)

After Carlos looked over the application guide, Yolanda said to him, "There is no way you can prepare for every question you will find on every application. If you don't understand something, ask the person who gave you the application. Actually, asking questions can make a good impression because it tells the person that you really care about doing a good job."

Activity C Number your paper 1 to 5. Then write the word or phrase from the "Possible Answers" box that answers each question. Use each answer only once.

Possible Answers		
Mary Smith, mother	$6 per hour	Yes
Administrative Assistant	Yes, Smith & Son	

1. Kind of work desired.
2. In case of emergency, whom should we notify?
3. Is all the information on this application true?
4. Have you ever been employed by a similar concern?
5. Final rate of pay.

N/A

Not applicable; used on job applications when a section does not apply to the person looking for a job

When you begin to fill out an application, there are six important things to remember. When you finish, check your application to make sure that you have done all six.

---

1. Read the application first. Follow the directions and print clearly. Use a pen. Use capital letters where appropriate and lowercase letters otherwise—as shown in this example.

Medina	Carlos	J.
(PRINT) Last name	First name	Middle initial

2. Be sure to fill in all blanks. If something does not apply to you, put **N/A** (for Not Applicable) on the blank line.

3. Check to make sure that your application is neat and easy to read. If you have to make a correction, be as neat as possible. Use an erasable pen or correction fluid to make your correction neater.

4. Make sure that all information is correct. Use your fact sheet whenever necessary. Check to make sure that you have the correct spelling of the names of people, streets, cities, and states. Make sure that the street numbers, ZIP codes, and telephone numbers are also correct.

5. Be honest about all the information that you put on an application.

6. If possible, ask someone else to check the final version of your application.

Keep a job application neat by keeping it in a folder until you return it to the employer.

Dictionary

To make sure that you spell words on your fact sheet correctly, check the spelling in a dictionary.

Remember that a dictionary not only lists the spelling of words, it also tells how to pronounce them and gives their meanings. The words listed in a dictionary appear alphabetically. Each word in a dictionary is called an *entry*. The entry word appears in boldface type and is divided into syllables. The phonetic spelling of the word appears after the entry word and helps you pronounce it. The abbreviations that follow the phonetic spelling tell you the part of speech of the entry word. The definition of the word follows the part of speech.

To find words in the dictionary, use the guide words at the top of each page. These name the first and last words on the page.

Use a dictionary to respond to these items.

1. Write the phonetic spelling of the word *applicable*.

2. The word *experience* acts as two parts of speech. Name them.

3. Write the word *references* in syllables.

4. List all the meanings of the word *degree*. You may shorten the meanings.

5. Look up the word *signature*. Now write the guide words that appear at the top of the page.

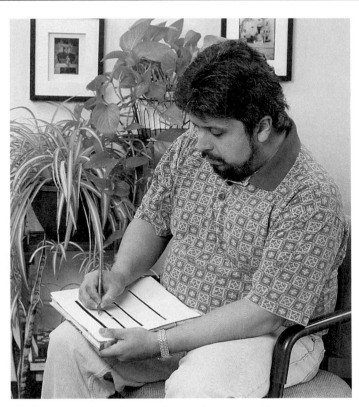

Carlos uses a fact sheet to fill out his job application.

Activity A Number your paper 1 to 10. If the statement is true, write *True* next to the number. If it is not true, write *False*.

1. A job application should be as perfect as you can make it.

2. If the directions on an application say to type, you could fill it out with a pen.

3. If something on an application does not apply to you, leave that section blank.

4. Some employers think that people who turn in messy applications will not be dependable.

5. Give your fact sheet to a potential employer.

6. You should use the same fact sheet for years.

7. Use capital letters only where appropriate.

8. Always fill in an application with a pencil.

9. Check the spelling of all words on your application.

10. Never ask someone else to check your application for you.

Other Types of Applications

Job applications are not the only forms you will fill out in your lifetime. You will have to fill out an application to get a passport, open a checking or savings account, or join a health club. Most forms begin by asking your name, address, and telephone number. Applications differ in what they ask for next.

Judy learned about the different kinds of applications before her vacation last year. She was going to Italy to see her relatives. She needed some extra money for her trip. She had to fill out a passport application and a loan application before she left.

A passport is an important document that a government issues to citizens when they travel to foreign countries. Judy found the form on the Internet at *www.travel.state.gov*. The application asked for personal information that was on her fact sheet. However, other questions asked about her height, her hair color, her eye color, and her place of birth. She also needed to supply two recent photos and had to pay a fee to process her application.

She went to City National Bank to fill out an application for a loan. This form asked for information about the money Judy had saved and the amount of rent she paid each month. Once again, Judy was glad she had her fact sheet with her.

Judy discovered that all applications tell a lot about a person, so it is best to present the neatest—and most honest—picture of yourself.

For Discussion

1. Why did Judy need a passport?

2. Name three things that most applications ask for.

3. Why do you think the loan application asked how much money Judy had saved?

Chapter 4 R E V I E W

Word Bank

fact sheet

human resources department

job application

N/A

place of birth

Social Security number

supervisor

Part A On a sheet of paper, write the correct word or words from the Word Bank to complete each sentence.

1. A _____ is a formal written request for a job.
2. A _____ is someone who is in charge of others.
3. The _____ is the part of a company that deals with employees.
4. A _____ lists information about you, including personal, career, and educational information, and references.
5. A nine-digit number used to identify Americans for government purposes is a _____ .
6. The _____ is the city and state or country where a person was born.
7. A person writes the abbreviation for not applicable, _____ , when a section does not apply to him or her.

Part B Number your paper 8 to 14. Write short answers to these questions.

8. What are two reasons for preparing a fact sheet before you apply for a job?
9. What four kinds of information should you include in your fact sheet?
10. Why should you include on a fact sheet the information that you know by memory?
11. If you are not sure how to spell a person's name, what should you do?
12. If you are not sure how to spell a street name or the name of a company, what should you do?
13. Why is it important to update your fact sheet every time you apply for a new job?
14. What six things should you do when filling out an application?

Part C Number your paper 15 to 18. Write the letter of the correct answer on your paper.

15. You should follow all _____ on an application.

    A directions   **C** capital letters

    B corrections   **D** assignments

16. Make sure you fill in all the _____ .

    A courses   **C** mistakes

    B numbers   **D** blank lines

17. If something does not apply to you, write _____ on the blank line.

    A your surname   **C** "nothing"

    B inc.   **D** N/A

18. References usually tell about _____ .

    A your age

    B your Social Security number

    C your skills in doing a job

    D your career goals

Part D Number your paper 19 to 25. Write the information you would supply for each of these items on a job application. Some items may not apply to you if you have never worked before. What should you write if something does not apply to you?

19. Place of birth

20. Job applied for or position applied for

21. List last or present employer first

22. Final rate of pay

24. Reason for leaving

25. Kind of work desired

Test-Taking Tip Try to answer all test questions as completely as possible. When asked to explain your answer, do so in complete sentences.

5

Applying for a Job by Telephone

Help-wanted ads in the newspaper often include telephone numbers for you to call. When you call these numbers, you need to know what to say and how to say it. How well you do during the telephone call often determines whether or not the company decides to interview you for a job opening.

In Chapter 5, you will learn how to prepare for a telephone call to ask about a job and what to say during the conversation.

Goals for Learning

◆ To know what information you need before applying for a job by telephone

◆ To know how to begin a telephone conversation positively when applying by telephone

◆ To learn what information to get and to give when applying by telephone

◆ To know how to end a conversation properly when applying by telephone

The telephone rang in the human resources department of Hilbert Electronics, a large company with many employees. Cynthia Dawson picked up the telephone and said, "Good morning. Human Resources, Hilbert Electronics. May I help you?"

"Yeah," said the voice at the other end. "I want a job."

Cynthia sighed to herself and thought, "Here we go again." Then she asked politely, "What job are you interested in?"

"This here job you got advertised," a woman's voice on the other end replied.

"Ma'am, we have 12 jobs advertised. Which one are you referring to?" Cynthia asked.

"The one for a stock clerk," the woman answered.

"Was that stock clerk position for the supply warehouse or for the docks?" Cynthia inquired.

"Well, I'm not sure. Wait while I find out where that newspaper went. Here we go. Guess I want the job in the supply warehouse," the woman answered.

"Then the person you need to speak to is Radia Horowitz," said Cynthia. "I'll transfer your call."

"I want to write that name down. Let me go get a pencil," said the woman.

After about three minutes of waiting, Cynthia hung up the phone. Then she turned to her friend Ming Lee and said, "I am really tired of talking to people on the telephone who do not have the slightest idea of how to make a call—especially a call applying for a job. Sometimes I wish I could give them some advice."

Ming Lee laughed. "I know just what you mean," she said. "Sometimes I think we could make a fortune if we wrote a handbook about how to apply for a job on the telephone."

"What a good idea!" exclaimed Cynthia. "We should write a handbook and send it to people who call us to apply for jobs but don't know how. They might not get a job here, but the handbook would help them the next time they make a call."

"Let's remind people to have all the information they need before they make a call," said Ming Lee.

"That's good," said Cynthia. "Let's start a list."

Ming Lee and Cynthia listed the information a person should have handy before calling to apply for a job. Here is what their list looked like.

Needed Information
1. The exact description of the job that was advertised
2. Where and when the job was advertised, including the name and date of the newspaper or job announcement
3. A fact sheet of information about education and work
4. Days and times when the applicant is available for a job interview
5. Telephone number where applicant can be reached if a call back is necessary

Helpful Hints
1. Cut out the ad from the newspaper, and have it available when you place the call.
2. Have paper and pencil available to write information given during the call—such as the date, time, and place for an interview.

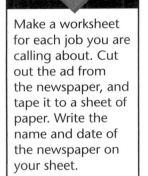

Make a worksheet for each job you are calling about. Cut out the ad from the newspaper, and tape it to a sheet of paper. Write the name and date of the newspaper on your sheet.

It was clear to Cynthia and Ming Lee that applicants have to do some work before they dial a telephone number to apply for a job. If you want to make a **good impression** during a telephone call, you will also have to have with you all the information you need. If you prepare before making the call, you will impress the people to whom you speak. They might think that you pay attention to details and organize your thoughts. This is just one way to make your first contact with a future employer a positive one.

Activity A Number your paper 1 to 6. Write short answers to these questions.

1. Why is it necessary to state the exact job for which you are applying?

2. How will a fact sheet help you during a telephone call to apply for a job?

3. Why should you tell where and when you saw the job advertised?

4. If you are asked when you can come in for an interview, why is it important that you answer immediately?

5. Why should you give a business your telephone number?

6. How does being prepared make a good impression?

Activity B On a sheet of paper, list the information you would need before you make a call to apply for the following job that was advertised in the *Pittsfield Chronicle* on November 23. Be sure to refer to Ming Lee and Cynthia's list.

STOCK CLERK to work in supply warehouse. No exp. nec. Should be good in math. Needs computer exp. Call Mr. Neal at 716-555-0800.

Interviewer

The person doing the hiring

If possible, practice your telephone call with a tape recorder. Then listen to the conversation and write down what you do well and what you need to improve.

"What do you think ought to come next?" Cynthia asked Ming Lee.

"Well, one of the things I hear from the people in the human resources department is that callers don't identify themselves. Then it takes some people a long time to get around to saying why they are calling," answered Ming Lee.

"You are absolutely right," Cynthia agreed. "Those are two complaints I have heard, too."

Cynthia and Ming Lee decided that they would make a list of some easy-to-understand steps about making telephone calls in answer to job ads.

> **Steps for Answering Ads by Telephone**
>
> 1. Say your first and last name in a clear, distinct voice.
> 2. Then say why you are calling. For example, you could say, "I am calling in answer to your ad for a stock clerk that appeared in Sunday's *Pittsfield Chronicle*."
> 3. If someone puts you on hold or transfers you to another person, wait. Then, when the second person answers, repeat steps 1 and 2.

Cynthia and Ming Lee realized that once a telephone interview begins, it is hard to know what the **interviewer** will ask. However, they did think that some general guidelines might be helpful. For example, the first thing an applicant should remember is to try to make a good impression. To do that, the applicant must remember certain things about language and behavior.

Activity A With a classmate or friend, practice beginning a telephone call in response to the ad below. Refer to the three rules that Cynthia and Ming Lee wrote.

STOCK CLERK
wanted for dock warehouse.
No exp. nec.
Call Mr. O'Leary,
716-555-7463.

> If you reach an answering machine, speak slowly. Spell your name if it might sound confusing. Give your telephone number. Briefly explain the reason for your call.

When you practice, use these situations.

1. Mr. O'Leary is the person who answers the telephone.

2. Mr. O'Leary's assistant answers the telephone.

3. Mr. O'Leary answers the telephone, but he transfers you to Mrs. Santos in the human resources department.

4. The ad tells you to ask for extension 513, but does not give the person's name at that extension.

5. When you call the number in the ad, you reach an answering machine.

Activity B Call a friend or relative. Ask that person to tell you whether your voice is clear and easy to understand. Take notes on any comments or suggestions that he or she gives you.

Vocabulary Builder

Always Be Polite

One way to create a good impression is to address people whose name you do not know as *ma'am* or *sir*. Always use *yes* instead of *yeah* or *OK*.

Each underlined word in these sentences can be replaced with a more polite word. For example, *Yes, we have that product* is more polite than *Yeah, we got that.*

Rewrite the following sentences by replacing each underlined word with a word that is more formal or polite.

1. <u>Lady</u>, we do not have that part.

2. <u>Dude</u>, would you repeat that number?

3. <u>Hey man</u>, are you interested in that new car?

4. "<u>Honey</u>, what would you like to order?" asked the waitress.

5. "<u>Yep</u>, I can do that job quickly," Miguel said.

Activity C On a sheet of paper, make three columns. Label them *Good, Bad,* and *Could Be Improved*. Then, write what is *good* about this conversation, what is *bad,* and what *could be improved* in the correct column.

Joseph Fritz: Hello, this is Joseph Fritz. I'd like to speak to
(the caller)   Mr. O'Leary.

Marcia Hunt: Hello, this is Marcia Hunt, John O'Leary's assistant.

Joseph Fritz: I want to speak to Mr. O'Leary.

Marcia Hunt: May I ask the reason for your call?

Joseph Fritz: Yeah, I'm calling about a job. What else?

Marcia Hunt: What job is that, sir?

Joseph Fritz: Stock clerk.

Marcia Hunt: Is that the stock clerk at the supply warehouse or at the dock warehouse?

Joseph Fritz: *(a little annoyed)* The dock warehouse—if that makes any difference.

Marcia Hunt: What are your qualifications for this job?

Joseph Fritz: I don't know. I never had a job like it before.

Marcia Hunt: *(sounding bored)* Did you graduate from high school?

Joseph Fritz: Yeah, but can I talk to Mr. O'Leary now?

Marcia Hunt: *(coldly)* Unfortunately, Mr. O'Leary is not available right now, but if you give me your telephone number, I'll have him call you if he wants any more information.

Joseph Fritz: Yeah, OK. Area code 210-555-4952.

Marcia Hunt: Thank you. *(hangs up)*

The Wrong Way

After Mr. O'Leary reads the notes of the conversation between his assistant and Joseph Fritz, do you think he'll call Joseph back? Unfortunately, Joseph probably lost the chance to get the job because of the mistakes he made.

- Joseph did not repeat his name to Marcia or use the word *please*.

- He neglected to tell Marcia his reason for calling. She had to ask him.

- He did not say where he had seen the ad for the stock clerk's job.

- He did not tell Marcia any qualifications he might have for the job.

- He was rude in answering Marcia's questions.

- Overall, Joseph gave the impression that he did not care about the job.

- Moreover, because Joseph did not give all the information he should have given to Marcia, he did not make a good impression.

What should Joseph have said during this telephone call? What might have helped him make a good impression?

Spelling Builder

Capital Letters

Suki was getting ready to write a letter of application to a local business. However, she did not know which words in the business's name and the product's name to capitalize.

Remember that the names of businesses are proper nouns and should begin with capital letters. For example, capitalize *Bank of New York* or the *Dettman Clothing Factory*.

Capitalize brand names of products, but begin the common noun that follows a brand name with a lowercase letter. For example, for Connally's china, capitalize the *c* in Connally but not in the word *china*.

Number your paper 1 to 5. Correct the mistakes in capitalization in the following phrases.

1. Craine's mobile technology, inc.
2. Angus Beef
3. Homestead Dairy and cheese Company
4. Pickens Cars
5. vegetable delight restaurant

Joseph should have followed these steps during his telephone conversation.

1. Politely repeated his name and reason for calling to each person with whom he spoke.

2. Answered the questions about qualifications by listing his **personal qualifications,** or qualities that would show he was a good person to hire. For example, he could have said, "I had a good attendance record at school. I enjoy working with numbers, and I know how to keep very accurate records. I follow directions well."

3. Used correct English, not **slang** such as *yeah.*

4. Used the last name of the person to whom he was speaking. Calling a person by name (when you know it) is polite and makes a good impression.

5. Asked for information he might need about the job. For example, he could have asked about the location of the job, the hours, and the type of work. (Some people prefer to discuss salary in person rather than over the telephone.)

6. Finally, he should have found out whether he could have an interview; if so, he should have asked for a specific time and place.

When job applicants call Hilbert Electronics, they speak to Ming Lee first. You should make a good impression on everyone you talk to when applying by telephone.

Joseph never reached steps 5 and 6 because Marcia ended the telephone call. She lost interest in talking with him and probably decided that Joseph was not the kind of person the company wanted to hire. Assistants like Marcia often rule out job applicants who do not make a good impression.

Where To Find It

Using a Thesaurus

Have you ever thought of an idea but could not find the exact word to say what you mean? A thesaurus might help you find that word. It contains synonyms and sometimes antonyms.

Entry words in a thesaurus appear in alphabetical order, much like they do in a dictionary. The word's part of speech and its definition follow the entry word. A list of synonyms comes next. Synonyms usually appear in italics. Antonyms are usually in boldface type.

When you use a thesaurus, look for synonyms you know. If you decide to use an unfamiliar word, check its meaning in a dictionary to be sure it matches the idea you want to express.

Using a thesaurus, find synonyms for the following words and list them on your paper. Then choose the best synonyms to use in the sentences to replace the italicized words. If none have the right meaning, keep the original word. Write the new sentences on your paper.

1. meet (verb)
2. employer (noun)
3. job (noun)
4. honest (adjective)
5. talk (verb)

A Will you *meet* with that *employer* about a *job?*

B Companies value *honest* people.

C Interviewers *talk* to people about employment.

A Better Conversation

A better way for Joseph to handle the call would be this.

Marcia Hunt:	This is Mr. O'Leary's office, Marcia Hunt speaking.
Joseph Fritz:	Hello, Ms. Hunt. My name is Joseph Fritz. I am calling in answer to your ad in Sunday's *Pittsfield Chronicle* for a stock clerk in your dock warehouse.
Marcia Hunt:	Just one minute; I'll put you through to Mr. O'Leary.
Mr. O'Leary:	This is John O'Leary.
Joseph Fritz:	Good morning. Mr. O'Leary, my name is Joseph Fritz. I'm calling in answer to your ad in Sunday's *Pittsfield Chronicle* for a stock clerk in your dock warehouse.
Mr. O'Leary:	Fine, Mr. Fritz. What are your qualifications for the job?
Joseph Fritz:	Well, sir, I'm good at keeping accurate records. In fact, I kept records of the stock in a grocery store last summer. I also got good grades in math in school, and I had a perfect attendance record in high school.
Mr. O'Leary:	Did you graduate?
Joseph Fritz:	Yes, Mr. O'Leary. I graduated in June. Can you tell me something about the job, sir? What would I be doing?

Mr. O'Leary:	You would keep records of all incoming stock received at our dock warehouse. You would also be responsible for letting the manager know when to order more stock.
Joseph Fritz:	I know I could handle that, sir. Where is the warehouse located?
Mr. O'Leary:	It's at 110 Water Street.
Joseph Fritz:	Yes, I know where that is.
Mr. O'Leary:	You sound like someone I would like to talk to, Mr. Fritz. Would it be possible for you come for an interview with me tomorrow at 10:00 A.M.?
Joseph Fritz:	Yes, sir. Where are your offices located?
Mr. O'Leary:	My office is in the Steel Building on the corner of Maple and Evergreen Streets, Suite 553.
Joseph Fritz:	(*reading his notes*) That's the Steel Building, Maple and Evergreen Streets, Suite 553, at 10 o'clock tomorrow morning.
Mr. O'Leary:	That's correct.
Joseph Fritz:	Thank you, Mr. O'Leary. I'll be there. Good-bye.

Joseph's organization and courtesy impressed Marcia. That could be the reason she transferred the call quickly. Joseph's polite manner, experience, and personal qualifications impressed Mr. O'Leary, too, which may be why he set up an interview with Joseph.

Activity A Number your paper 1 to 8. If the statement is true, write *True* next to the number. If the statement is not true, write *False*.

1. Always keep your **tone** of voice polite and patient.

2. Give your name and the reason for calling to the first person who answers the phone. After that, just give your name.

3. Use the name of the person to whom you are speaking.

4. Write all the information given, and read it back to make sure that it is correct.

5. Never ask questions about the job during an interview on the telephone. Wait to ask questions about the job until you can speak to the interviewer in person.

6. If you don't have any work experience for the job advertised, list the personal qualifications that you think would help you do a good job.

7. Never use slang. Use correct English.

8. If you know the name of the person, you may use it when you are speaking.

In addition to making certain he had written all the information correctly, Joseph Fritz thanked Mr. O'Leary before saying good-bye. Cynthia and Ming Lee think that the way you end a conversation is almost as important as the way you begin it. People often remember the last thing they hear.

Also remember that you should never make a conversation longer than it has to be. Don't risk making the person you are talking to impatient and annoyed. Instead, save questions about details for the job interview.

Activity B Number your paper 1 to 10. If the statement will help make a good impression, write *Good* next to the number. If the statement will help make a bad impression, write *Bad.* Be prepared to explain why you labeled the statement *Good* or *Bad.*

1. "Okay. Yeah, I'll come."

2. "Yes, sir. I'll be there."

3. "Don't talk so fast. I can't get all this stuff down."

4. "Last summer I didn't have a job, but now I think I should have. The experience would have been good. Actually, my mother wanted me to get a job."

5. "Gee, this is great! Of course, I'll come in for an interview. See you then."

6. "Would you mind going a little slower? I want to make sure that I get all this information down correctly."

7. "Thank you very much. I'll see you tomorrow morning at 10 o'clock in your office."

8. "I don't know nothing about your company."

9. "I ain't got any experience."

10. "Would you please give Mr. O'Leary my name and telephone number, Ms. Hunt?"

Accent the Positive

Rob looked through the newspaper ads for a job. He has never had a full-time job, and he told his sister Kim that he does not think he has any skills.

"Why would anyone want to hire me?" asked Rob.

"Stop and think a minute," said Kim. "What do you do well, and what things do people like about you?"

"My science teacher says that I never give up, even when the problems are tough," said Rob.

"Okay. That means that you are persistent. Employers like that in an employee," said Kim.

"My English teacher says that she likes my friendliness and patience with other students. She knows I am always on time for class," said Rob.

"That means that you are on time, friendly, and patient. Those are all important qualities for an employee," said Kim.

"But if I tell employers these things, won't they think I am bragging?" asked Rob.

"Not at all," said Kim. "If you do not tell them what you do well, no one else will."

For Discussion

1. What good personal qualifications does Rob have?

2. Why would an employer believe that these skills are important?

3. Why is Rob unsure about telling an employer about his personal qualifications?

4. Why is it important to tell an employer your personal qualifications?

5. If Rob has won an award for the most-improved science student, should he tell an employer? Why or why not?

Chapter 5   R E V I E W

Part A On a sheet of paper, write the correct word or words from the Word Bank to complete each sentence.

1. Qualities about a person that will be valuable on the job, including honesty and courtesy, are _____ .

2. _____ is language that is not formal or proper.

3. When you make a _____ , other people think well of you because you are polite and use proper behavior.

4. _____ is a way of speaking or writing that expresses a certain mood, style, or feeling.

5. An _____ is the person doing the hiring.

Part B Number your paper 6 to 15. Then rewrite these activities in the order in which you would probably do them when applying for a job by telephone.

- Give the qualifications I have for the job.
- Identify the job for which I am applying.
- Give my personal qualifications.
- Have my fact sheet and a pencil and paper handy.
- Give my name.
- Give the reason for my call.
- List the days and times I am available for an interview.
- Thank the person for his or her assistance and time.
- Repeat my name and the reason for my call if someone transfers the call.
- Tell where I saw the job advertised.

Part C Number your paper 16 to 18. Then write short answers for these questions.

16. What should you say if an interviewer asks about your qualifications and you do not have any work experience?

17. Why should you avoid using slang or incorrect English when you call about a job?

18. Why should you repeat directions the interviewer gives you?

Part D Number your paper 19 to 22. If the statement is true, write *True* next to the number. If the statement is not true, write *False*.

19. Making a good impression is important when you call about a job.

20. It is not important to be polite to the person who first answers the telephone.

21. You cannot talk too much during a telephone call. The more you say about yourself, the more the employer will like you.

22. Even if you know the last name of the person to whom you are talking, it is not a good idea to use it.

Part E On your paper, write the letter of the correct answer.

23. Which of the following words should you always use when calling about a job?

    A please   **B** yeah   **C** dude   **D** ain't

24. What tone of voice should you use in a telephone call to a business?

    A angry   **B** informal   **C** polite   **D** sad

25. Which of the following does NOT belong on a worksheet you use to place a telephone call?

    A exact description of the job you are calling about

    B how you found out about the job

    C the name of your best friend

    D times you are available for an interview

Test-Taking Tip When taking a true-false test, look for words such as *many, some, sometimes, usually,* and *may*. These words mean that the statement can have exceptions.

Being Interviewed

6

If you get an interview at a company, you have a good chance of getting a job there. That is why it is so important that you make a good impression at the interview. Of course, your chance to make a good impression begins long before the interview actually takes place and continues until the moment you leave the interview.

In Chapter 6, you will learn what to do before an interview, what to do during an interview, and what to do at the end of an interview.

Goals for Learning

◆ To know how to dress for an interview

◆ To understand the importance of neatness and cleanliness for an interview

◆ To be able to answer questions correctly and completely during an interview

◆ To know how to speak clearly during an interview

◆ To understand the importance of nonverbal signals in an interview

Barry Cohen was very nervous the day before his job interview. His teachers, his parents, and his friends had all warned him that how he acted and looked would have a lot to do with whether or not he would get the job.

Barry really wanted this job. It was the kind of work he liked. The pay was good, and the company had good benefits. There was no doubt in his mind that the company would be a good place to work.

It made sense to Barry to do everything he could to make a good impression. As he thought about the interview, he decided that he should concentrate on three areas: how he looked, how he answered the interviewer's questions, and how well he **communicated** or let others know how he felt.

Barry's mother told him, "When you are applying for most jobs, you should wear business clothes such as a jacket and a tie." Then she reminded him that everything he planned to wear should be clean and free of stains. As a result, Barry took his suit to the cleaners, and he made sure that he had a clean shirt and tie. He even polished his shoes.

It's important to make a good impression in an interview.

Makeup that looks natural makes a better impression than makeup that is applied too heavily. Very unusual lipstick or eye shadow may make a bad impression.

Then on the morning of the interview, Barry got up early enough to shave, shower, and wash his hair. Here are some other hints to help you prepare for an interview.

Helpful Hints for Preparing for an Interview
• Trim your hair and comb it neatly.
• Trim and clean your fingernails, use deodorant, and brush your teeth.
• Don't wear too much jewelry. Many chains or long, dangling earrings are not businesslike.
• Wear clean clothing that makes you look serious about working.
• Avoid wearing loud colors. You want people to focus on you and your answers, not on what you are wearing.
• Be as neat as possible. Iron the clothes you will wear. Replace missing buttons and mend any tears.
• When you are dressed and ready to go to the interview, check the way you look in a mirror. You could even ask someone else how you look.

Because the people who interview you will judge you by your appearance first, you need to look good. Just remember that looking good for a job interview is not the same as looking good for a dance or some other social event.

Activity A On your paper, draw the following chart and label the three columns. Then write each of these items in the correct column.

Preparing for an Interview		
Two or Three Days Ahead	The Night Before	That Morning

brush teeth	press clothes
get suit cleaned	use deodorant
iron shirt or blouse	shine shoes
replace buttons	clean and file nails
shower	wear small amount of jewelry
shave	check appearance in a mirror
wash hair	make needed repairs
get a haircut	

Where To Find It

Using the Internet to Get Directions

Imagine that you schedule an interview with the manager of City National Bank. The bank is in another part of the city, and you are not sure how to get there.

You could use a map, but it's easier to use the Internet. Special map Web sites will give you directions from your home to the location you want. They will also tell you the distance and the amount of time it will take to drive there.

Select driving directions; then enter the starting and ending points of your trip. The program will give you written directions and allow you to print a map.

Go to one of the map programs on a computer. Find and print out directions to the following places.

1. from your home to your school
2. from the nearest library to your school
3. from your school to the nearest shopping mall

Receptionist

A person whose job it is to greet the public, answer questions, direct people to offices, etc.; the receptionist is often the first contact people have with a company

Barry sat nervously in the waiting room. He had thrown away his chewing gum before he got to the office. One of his teachers had said that chewing gum during an interview made a bad impression. Finally, the **receptionist** said to him, "Ms. Mendez will see you now, Mr. Cohen." Barry walked into Ms. Mendez's office and then introduced himself.

"Hello, Ms. Mendez. My name is Barry Cohen, and I have an interview at 10 o'clock." He waited until Ms. Mendez invited him to sit down. Then he sat patiently until she asked the first question.

Allow extra time to get to your interview. If you arrive late, you will make a bad impression.

During the interview, Barry listened carefully to each question. He thought about his answers and made sure he answered each question completely. He answered in a clear, easy-to-understand voice, and he looked at Ms. Mendez as he spoke. If he needed to be sure of a date or an address or the spelling of a name, he checked his fact sheet or résumé, which he had brought with him.

When the interview was over, Barry politely thanked Ms. Mendez for the interview and handed her a copy of his résumé. Then he asked when he might hear from her.

Barry believed that he had handled the interview well. As an extra show of thanks, Barry sent Ms. Mendez a thank-you letter.

Barry knew that writing a thank-you letter after an interview could improve his chances of getting a job. He remembered to include

Writing Tip

Always use the interviewer's title and last name in a thank-you letter. For example, use *Dear Mr. Johnson,* not *Dear Fred.*

- the title of the job for which he interviewed
- a reminder to Ms. Mendez of his interest in the job
- several ways that his personal qualifications fit the job.

Barry ended his thank-you letter with a statement that he hoped to hear from Ms. Mendez soon. He mailed the letter the day after his interview.

Activity A Number your paper 1 to 5. Then list at least five things that Barry did that probably impressed Ms. Mendez.

Although there is no way you can guess all the questions an interviewer will ask you, remember that the aim of most questions is to determine how well you can do the job. You should always answer truthfully and completely. If you do not know the answer to a question, say so politely.

During an interview, communication is very important. There are several ways people express their ideas, including through their words and their attitudes. However, people can communicate without using words. The expression on a person's face and the way that he or she moves can send messages to another person. This **nonverbal communication,** or body language, usually includes how people sit or stand and how they look at others.

Alice Blue, the person Ms. Mendez interviewed after Barry, did not get the job because she did not express important information well. Alice came into Ms. Mendez's office with her head down and plopped into the chair nearest to the door. She mumbled the answers to the questions and sometimes used poor grammar and slang. When the interview was over, Alice left without saying anything. Alice did not get the job because she did not answer the questions carefully and her manners were poor.

On the other hand, Barry did get the job because he understood the importance of communication. He knew that how well he communicated could make the difference between getting a job and not getting it. He acted as if he really wanted the job.

Activity B Number your paper 1 to 5. Write the letter of the best answer on your paper. Listed below and on page 106 are situations that could happen during a job interview. Be prepared to explain why your choice is the best answer.

1. The interviewer asks you why you want the job. You answer,

    A "I need the money."

    B "I'm interested in this kind of work."

    C "My father told me to get a job."

    D "Well, I was fired from my last job."

2. The interviewer asks you a question to which you do not know the answer. You say,

    A "I read about that somewhere. It was in some magazine, I think."

    B "Whatever you think."

    C "I'm sorry. I don't know the answer to that question."

    D "I dunno."

3. The interviewer tells you this job requires you to work one Saturday a month. You say,

    A "I can manage that."

    B "You've got to be kidding. I don't want to work on Saturdays."

    C "I play baseball on Saturdays."

    D "I hope that doesn't mean I have to get up early."

Vocabulary Builder

Good and Well

When someone asks you how you feel, should you say "I feel good," or "I feel well"?

Remember that *good* can only be an adjective, a word that describes a noun. *Well* can be either an adjective or an adverb. When you say you are *well,* you are saying that you feel healthy. *Well* is also an adverb to tell how something is done.

In an interview when someone asks how you are, the correct answer is "I feel *well,* thank you."

Number your paper 1 to 3. Select either *good* or *well* to complete the following sentences.

    1. I play (good/well).

    2. The (good/well) copy is on the printer.

    3. I do not go to the doctor when I am (good/well).

4. The interviewer asks you how your English grades were in school. You say,

   A "I ain't never got nothin' lower than a C."

   B "I have good grades in English."

   C "I do good in English."

   D "I hated my English classes."

5. The interviewer asks you why you were fired from your last job. You

   A get angry and snap, "None of your business!"

   B look down at the floor and mumble, "I don't know."

   C look at the interviewer and say, "The company downsized, and I was laid off."

   D start to cry and say, "Everyone hates me."

Spelling Builder

Correct Pronunciations

When you interview for a job, you will make a better impression if you pronounce words correctly. Some common words that people often misspell and pronounce incorrectly are *congratulate, February,* and *government.* Most people pronounce these words incorrectly because they do not know how to spell them.

Read aloud the following sentences. Then copy each italicized word onto your paper and underline the letters in each word that are often forgotten or incorrect.

  1. I finished my class in *February.*

  2. I worked in a *government* office for three years.

  3. My employer *congratulated* me when I was hired.

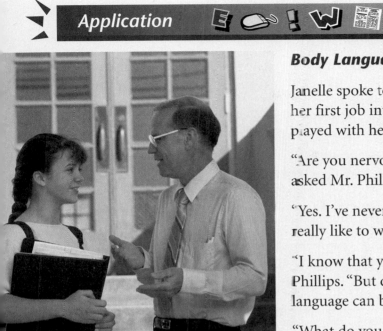

Body Language

Janelle spoke to her teacher, Mr. Phillips, about her first job interview. As she talked with him, she played with her braid.

"Are you nervous about this interview, Janelle?" asked Mr. Phillips.

"Yes. I've never had an interview before, and I'd really like to work for this company," said Janelle.

"I know that your skills are excellent," said Mr. Phillips. "But do you know how important body language can be in an interview?"

"What do you mean?" asked Janelle.

"Body language is how you act. If you bite your fingernails during an interview, for example, the interviewer will see that you are nervous. The interviewer may think you could not handle the job."

"What other kinds of body language might keep me from getting a job?" asked Janelle.

"Not making eye contact with the interviewer may make the person think that you are not telling the truth," said Mr. Phillips. "Be aware of body language, try to relax, and do your best. Good luck on Tuesday."

For Discussion

1. What did Mr. Phillips say body language is?

2. Why is body language important to some interviewers?

3. What examples of body language did Mr. Phillips mention to Janelle?

4. What bad impressions can body language create?

5. How does Mr. Phillips say Janelle can avoid body language mistakes?

Chapter 6   R E V I E W

Part A On a sheet of paper, write the correct word or words from the Word Bank to complete each sentence.

1. The job of a _____ is to greet the public, answer questions, and direct people to offices.
2. Body language, or _____ , includes how people sit or stand and how they look at others.
3. To _____ is to let other people know how you feel about something.

Part B Number your paper 4 to 10. Then write the correct answer from the box that completes each statement. Use each answer only once.

cleaners	hair	time
ahead	clean	teeth
polish	communicate	

4. When you go for a job interview, everything about you should be _____ .
5. This statement means that you must plan _____ .
6. If you plan to wear clothing that cannot be washed, allow _____ to send the clothing to the _____ .
7. _____ your shoes.
8. Shampoo your _____ .
9. Be sure to use deodorant and brush your _____ .
10. An interviewer knows that you care about getting the job when you _____ well.

Part C Number your paper 11 to 16. If the statement is true, write *True* next to the number. If the statement is not true, write *False*.

11. When you need to repair something that you plan to wear to an interview, mend it neatly.
12. If you have an interview during lunch hour, be sure to bring food. Offer it to the interviewer.

13. Broken nails look okay.

14. Don't ask other people how you look.

15. The color of your clothes is not important at all.

16. Always wear jeans to an interview, no matter what job you would like to have.

Part D Rewrite these sentences, correcting any errors.

17. Ain't I got an appointment?

18. My name be Patrick.

19. I doesn't know that.

20. Yeah, okay.

21. I think that you and me will get along fine.

22. What for do you wanna know that?

Part E On your paper, write the letter of the correct answer.

23. When an interviewer asks how you are, your reply should be _____
   A "None of your business."   **C** "I am good."
   B "I ain't so good today."   **D** "I am well."

24. How would you introduce yourself to Mr. John Estevez?
   A "Hey, Jack."   **C** "Hello, John."
   B "Hello, Mr. Estevez."   **D** "What's up, Mr. Estevez?"

25. Which of the following should you do during an interview?
   A thank the interviewer for taking the time to interview you
   B chew gum, since it will make your breath smell better
   C play with your car keys to keep from getting nervous
   D look down at the floor as often as possible

Test-Taking Tip To prepare for a test, study in short sessions rather than one long session. In the week before the test, spend time each evening reviewing your notes.

7 Starting a New Job

Knowing what to expect when you start a new job will help you make a good impression on your supervisor and fellow workers. The best advice is to read and follow all instructions carefully. If you have questions, ask your supervisor. Asking a few questions is better than making mistakes during your first weeks on a new job.

In Chapter 7, you will get some good advice that will help you get through the first weeks of a new job. You will also learn the areas that the company will examine to evaluate your performance. If you know what to expect, you will find it easier to be successful.

Goals for Learning

◆ To learn how to fill out a W-4 form

◆ To understand the importance of a company's rules and regulations

◆ To find areas within a company building

◆ To understand the structure of a company

◆ To learn the main points of a job evaluation

W-4 form

An IRS form that decides the amount of money taken out of your paycheck for income tax

Internal Revenue Service (IRS)

The government agency charged with collecting taxes

Withholding

An amount of money subtracted from your paycheck and given to the IRS as part or all of your income tax

Allowances

Items that determine the amount of money to be withheld for a person's income tax

Although Shaun Owens and Bill Yee had never met, they reported to work at the same time for their first day at Beacon Industries. By the end of the first week, Shaun no longer had a job, but Bill was doing fine. What happened to them could also happen to you. Take a look at their first day.

Ms. Jackson, the head of human resources at Beacon Industries, asked Shaun and Bill to fill out a **W-4,** an **Internal Revenue Service (IRS)** form. Federal law says that you must complete this form when a company hires you. A W-4 tells an employer how much money you want held back from your wages for federal income tax. The company holds back from each of your paychecks some of the taxes that you will owe the government at the end of the year. The company keeps all W-4s to verify that it is **withholding** federal income tax according to your instructions.

Shaun made a mistake on three forms. On the fourth try, he made another mistake. It would have caused the employer to take out more money from Shaun's wages than was necessary. Bill, however, filled out his form correctly the first time because he read and understood the instructions. Reading tax forms of any kind can be confusing, but some practice will help you understand them.

Understanding the following words on a W-4 form will also help you the next time you have to complete one.

Withholding on a W-4 form is the amount of money that the company subtracts from your salary. You pay this part of your salary directly to the IRS as part or all of your income tax.

Allowances are things the government will consider when deciding the amount of money to withhold from your salary as income tax.

Dependents

Children or other people who may not work and who count on you for more than half of their needs

Spouse

Your husband or wife

Exempt

To free from a duty or rule; means money does not have to be withheld

Deductions

Expenses considered when determining taxable income; you do not have to pay income taxes on such expenses

You can claim from zero to several allowances. For example, you can claim one allowance for yourself. The W-4 form describes other allowances. The more allowances you claim, the less money your employer will withhold from your paycheck. Follow the directions on the W-4 form.

Dependents are an allowance. Dependents are children or other people who do not work and who rely on you for food, shelter, and clothing. You can claim another allowance for your husband or wife (your **spouse**). You can claim additional allowances if your spouse does not work.

On the W-4 form, **exempt** means that the company does not have to withhold money as taxes from your pay. Some students can be exempt from withholding. If you have a green card you could be exempt.

A **deduction** is an expense considered when determining taxable income. For example, you do not pay taxes on some expenses such as donations to charities, home mortgage interest payments, and state and local taxes.

Activity A Number your paper 1 to 6. Then match each income tax term in the first column with its meaning or explanation in the second column.

Terms	Meanings
1. spouse	A expenses the government considers when deciding what amount of money will be withheld from your paycheck
2. allowance	B expenses for which you do not pay taxes
3. dependents	C your husband or wife
4. deductions	D the part of your paycheck paid to the IRS as income tax
5. withholding	E people who count on you for food, clothing, and shelter
6. exempt	F means that money does not have to be withheld from your wages

Personal Allowances Worksheet (Keep for your records.)

A Enter "1" for **yourself** if no one else can claim you as a dependent . . . . **A** _____

B Enter "1" if: {
- You are single and have only one job; or
- You are married, have only one job, and your spouse does not work; or
- Your wages from a second job or your spouse's wages (or the total of both) are $1,000 or less. } . . **B** _____

C Enter "1" for your **spouse**. But, you may choose to enter -0- if you are married and have either a working spouse or more than one job. (Entering -0- may help you avoid having too little tax withheld) . . . . **C** _____

D Enter number of **dependents** (other than your spouse or yourself) you will claim on your tax return . . . . **D** _____

E Enter "1" if you will file as **head of household** on your tax return (see conditions under **Head of household** above) . . **E** _____

F Enter "1" if you have at least $1,500 of **child or dependent care expenses** for which you plan to claim a credit . . **F** _____
(**Note:** Do **not** include child support payments. See **Pub. 503**, Child and Dependent Care Expenses, for details.)

G **Child Tax Credit** (including additional child tax credit):
- If your total income will be between $18,000 and $50,000 ($23,000 and $63,000 if married), enter "1" for each eligible child
- If your total income will be between $50,000 and $80,000 ($63,000 and $115,000 if married), enter "1" if you have two eligible children, enter "2" if you have three or four eligible children, or enter "3" if you have five or more eligible children. **G** _____

H Add lines A through G and enter total here. (**Note:** This may be different from the number of exemptions you claim on your tax return.) ▶ **H** _____

For accuracy, complete all worksheets that apply. {
- If you plan to **itemize or claim adjustments to income** and want to reduce your withholding, see the **Deductions and Adjustments Worksheet** on page 2.
- If you are **single**, have **more than one job** and your combined earnings from all jobs exceed $35,000 **or** if you are **married** and have a **working spouse or more than one job** and the combined earnings from all jobs exceed $60,000, see the **Two-Earner/Two-Job Worksheet** on page 2 if you want to avoid having too little tax withheld.
- If **neither** of the above situations applies, **stop here** and enter the number from line H on line 5 of Form W-4 below. }

- - - - - - - - - - - - - - - - Cut here and give Form W-4 to your employer. Keep the top part for your records. - - - - - - - - - - - - - - - -

Form **W-4** Department of the Treasury Internal Revenue Service	**Employee's Withholding Allowance Certificate** ▶ **For Privacy Act and Paperwork Reduction Act Notice, see page 2.**	OMB No. 1545-0010 2003

1 Type or print your first name and middle initial	Last Name		**2** Your social security number

Home address (number and street or rural route)

3 ☐ Single ☐ Married ☐ Married, but withholding at higher Single rate.
Note: If married, but legally separated, or spouse is a nonresident alien, check the Single box.

City or town, state, and ZIP code

4 If your last name differs from that on your social security card, check here. You must call 1-800-772-1213 for a new card. ▶ ☐

5 Total number of allowances you are claiming (from line **H** above **or** from the worksheets on page 2) . . . . . . **5** _____

6 Additional amount, if any, you want withheld from each paycheck . . . . **6** $ _____

7 I claim exemption from withholding for 2003 and I certify that I meet **both** of the following conditions for exemption:
- Last year I had a right to a refund of **all** Federal income tax withheld because I had **no** tax liability.
- This year I expect a refund of **all** Federal income tax withheld because I expect to have **no** tax liability.

If you meet both conditions, write "Exempt" here . . . . ▶ **7** _____

Under penalties of perjury, I certify that I am entitled to the number of withholding allowances claimed on this certificate, or I am entitled to claim exempt status.

Employee's signature
(Form is not valid unless you sign it.) ▶ _____ Date ▶ _____

8 Employer's name and address (Employer: Complete lines 8 and 10 only if sending to the IRS).	**9** Office code (optional)	**10** Employer identification number

Activity B On a separate sheet of paper, write the information you would fill out for items 1, 2, and 3 on the W-4 form shown on page 114.

1. Your full name, home address (including the number and street or rural route), city or town, state, and ZIP code

2. Your Social Security number

3. Your marital status: Single; Married; Married, but withhold at higher single rate

See whether you could do as well as Bill did filling out a W-4 form. Read the directions on the W-4 form on page 114. Then answer the questions in Activity C.

Activity C Number your paper 1 to 5. Then write short answers for these questions about a W-4 Personal Allowances Worksheet. Refer to the W-4 form on page 114.

1. On line A, can you claim yourself if your parents claim you as a dependent? When can you claim yourself?

2. You and your spouse work; what do you enter on line C?

3. You are single and earned $1,987 on a second job. What do you enter on line B?

4. You have one job; your spouse does not work. Where do you enter the number 1?

5. You have two children, ages three and five, who live with you. Your spouse works. What number do you enter on line D?

Your salary, your number of dependents, and your expenses will all determine how you complete a W-4 form. Because tax laws change often, you may need to change the amount of money withheld from your paycheck from time to time. If you do not understand how to complete this form, ask your employer or someone in the human resources department of your company. You may also call the IRS to get help or to get the latest information.

Regulations

Rules of behavior

Time card

A card used with a time clock to record an employee's starting and quitting times during each day on the job

Status

The condition or rank of an employee

Probation

A period of time during which workers prove that they can do a job

Once Shaun and Bill filled out their W-4 forms, Ms. Jackson gave them a list of the company's rules. She told them to read the list carefully because the company could fire any employee who broke the rules.

Company Rules and **Regulations**
Beacon Industries

Employee Rules

1. Working Hours

   Working hours are 8:30 A.M. to 5:00 P.M. You may take two 15-minute breaks daily. Your lunch period runs from noon to 12:30 P.M. All employees must punch the time clock at the start and finish of each day and also before and after the lunch break. You are responsible for your own **time card.** Do not punch another person's time card. The number of hours on your time card determines your pay.

2. Employee **Status**

   All new employees will be on **probation** for the first six months they work at Beacon Industries. The human resources department can place an employee on probation at any time if his or her work is less than satisfactory for any given evaluation period.

3. Wage Policies

   An employee will receive a pay raise and be removed from probation after six months of satisfactory service. The company gives pay raises annually. Employees are paid each Friday for the work done the week before.

Activity A Number your paper 1 to 5. If the statement is true, write *True* next to the number. If the statement is not true, write *False.*

1. At Beacon Industries, you can eat lunch whenever you want as long as you don't take more than 30 minutes.

2. You must be at work by 8:00 A.M., and you may leave at 5:00 P.M.

3. You get one 15-minute break every day.

4. You must punch the time clock four times each day.

5. You can punch another person's time card if he or she is in a hurry.

Activity B If you begin work on Monday, March 5, when will you get your first paycheck? Remember, according to the rules and regulations, the company pays you each Friday for the work that you did the week before.

Spelling Builder

Taxing Terms

When you fill out your W-4 form, you will see some terms that may be difficult to spell such as *government, exemption,* and *withholding.*

Look at each word carefully. You can see the words from which they are made. Remembering these base words will help you spell them correctly.

For example, the word *government* includes the base word *govern,* meaning "to rule." Many people forget to pronounce the *n* in *government,* so they misspell the word.

When you spell the word *exemption,* remember the base word *exempt.* Because *exempt* ends in *-t,* you must keep the *-t* in *exemption.*

Withholding is a combination of *with* and *holding.* Keep both *-h's* to spell *withholding* correctly.

Number your paper 1 to 5. List the base word in the following words. Then think of a short rule to help you remember how to spell these words.

1. dependent
2. allowance
3. adjustment
4. deduction
5. itemize

More Regulations

Shaun and Bill continued to read the company's rules. With discouragement in his voice, Shaun said, "This company has rules about everything. You can't do anything around here!"

"I think the rules make sense," Bill said. "Beacon has a business to run. You can't expect to do just what you want to," he added. "These rules seem fair to me."

General Rules and Regulations

1. Be at your **workstation** by 8:30 A.M. If you are sick, call your manager by 8:30 A.M. Constant absence and lateness are grounds for dismissal.

2. For everyone's health and safety, do not smoke inside the building.

3. Do not use the telephone for personal business except in an emergency.

4. If your manager rates your work unsatisfactory, you will have six months to improve your rating. If you do not improve, the company will dismiss you.

5. Any employee found guilty of **sexual harassment** is subject to automatic dismissal and possible criminal charges.

Activity C Number your paper 1 to 5. Then write short answers to these questions.

1. It takes you half an hour to get to work. You are due at your workstation at 8:30 A.M. You can get a bus that leaves your corner at 7:40 A.M., another that leaves your corner at 7:50 A.M., and another that leaves your corner at 8:00 A.M. Which bus or buses should you take to get to work on time? Why?

2. If you are sick and cannot go to work, what should you do?

3. Why are employees not allowed to smoke in the building?

4. Why might it be a good idea to tell your family and friends not to call you at work unless there is a real emergency?

5. In June your manager rates your work as unsatisfactory. By what month must you bring up that rating? What will happen if you don't improve your rating?

When Shaun and Bill filled out their W-4 forms, each of them received a set of safety rules. Ms. Jackson told them to read the rules before they did anything else. Here are the rules Shaun and Bill received.

Beacon Industries

Safety Rules

1. Unless you are working with a manager, do not operate any machinery. You must be properly trained to run the equipment.

2. Be sure that all safety devices are in place before operating any machine.

3. In case of a breakdown or faulty operation, shut off all machinery and report to your department manager.

4. Do not wear open-toed shoes, neckties, rings, loose clothing, or jewelry of any kind. Keep your hair short or contained; long hair poses a safety risk because it can become caught in the machinery.

5. Keep your jacket or coat and valuables in your assigned locker.

These rules come under the U.S. Occupational Safety and Health Administration (OSHA).

Activity D Number your paper 1 to 5. Then complete these safety rules for Beacon Industries.

1. Do not try to use any machine unless _____.

2. In case the machine breaks, _____ and _____.

3. If the machine is not working right, _____ and _____.

4. Do not wear _____, _____, _____, _____, or any kind of _____.

5. Store your jacket, coat, and any valuables in your _____.

Where To Find It

IRS Online

If you need information about federal taxes, you may find the answers on the Internet at the IRS Web site (*www.irs.gov*).

The home page features a list of topics that make finding answers easy. Some of these topics include frequently asked questions (FAQs), forms you might need to fill out, books and information published by the IRS, information on how to file your taxes, and many other topics.

Using a computer with Internet access, go to the IRS Web site (*www.irs.gov*), and write down the answers to these questions.

1. What is one frequently asked question on the IRS Web site?

2. What three forms can you download from the Web site?

3. What is the IRS e-mail address for taxpayers who have questions?

After Shaun and Bill read the company rules, they went to their workstations. Because Beacon Industries is in a large building, Ms. Jackson gave them a floor plan, or a map, to help them find their way. Shaun would work in area B, and Bill would work in area D.

Here is a copy of the floor plan they received.

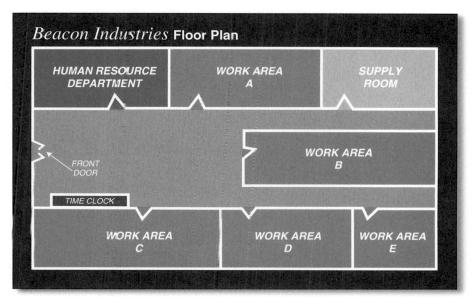

Beacon Industries **Floor Plan**

HUMAN RESOURCE DEPARTMENT

WORK AREA A

SUPPLY ROOM

FRONT DOOR

WORK AREA B

TIME CLOCK

WORK AREA C

WORK AREA D

WORK AREA E

Activity A Number your paper 1 to 5. Then write short answers to these questions.

1. Why do you think the time clock is near the front door?

2. To go from work area C to work area E, which way would you turn when you walked out of the door of work area C?

3. Which work area is farthest from the human resources department?

4. Once they punch the time clock, which workers will get to their work area first?

5. Which work area is the largest?

Ms. Jackson also gave Bill and Shaun an **organizational chart.** It listed the names of employees and their job titles. Bill works in the construction department. He could see that Phil Cummins is his manager and that Dan O'Leary is Phil's assistant. Bill would work with Amie LaRue and K. C. VanDoerst.

Ignoring the floor plan, Shaun walked out of the human resources office and into the supply room. Embarrassed, he quickly pulled out the floor plan to find his work area. He had lost the organizational chart, so he didn't know the name of his manager or any of his co-workers.

Shaun did glance at the rules before he walked around his workstation. He saw a switch on a piece of machinery. When he pushed it, he heard a loud noise. Then his manager yelled, "Turn off that machine! It's jamming!"

Shaun's manager, Mr. Lee, was upset that Shaun had pushed the switch. "Look," he told Shaun, "the rules say not to touch anything unless a manager shows you how!"

Using the floor plan, Bill made it to his department. He read the safety rules and organizational chart. He found his manager, Mr. Cummins, and told him he was ready to learn to use the machines. Bill made friends easily because he recognized names from the chart.

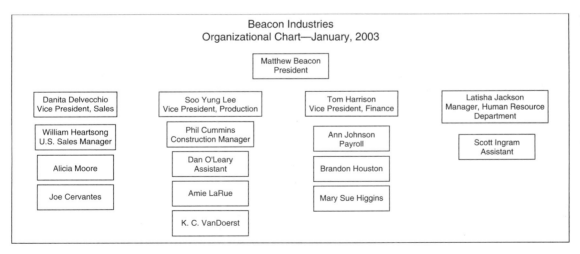

Beacon Industries
Organizational Chart—January, 2003

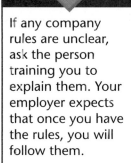

If any company rules are unclear, ask the person training you to explain them. Your employer expects that once you have the rules, you will follow them.

Activity B Number your paper 1 to 10. Then write short answers to these questions about the organizational chart on page 122.

1. Who is the president of the company?
2. What is Latisha Jackson's title?
3. Who is the manager of the department in which K. C. VanDoerst works?
4. Who is Latisha Jackson's assistant?
5. Name the three vice presidents of Beacon Industries.
6. Name a person who works in the Sales Department.
7. Who is in charge of payroll?
8. Who is Danita Delvecchio's immediate supervisor?
9. Copy the organizational chart on your paper. Add Bill Yee to the chart.
10. Who is Alicia Moore's manager?

The Outcome

All week Shaun did just what he felt like doing. He arrived at work late, and one day he never showed up. He did not call Mr. Lee to say that he would be out that day. Worst of all, however, he did not learn how to use the machines properly. In fact, he caused one to break down. It took two days to get it repaired, and the delay cost the company a lot of money.

Bill, on the other hand, did just what he was told to do. He paid attention and learned fast. He followed the rules, got to work a few minutes early every day, and was never absent. He was polite and helpful. Even though Bill made a few mistakes, Mr. Cummins could see that Bill was trying to do well.

At the end of the week, Mr. Lee fired Shaun. Bill was off to a good start. Some of his coworkers invited him to join the company baseball league. Mr. Cummins told him he was doing a good job.

Performance

The act of doing your job

Evaluation

A rating of how well a worker does a job; many companies use a form to tell employees on a regular basis how they are doing

Promotion

A raise in rank or position; it may include a pay raise

Nearly all companies judge the **performance** of their employees on a regular basis. An employee's immediate supervisor usually does this type of **evaluation.** How well employees do on an evaluation can determine whether or not they keep their job, get a **promotion,** and/or get a pay raise.

It is helpful to know some guidelines about how your manager will judge your work. While these guidelines vary from one business to another, most have some common areas that managers consider when they judge an employee's performance. Most companies judge a worker's performance in the following six areas.

Guidelines for Judging Job Performance

1. **How well do you know your job?**
   You work well by yourself and with others. You do not need to be reminded about company rules and regulations. You do not need to be told over and over again what to do.

2. **What is the quality of your work?**
   You make only a few mistakes, and you finish each job.

3. **How much work do you produce?**
   You work at a good pace, and you stay on schedule.

4. **How dependable are you?**
   You follow directions and regulations, and you regularly report to work on time.

5. **What kind of attitude do you have?**
   You are cooperative, and you take pride in the job you do. You get along with other workers.

6. **How is your attendance?**
   You come to work regularly and report to your workstation on time.

You will be a good employee if you learn to do your job well, work accurately, and do what is expected. You also need to be dependable, have a positive attitude, and go to work regularly and on time. If you are this kind of employee, the company won't fire you, and you will probably get raises and promotions.

Activity A Number your paper 1 to 10. After reading the following descriptions of 10 workers, write the area in which each seems weak. Use the questions from "Guidelines for Judging Job Performance" on page 124.

1. Nathan comes to work regularly, but he was late 14 times in the past month.

2. Maya is careless. Her manager often has to redo her work.

3. Ella does what she wants when she wants to do it. She can work well, but often ignores rules.

4. Rosa misses a lot of time from work, and she never calls to let her manager know that she won't be coming in that day.

5. Selma becomes annoyed when her manager points out something she is doing wrong. She then takes her anger out on the people around her.

Vocabulary Builder

Decoding an Employee Handbook

Your employee handbook might contain the following sentence:

"If your *attitude* is not *cooperative* and your *performance* is not *satisfactory,* we will have *grounds* for your *dismissal.*"

What does this mean?

To put this sentence into words you can understand, look up the word *attitude* in a dictionary or a thesaurus. You may find *way of acting* or *outlook.* A dictionary defines *cooperative* as *working together with others.* A dictionary may give several synonyms for *grounds.* In this sentence it means *reason.*

Using a dictionary or a thesaurus, find a synonym for each of the following words: *performance, satisfactory,* and *dismissal.* Write the synonyms on your paper.

---

6. Mary has worked for the company for six months. She never seems to know what she should do. She always has to wait until her boss tells her what to do next.

7. B. J. works at a job where he is expected to turn out a certain number of items each day. He takes several long breaks throughout the day.

8. Raul is well liked by his immediate supervisor and his coworkers. However, he does not pay attention to directions, and he makes a lot of mistakes.

9. Isaac does a good job most of the time. However, he works for a company that asks its employees to work odd shifts and overtime during busy times. Isaac never agrees to work an odd shift, nor does he work overtime.

10. Jamal works on a computer with Internet access. Even though his supervisor has asked Jamal not to search the Web during business hours, Jamal continues to do so. Because of this, Jamal's work has been late.

Cooperation and a positive attitude are important in all jobs.

Wages or Salary: What's the Difference?

When Ted started looking for a new job in sales, he noticed that some businesses offered a salary, while others listed an hourly wage. Some businesses also paid a commission. Because he was confused about the difference in pay, he talked to his Uncle Bob who has worked in sales most of his life.

"Uncle Bob, what is the difference between a wage and a salary?" asked Ted.

"Ted, wages are usually an hourly or daily rate of pay. A salary is the same amount of income paid regularly, like every two weeks."

"How are they different?" asked Ted.

"Well, a salary does not change if you work more or fewer than 40 hours a week. Wages pay you only for the time you work," said Uncle Bob.

"What about commission?" asked Ted.

"Do you remember when you worked as a restaurant server and you earned tips from customers? Usually a tip is a percentage of the customer's bill. A commission is a percent of the value of what you sell. Your employer pays you a percentage of your total sales," he said.

"So I really need to know how much I can expect to sell to see whether I want to work on commission or on a higher salary," said Ted. "Thanks, Uncle Bob."

For Discussion

1. What is the difference between a wage and a salary?

2. What is a commission?

3. What are some benefits of a salary?

4. What is a drawback of wages?

5. What must Ted consider before accepting a job that pays a commission rather than wages or salary?

Chapter 7 R E V I E W

Word Bank

allowances
deductions
dependents
evaluation
exempt
Internal Revenue Service
probation
promotion
sexual harassment
spouse
status
time cards
W-4 form
withhold
workstation

Part A Number your paper 1 to 15. Then write the correct answer from the box that completes each sentence. Use each answer only once.

1. Everyone who works fills out a _____.

2. This form is used to decide how much your employer will _____ from your paycheck.

3. Money subtracted from your pay goes to the _____ for your income tax.

4. Your _____ is your husband or wife.

5. Children who count on you for over half of their needs are _____.

6. If you are _____ from withholding, you are free from this requirement.

7. Your job performance determines your _____.

8. Most companies allow employees a period of _____ to prove they can do a job.

9. At the start of a day most employees punch their _____.

10. You can use a floor plan to find your _____.

11. An employee found or proved guilty of _____ could be fired and could face criminal charges.

12. Most companies rate job performance in a yearly _____.

13. The government considers _____ when deciding the amount withheld from your salary as income tax.

14. You do not pay taxes on _____ such as donations to charities, home mortgage interest payments, and local taxes.

15. A worker's _____ is the condition or rank of an employee.

Part B On your paper, write the letter of the correct answer.

16. Julio is married and has two children. His wife does not work outside the home. How many allowances can Julio claim on his W-4 form at Beacon Industries?

   A 3   **B** 1   **C** 2   **D** 4

17. What does a company do with its employees' W-4 forms?

    A throws away the forms in January

    B saves the forms

    C sends the forms to the IRS

    D throws away the forms after April 15

18. Which of the following employees would probably be fired from Beacon Industries?

    A Jamal called his supervisor when he was sick on Friday.

    B Mitsu had to fill out a new W-4 form because she moved.

    C Susan was caught in traffic and was late.

    D Tom was found guilty of sexual harassment.

Part C Number your paper 19 to 25. If the statement is true, write *True* next to the number. If it is not true, write *False*.

19. Employees are never evaluated on whether or not they follow company rules and regulations.

20. Your attitude can affect your performance review.

21. The way you get along with the other employees may affect your performance review.

22. An organizational chart lists employees' names and their titles.

23. Your immediate supervisor is often the person who does your performance review.

24. On a performance review, how well you do your work will not count as much as how much work you do.

25. An organizational plan can help you find your workstation.

Test-Taking Tip Always pay special attention to key words in a set of directions—words such as *first, second, third,* or *most important, least important, all,* or *none.*

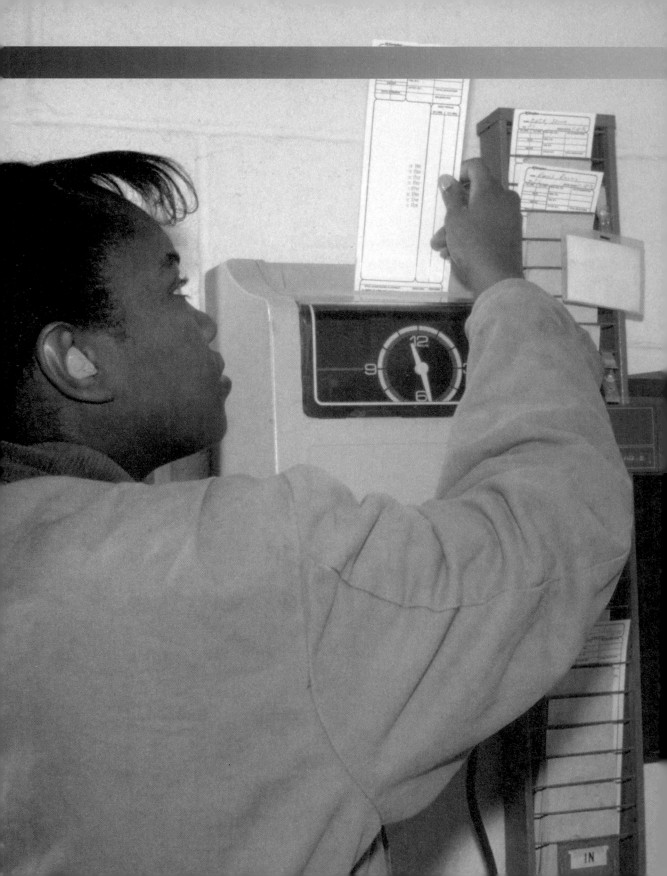

8 Following Directions

The first weeks of a new job usually include learning many new tasks—everything from filling out time cards to taking care of machinery. If you know how to follow directions carefully, you will do very well.

In Chapter 8, you will learn that following directions is an important part of being successful in a new job. You will also discover some "tricks" such as note taking that will help you remember important directions.

Goals for Learning

◆ To be able to fill in a weekly time card

◆ To understand how to read a work schedule

◆ To understand the importance of reading and following both written and oral directions carefully

◆ To learn how to take notes to help you remember the details of important tasks

Pay week

One pay period of seven days

The first week on her first job was wonderful for Violet. The manager of her department assigned Tony Fusco to be her "buddy." His job was to help her through any new situation—such as filling out company paperwork and learning to use the sorting machine. With Tony's help, Violet did very well on her first day.

When she got to work on the second day, she realized that no one had shown her how to fill in a time card. Just then Tony came through the front door. "Hi, Violet," he said. "I'm glad I ran into you this morning. I forgot to show you how to fill out a time card yesterday."

Tony showed Violet his time card from the week before. This is how it looked.

Hall Distribution Company				*Time Report*
Name: Tony Fusco		Position: Sorting Machine Operator		
Date: 12-7-03		No.: 229		
Date	Time			
07-DEC	A 7:50	P 4:32	8:00	8:00
08-DEC	A 7:52	P 4:30	8:00	16:00
09-DEC	A 7:56	P 4:00	7:30	23:30
10-DEC	A 7:50	P 12:00	4:00	27:30
11-DEC	A 7:50	P 2:01	5:30	33:00

The time card seemed pretty simple. Still, Violet was unsure what to put next to the word *Date*. Tony explained that at their company the **pay week** started on Monday. Since today was Tuesday, the first date Violet should put in was yesterday's date. Tony told Violet to start a new time card every Monday.

Violet also wanted to know what the word **position** meant. Tony explained that was the name of Violet's job. "Oh, that's easy," she said. "I'm a sorting machine operator."

"Right," said Tony. "In the space next to the abbreviation *No.*, write in your employee number—238. That's another way for the human resources department to identify you. Do you have any other questions?"

"What is this card for? What do I do with it?" Violet asked, showing Tony her swipe card.

Tony said, "That is our security card. Always carry it with you. It prevents strangers from entering the building. Company employees may enter most places in the building but not the accounting office." He continued, "At my last job, we didn't have to fill out time cards. We had a swipe card for security that also recorded the hours we worked."

"Thanks for your help, Tony," said Violet.

Activity A Number your paper 1 to 3. Write short answers to these questions.

1. Why would Hall Distribution want to keep track of Violet's hours?

2. What should Violet write in the space next to the abbreviation *No.*?

3. Why do you think the swipe cards won't allow most employees at Hall Distribution into the accounting department?

Work schedule

A plan that shows the exact hours or shift each employee will work during a given pay period

Shift

A scheduled period of work or duty; for example, a shift could be from 9 A.M. to 5 P.M. or from 7 P.M. to 3 A.M.

Write down your work schedule. Keep it in your wallet or purse.

As they walked to their work area, Tony told Violet to check the **work schedule.** The supervisor posted it on Thursday afternoon for the following week. "This is not a nine to five place," he told her. "Our hours vary depending on the workload. Some weeks you may have to come in earlier or later than usual because we have an extra **shift** working."

On Friday morning, Violet went to the bulletin board in her work area. She checked the work schedule. This is what she saw.

WORK SCHEDULE—WEEK OF 1/14	
	Begin Shift
Canos, Anika	3:30 P.M.
Carting, Ed	6:00 A.M.
Chung, Rose/Robinson, Bob	6:00 A.M.
Deever, Violet	6:00 A.M.
Fusco, Tony	8:30 A.M.
Glassman, Sylvia	8:30 A.M.
Moore, Simon	8:30 A.M.
Wu, Ai-Ling	8:30 A.M.

Starting Monday, Violet would begin work at 6 A.M.—two hours early. She would finish work at 2:30 P.M.

On Monday, when Violet reported to work a few minutes before 6, her supervisor was happy. He told her that new people often forget to check the work schedule. That means they lose pay because they arrive to work late. For example, if Violet had reported to work at 8 A.M. instead of 6, she would have lost two hours of pay.

Notice that the line at the top shows the week this schedule covers. At the left are the employees' names. In the right-hand column are the times they are to report to work. Notice that two names in the left column—Bob Robinson and Rose Chung—appear on one line. This means that Bob and Rose are **job sharing.** Job sharing is a situation in which two people divide one job between them. Each person works part-time. Job sharing allows a person time to care for a young child or an elderly parent or to work another part-time job. In this case, Bob works all day Monday and Tuesday and on Wednesday morning. Rose works Wednesday afternoon and all day Thursday and Friday.

You might also notice that Hall Distribution operates three shifts—one at 6 A.M., one at 8:30 A.M., and one at 3:30 P.M.

Activity A Number your paper 1 to 10. Then write short answers to these questions about the work schedule on page 134.

1. List the start times for the three shifts.
2. Do Violet and Tony work on the same shift this week?
3. Who works on the same shift with Tony?
4. Who works on the same shift with Violet?
5. Who works on the 3:30 P.M. shift?
6. What week does this schedule cover?
7. How many workers does this schedule include?
8. At what time should Simon Moore report to work?
9. Why are Bob Robinson and Rose Chung's names on the same line?
10. In what kind of order do the names on this schedule appear?

Activity B Figure out the time each shift ends if each employee works an $8\frac{1}{2}$-hour shift.

Activity C The work schedule on page 134 changed for January 16 because of a problem with the equipment. Fusco, Glassman, and Moore were to report four hours later than scheduled. Deever, Carting, and Robinson/Chung were to report three hours later than scheduled. Wu was to report two hours and thirty minutes earlier than scheduled. Canos was to report three hours and forty-five minutes earlier than scheduled. Rewrite the work schedule for January 16.

Vocabulary Builder

When Will You Get Paid?
When a company offers you a job, the employer will tell you whether you will receive your pay *weekly, biweekly, monthly,* or *twice a month*.

If your employer pays you *weekly*, you will be paid every week. *Biweekly* pay means that your employer pays you every two weeks. *Monthly* pay is the amount you will earn each month.

Number your paper 1 to 4. If the statement is true, write *True* next to the number. If the statement is not true, write *False*.

1. If you are paid *biweekly*, you will receive your pay twice a week.
2. If you are paid *monthly*, you will receive 14 checks each year.
3. *Weekly* checks are given out 365 times a year.
4. If you are paid monthly, your paycheck would contain more money than it would if you were paid weekly.

Violet followed directions well during her first week on the job. When she was unsure about something, she asked someone she could trust, like Tony. She knew that reading and following directions would help her make as few mistakes as possible.

Violet's job required lifting and moving heavy boxes. Her supervisor gave her these safety rules to follow.

Lifting and Moving Boxes

1. Check the area in which you will be moving the boxes.

2. Clear the floor of all objects that might cause you to trip.

3. Make sure the boxes will fit through doorways.

4. To lift, squat close to the box with one foot beside it and one foot behind it. Grasp the box in both palms and fingers. Keep both arms close to your body. Lift the box by straightening both legs.

5. To put the box down, reverse the lifting procedure. Let one side of the box touch down first so that you do not trap your hands under the box. If you have to shift position, first set the box down on a sturdy support.

WARNING: Employees must follow these procedures. If you do not and you injure yourself, the company's medical insurance may not cover your medical costs.

The United States Occupational Safety and Health Administration (OSHA) provided these directions.

Activity A Number your paper 1 to 5. Put these instructions in the correct order. Write the letter next to the number.

A. Check to see whether the doorways are big enough for the boxes.

B. When putting the box down, let one side of the box touch first so that you will not trap your hands under the box.

C. Check the area in which you will be moving with the box.

D. Squat close to the box. Put one foot beside the box. Put the other foot behind it. Hold the box in both hands close to your body. Lift the box by straightening both legs.

E. Clear the floor and the surrounding area of anything that is in your way.

Activity B Write a short answer to these questions.

1. The warning at the end of the directions states, "Employees must follow these procedures. If you do not and you injure yourself, the company's medical insurance may not cover your medical costs." Rewrite the statement in your own words. Make sure that you keep the meaning of the statement the same.

2. Violet bent over to pick up a heavy load. When she tried to straighten her legs, she injured her back. What didn't Violet do?

Follow the directions for lifting heavy boxes.

During the second week, Violet's supervisor gave her a small booklet. He explained, "These are directions for keeping your machine in the best possible running condition. Read them and make sure you follow them. If you have any questions, just ask me."

Violet read the directions carefully. Then she made herself a **schedule.** After you read the directions, ask yourself why Violet made a schedule.

Caring for the Sorting Machine

- Always turn the machine off when you leave the work area.
- Oil the starter once a week.
- Oil the rotary wheels once a day.
- Oil the tray lifts once a month.
- Before using the machine each day, dust it with an oiled cloth.
- Do not try to repair the machine yourself. If something goes wrong, notify your immediate supervisor as soon as possible.

Violet made a schedule because there were some things she had to do every day. Other things she had to do once a week. Still others she had to do once a month. Her schedule helped her keep track of the different things she had to do.

Here is her schedule.

First (every day): Dust with an oiled cloth.

Second (every day): Oil the rotary wheels.

Monday: Oil the starter.

First Monday of the month: Oil the tray lifts.

Reminder 1: Turn OFF the machine when you leave work area.

Reminder 2: If anything goes wrong, call a supervisor.

Violet posted her schedule in her workstation. She checked off tasks as she completed them. She was smart not to trust her memory with something so important.

Find the directions
for setting a VCR
or running a
microwave. Then
take notes from
the directions.

Activity C Number your paper 1 to 10. Then after you read
the directions in the box, write short answers to the following
questions.

Using the Copying Machine

- Push *Start* button.
- When the orange light under the *Start* button stops
  blinking, insert paper. Make sure you match the paper size
  to the proper tray.
- Use a stack of paper no more than three inches high.
- Place the item you need to copy facedown on glass.
- Close lid.
- Push *Quantity* button until number of copies
  desired appears.
- Push *Print* button.
- Remove finished copies from tray at the lower left side of
  the machine.

---

1. How high can the stack of paper be in the paper tray?

2. What number should appear by the *Quantity* button?

3. Where do you put the paper?

4. How do you insert the item you need to copy?

5. Where will you find the finished copies?

6. When do you put the paper in?

7. What do you press to start copying?

8. Can you use more than one size paper in this machine?

9. Is it better to copy with the lid open or closed?

10. Where is the orange light?

Activity D Number your paper 1 to 10. Read these directions for using a computer printer. Then write *True* or *False* for each of the following statements.

Guidelines for Using the Printer

- Load all paper, cards, or envelopes in the tray at the base of the printer.
- For plain paper, load print side down. The package indicates the print side.
- For letterhead, load letterhead side down and forward in the tray.
- For glossy paper, load the glossy side down.
- Load only one type of paper at a time. Do not mix glossy, plain, and letterhead.
- To print index cards or postcards, align the right side of the card with the left side of the raised card guide.
- Load all envelopes flap side facing up and forward.
- Never use more than $\frac{1}{2}$ inch of paper, $\frac{1}{4}$ inch of cards, or 20 envelopes at one time.

---

1. Put paper print side down in the tray of the printer.

2. For glossy paper, put the glossy side down.

3. Load as many kinds of paper at one time as you will need.

4. You cannot use postcards in this printer.

5. Plain paper has a small arrow on the first page to show which side is the print side.

6. Never use more than $\frac{1}{8}$ inch of cards at one time.

7. Load paper at the top of this printer.

8. When you print on letterhead, put the letterhead side down and back.

9. Use no more than 20 envelopes at one time.

10. This printer will not print envelopes.

Oral directions

Instructions given by talking; spoken rather than written orders

Key words

Important words that give the main idea; clues to help people remember information

Writing Tip

If your notes are hard to read, recopy them or type them on a word processor. Do this as soon as possible so that you can remember what you wrote.

During her first few weeks on the new job, many people gave Violet directions by speaking to her. These were **oral directions.** Violet quickly realized that she was having trouble remembering everything people told her. As a result, she got herself a small notebook and kept it—along with a pencil—in her pocket. When someone began to tell her directions, she would take the notebook out and begin taking notes.

At first Violet tried to write every word that someone said. But this took too much time. Sometimes she would miss part of what someone was telling her because she was so busy writing. She learned that she did not need to write every word people said—just the most important, or **key words,** to help her remember what they had said. She found that taking notes helped her and saved her from asking the same questions over and over again.

At the beginning of Violet's fourth week, for example, Tony told her, "When you start the sorter, set the dial on 5. Once it is working smoothly, move the dial slowly to 7. Never move the dial past 7 unless the supervisor tells you to."

This is what Violet wrote in her notebook.

> Set 5; when working smoothly, move slowly to 7. Never past 7.

She included all the important ideas and left out those things she would remember once she saw what she had written. For example, when she saw "Set 5," she knew she would know to set the sorter correctly when she started it.

Later that same day, her supervisor had told her, "The paper loader should never get below 1,000. Refill the loader at about 1,500." Violet wrote this in her notebook.

Refill paper loader—1,500

That was all she needed to write down because it was the most important information.

Activity A Have a partner read aloud the information in the box. Write down the key words or ideas from these oral directions on a sheet of paper. The words should be what you would need to remember the directions.

"When the mail comes in, the first thing you want to do is sort it according to office. You will find a list of the offices in the company directory that is on the counter next to the mail bin. After you sort the mail, deliver it. The first mail you deliver is to Mr. Gaudet, the president. The order after that is up to you, but do not waste time. Deliver all the mail within 20 minutes. Ask the secretary in each office to initial the mail sheet when you drop off your delivery. Bring that sheet back with you and put it in the file under *Mail Sheets*. Put the most recent sheet in the front of the file."

Where To Find It

Table of Contents

Have you ever wondered whether a book had a chapter about the information you needed? One quick way to find out is to check the table of contents. The table of contents always appears in the front of the book, usually after the title page.

The table of contents lists the chapter names and the page numbers of the chapters.

At the library, find a book about a career that interests you. Then complete the following activity.

1. Write the book title.

2. List three chapter titles and their page numbers.

3. Go to one of the three chapters. Read the headings on the first few pages of the chapter. Write a sentence telling what kind of information the chapter includes.

Activity B Write the following sentences on your paper. Underline the key words you would use in taking notes.

1. To take better notes, improve your listening skills.

2. Listen for transition words such as *then, next, first,* and *second.* Transition words help you organize your thoughts.

3. Put the date at the top of each page of notes.

4. Write notes in phrases rather than in complete sentences.

5. Develop your own shorthand. For instance, use *U.S.* for *United States, w/o* for the word *without, ea.* for *each,* and *in.* for *inch.*

6. Use a highlighter to mark important notes.

7. Circle unfamiliar words and ask about them later.

Spelling Builder

Through, Though, and Thorough

Have you ever read the word *through* and mistaken it for *though* or *thorough*? These three words have similar spellings. It is easy to misspell them or read them incorrectly.

For example, if you are giving directions, they must be *thorough,* or very carefully given. Then you must read *through* the directions, or read them from the beginning to the end. You may understand them, *though,* or in spite of the fact that, they could still be unclear.

When you spell these words, think about them. First ask yourself what the word means. Then pronounce it out loud to help you spell it correctly.

Copy the following sentences on your paper. Choose the correct word in parentheses to complete the sentence.

1. Please do a (thorough, through, though) search of your desk to find the missing time card.

2. Even (thorough, through, though) you are busy, please answer the phone.

3. If you walk (thorough, through, though) these doors, you will find your workstation.

4. You should be (thorough, through, though) when you inspect the parts.

5. Call your supervisor when you are (thorough, through, though) doing a (thorough, through, though) inspection.

How Much Will I Earn?

Mike just got a job with a manufacturing company. As he filled out his paperwork, he spoke with Ms. Wu from the human resources department.

"We issue paychecks every other Friday. The pay will cover the two weeks ending on the Friday before the payday," Ms. Wu explained.

"How much will I earn each pay period?" asked Mike.

"You are earning $8 per hour, so if you work 40 hours each week, you will earn $640 every two weeks. Keep in mind that's your pay before we take out taxes," said Ms. Wu.

"That's twice as much each payday than my last job!" said Mike.

"But didn't your last employer pay every week?" asked Ms. Wu.

"Yes," said Mike.

"Then you need to multiply your last pay by two to compare it with your paycheck here," said Ms. Wu.

"Oh, I forgot," said Mike.

For Discussion

1. If Mike got a raise to $9 per hour, how much would he make in a 40-hour week?

2. Would Mike's paycheck always be the same if he were paid monthly?

3. Will Mike's paycheck be larger or smaller after his employer takes out taxes?

4. How would Mike figure out how much he will make in a year?

5. If Mike makes $640 every two weeks, how else could he determine his yearly income?

Chapter 8 REVIEW

Word Bank

job sharing

pay week

position

shift

Part A On a sheet of paper, write the correct word or words from the Word Bank to complete each sentence.

1. A _____ is a pay period of seven days.
2. A _____ could run from 9 A.M. to 5 P.M.
3. A _____ is a job or job title.
4. In _____ , two people divide one job.

Part B Number your paper 5 to 9. Then write the information that an employee might fill in next to each number on this time card.

The Hall Distribution Company
EMPLOYEE TIME CARD

(5)

Employee's Name (print)   (6)

Position   (7)

For Week Beginning   (8)

Social Security Number   (9)

Employee's Signature

WORK SCHEDULE

Employee	Starting time
Anderson, Lee	7:30 A.M.
Chin, Adam	8:00 A.M.
Green, Hazel	9:00 A.M.
O'Leary, Daniel	9:30 A.M.

Part C Number your paper 10 to 13. If the statement about the work schedule above is true, write *True* next to the number. If it is not true, write *False*.

10. The company staggers the time its employees arrive and leave work.

11. Lee Anderson arrives at work two hours earlier than Hazel Green.

12. If the employees normally work an $8\frac{1}{2}$ hour day, Adam Chin would leave at 4:30 P.M.

13. Lee Anderson will leave work two hours earlier than Daniel O'Leary.

"First, wipe the grill with cooking oil before you turn it on. Set it at medium high for everything but fried potatoes. Set it at high for them. Every time you cook something, scrape the grill with the scraper and oil the grill again. Cook onions in the far left corner of the grill. That way they won't make everything else smell and taste like onions."

Part D Read the directions in the box and imagine that they are oral directions. Then write the key words or ideas on a sheet of paper. The words should be what you would need to remember the directions.

Part E Number your paper 14 to 17. Use your notes from *Part D* to write short answers to these questions.

14. What should you do before cooking anything?
15. At what temperature should you cook eggs?
16. How often should you oil the grill?
17. Why should you cook onions in the far left corner?

Part F On your paper, write the letter of the correct answer.

18. The employees at Springvale Hospital have security cards. The cards won't allow them into the Patient Records Room. Why not?
 A Patient records are private.
 B The cards don't work right.
 C Someone broke the lock and it needs to be fixed.
 D People who do not work there are allowed into that room.

19. Which of the following is NOT on a time card?
 A your name   C your employee number
 B your home address   D the date

20. What should you do if you are asked to lift a heavy box at work?
 A Refuse to do it.
 B Tell your supervisor to do it.
 C Follow the safety instructions issued by your company.
 D Pay your best friend five dollars to lift it.

Test-Taking Tip When a teacher announces a test, listen carefully. Write down the topics that will be included. Write down the names of any specific readings the teacher says to review.

9

Using Job-Related Resources

The more skills you have, the more valuable you will be as an employee. For example, understanding how to read and use technical manuals and the Internet will keep you up-to-date on the latest information. Print and electronic information will tell you about the latest developments in your field and will help you keep your skills current.

In Chapter 9, you will learn not only how to use technical manuals but also how to interpret charts, spreadsheets, graphs, and labels.

Goals for Learning

◆ To understand the importance of technical manuals

◆ To use the Internet to find technical information

◆ To understand information on a spreadsheet

◆ To be able to use an index

◆ To learn to read charts, graphs, and labels

Technical manual

A book that helps its readers understand or do something

Jimmie Eagle had been working for a large discount store for six months. He liked his job and was doing well. He got along well with his coworkers and the customers. He reported to work on time, and he was always friendly and helpful. His immediate supervisor, Mr. Hernandez, promoted him to assistant manager of the lawn and garden department.

Jimmie was excited about his promotion, but he was also a little worried. He was not sure that he would know how to do everything on his new job. He would have to find information in forms he did not know how to use.

Jimmie talked to Mr. Hernandez about his worries. Mr. Hernandez said, "Oh, Jimmie, don't worry. We offer training for new assistant managers. We will also send you to the training sessions that our suppliers offer. The first thing I'd like you to learn is how to put together and use the electric- and gas-powered lawn equipment that we sell." Jimmie was relieved. With training, he knew he could do a good job.

The first thing Jimmie learned was how to use, read, and understand **technical manuals.** Technical manuals are handbooks about certain skilled jobs. Most technical manuals tell about new tools, methods, and products. They explain how to do certain jobs. Most machines come with technical manuals.

Part of Jimmie's job was to put together and test lawn mowers. Customers preferred to buy an assembled lawn mower rather than put it together themselves. The store also had to make sure that the mowers worked after they were put together.

This is a section of a technical manual about lawn mowers that Jimmie read. It tells how to adjust the cutting height on push lawn mowers.

> Adjust both levers to the same height except when you use one of the two lowest cutting heights. At the two lowest cutting heights, raise the rear lever one notch higher than the front lever. This difference in height allows more air to get under the mower. Air movement is essential when you use a bag to catch clippings or when the clippings are thrown out the side chute.
>
> (Adapted from a manufacturer's home page)

As you were reading, you probably could tell that the company wrote the manual for someone putting together or using a lawn mower. The reader has two things to think about.

- How high does the user want to cut his or her lawn?

- Must the levers be at the same height or different heights to accomplish this?

Spelling Builder

Contractions

A contraction is one word created from two other words. One or two letters are usually left out, and an apostrophe takes the place of the missing letters. *Don't,* for example, is a contraction for *do not.* The apostrophe takes the place of the letter *o* in *not.*

Number your paper 1 to 5. Write the contractions in these sentences as two words on your paper.

1. We didn't complete the spreadsheet.
2. It's not your fault sales have declined.
3. They're sitting in the reception area.
4. You're responsible for this manual.
5. Who's coming for the training session?

Search engine

A location on the World Wide Web that allows you to search the Internet by using key words

Key word

A word or words that you can use to search on the Internet

When you read a technical manual, check the publication date to make sure that the information is recent. Out-of-date manuals are not helpful.

Activity A Number your paper 1 to 6. Read this section of a technical manual. Then write short answers to the questions that follow.

> Caution: Avoid injury or death. Engine exhaust fumes contain carbon monoxide. Exhaust fumes can cause serious sickness or death. If you feel dizzy or sick while the engine is running, turn it off immediately.
>
> To guarantee your safety, get a steady supply of fresh air:
>
> • Move outside before starting or running the engine.
> • Do not start or run the lawn mower inside a closed building.

1. What do these rules apply to?

2. What do exhaust fumes contain?

3. Where do exhaust fumes come from?

4. Why are exhaust fumes dangerous?

5. Where is the best place to start the lawn mower engine?

6. Why does a technical manual include safety information?

Jimmie knew that the safety information he found in the technical manual was very important. He made a sign with the safety information and placed it in the area where the store employees assembled equipment.

Then Jimmie wondered where he would find the information if he did not have the technical manual. His first thought was to check the Internet. "I wonder what information I can find about lawn mowers," he thought. He went to a computer with an Internet provider and selected a **search engine.** He typed in the **key words** *lawn mowers* and found a number of valuable Web sites.

Home page

A single page on the World Wide Web made by a person or company; it can serve as a main entrance to other information

Link

A connection you can click on to take you to another location on the Internet

First he found a site that rated all the lawn mowers on the market. The site not only had customer ratings for the lawn mowers but also included the features of each lawn mower. This site showed him how much people liked the brands his store carried. It compared these brands to the brands that other stores in the area sold. "I need to show this to Mr. Hernandez," thought Jimmie. He learned that their store carried the best lawn mowers. He knew that other salespeople in the lawn and garden department would want to share this information with their customers. It could improve lawn mower sales.

Next Jimmie visited the **home page** of the company that makes the lawn mowers that the store sells. A home page is the main Web page for a business. It is a starting point for all kinds of information about a company. The first home page topic he explored was *Training Sessions.* The site listed training sessions for home owners and salespeople. Jimmie found a session planned in a nearby city for later in the month. Jimmie knew that if he and his coworkers were better trained, they could do a better job of helping customers. "I need to mention this to Mr. Hernandez, too," Jimmie thought.

Next Jimmie clicked on the **links** connecting him to operating and assembling the lawn mowers. He was surprised to find complete assembly instructions as well as an operator's manual. "I should print out one of these for every model we sell," thought Jimmie. "Then if a customer comes in and says that he or she has lost the manual, I can either send the customer to the site or give him or her a copy. Customers will be happy that we offer that service."

Mr. Hernandez was pleased that Jimmie had explored the Internet and learned so much about their products. He asked Jimmie to write a memo to the other workers in the lawn and garden department. In the memo Jimmie shared what he had learned about the products. Because the employees now knew more about the products they sold, the lawn and garden department had a 10% increase in sales over the last year.

Activity B Use a computer with an Internet provider to search for sites with the key words *lawn mower*. Once you have found a list of sites, write a short answer to each of the following questions.

1. Write the names of three lawn mower companies that have home pages listed in your search results.

2. Write the Internet address of a site that rates different brands of lawn mowers.

3. What other key words might you use to find information about lawn mowing equipment?

Activity C Number your paper 1 to 10. Use the lawn mower Web site shown to answer the following questions.

1. What link would you click on to find what equipment is available in Mexico?

2. If you wanted to find a piece of equipment quickly, what would you do?

3. If you wanted a garden tractor, what link would you use?

4. How would you find a dealer on this Web site?

5. If you needed new tires for your tractor, where would you click on the Web site?

6. What would you click on if you wanted to ask a question?

7. Where would information on lawn trimmers be found?

8. What is the value of a Web site to a company?

9. What advantage does a Web site give to a buyer?

10. If you decided to buy a product but did not have enough money to pay for it, where would you go on the Web site?

At the end of the month, Mr. Hernandez handed Jimmie a
spreadsheet. He told Jimmie that the spreadsheet would help
them check stock and track sales for the month.

Many companies no longer use handwritten or typewritten
records. Instead, they use computers to track sales, keep records
of stock, and project future purchases. Special programs called
spreadsheets perform these and other related accounting tasks.
Many software companies offer spreadsheet programs.

Spreadsheets have many advantages over handwritten records.
You can look at information on sales, for instance, in many
different ways. You can track sales by month, by product, or
by salesperson.

A single page of a spreadsheet is called a **worksheet.** A
worksheet can have hundreds of boxes, called **cells.** Each
cell can hold letters or numbers that Jimmie can use to
examine, track, or project information for his company.
Each **row** has a number and runs straight across a page.

	A	B	C	D	E	F	G	H	I	J
1					Sheet 1					
2	Bulb Varieties	(Bulbs per Unit)	# Cost per Unit	Price per Unit	Unit Sales					Total Unit Sales
3					Week 1	Week 2	Week 3	Week 4		
4	T. Darwin Mix	10	$3.50	$6.95	50	52	45	42		189
5	T. Peacock Mix	10	$4.50	$8.95	62	60	55	51		228
6	T. Emperor Mix	10	$3.50	$6.50	75	73	65	60		273
7	N. King Alfred	05	$6.50	$12.95	35	30	25	25		115
8	N. Pheasant Eve	05	$5.50	$10.95	30	32	30	25		117
9										
10	Avg. Cost/ Price per Unit		$4.70	$9.35						
11	Total Unit Sales				252	247	220	203		922

Columns run down the page and are identified by a letter. The names of the columns are listed across the top of the worksheet page.

Cells have addresses, consisting of the column letter and row number. Knowing a cell's address allows you to move quickly through the worksheet.

When you fill in a spreadsheet, you can type words or numbers in the cells. You can also type in a **formula,** a way to add, subtract, divide, or multiply the numbers in the spreadsheet.

Each week Jimmie had to check the spreadsheets to see how much stock was on hand. He also checked to see how much stock was sold the week before. Some weeks the amount of a product on hand was smaller than the amount of stock the company expected to need in the next two weeks. When this happened, Jimmie told his immediate supervisor what to order.

With his spreadsheet, Jimmie and his supervisor could track what sold—and when. They could project, for instance, that there would be a demand for fertilizer in the spring and that a display of garden gloves would probably work well then, too. Jimmie and his supervisor also talked about what wasn't selling.

Spreadsheets track sales and stock on hand.

By keeping close watch over the spreadsheet to track sales and stock on hand and to project future sales, Jimmie and Mr. Hernandez made sure that they had enough stock to meet their customers' needs. At the same time, they made sure that they did not have a lot of unsold stock at the end of each season.

Activity A Number your paper 1 to 7. Write short answers to the following questions.

1. What is a spreadsheet?

2. What is a worksheet?

3. Where do you find a row on a spreadsheet page?

4. Where do you find a column on a spreadsheet page?

5. What does a cell contain? Where do you find it?

6. What could Jimmie and Mr. Hernandez learn from studying the spreadsheets for the garden department?

7. What do the spreadsheets for the garden department help Jimmie and Mr. Hernandez project?

Where To Find It

Reading a Road Map

When you look at a road map, you will find a boxed-in section that has a list of symbols and what they represent on the map. This is the key; it usually appears along the side of the map near one of the corners.

The key contains the scale of the map as well as many symbols. It shows the symbols for different types of highways, from dirt roads to divided highways. Other symbols on a key include those for airports, parks, rest areas, campgrounds, county seats, state capitals, and route numbers.

The key may also have symbols to show the distance between two points on the map.

Using a road map for your state, look at the key to find the symbols for each of the following. Then locate one of each, listing the city closest to it.

1. airport
2. park or campground
3. divided highway
4. state capital
5. county seat

Being able to read and understand graphs and **charts** was another important part of Jimmie's job. As an assistant manager, Jimmie had to understand all kinds of charts. A chart is a diagram that presents information in table or list form.

Jimmie talked to a salesperson from Grass Green Co. The salesperson had a chart of tools and prices. This chart was especially important because it listed the model numbers for all the equipment. For each tool, it also showed the salesperson the total quantity that the factory produced.

Grass Green Co. Production Chart — March 31, 2004			
Product	Deluxe	Budget	Commercial
lawn mowers	21,062	44,589	9,742
leaf blowers	658	246	52
rakes	17,932	35,749	19,298
shovels	42,003	46,703	8,732
snowblowers	450	982	291
snow throwers	219	62	1,873
Attachments	1,196	2,149	7,154

Each section on this chart lists a product: lawn mowers, leaf blowers, snow throwers, snowblowers. The company makes three models of each product: a deluxe model, a budget model, and a commercial model for gardening companies. The section marked Attachments lists all the additional parts (handles, bags, and hoses) for each model of each product.

Activity B Number your paper 1 to 5. Then write short answers to these questions.

1. According to the chart, how many deluxe leaf blowers were made?

2. How many commerical shovels were made?

3. How many budget model lawn mowers were made in March?

4. Which item did Grass Green produce the most of in March?

5. How many commercial rakes were made in March?

Jimmie and Mr. Hernandez looked at information presented in many ways. Sometimes they looked at bar graphs. A **bar graph** is a drawing that uses lines and shaded areas to present and compare information. You use the information in a spreadsheet or on a chart to create the bar graph.

As Jimmie and Mr. Hernandez reviewed their spreadsheet for the month of April, they found that the store returned a lot of bags of fertilizer because the bags were open or torn. They wanted to find out whether the problem was with one supplier or more than one. Jimmie used the information in his spreadsheet to develop this bar graph.

Rate of Returned Fertilizer Shipments

The store returned the fewest bags to the Grow It Co. and returned the most bags to the Johnson Co. Jimmie and Mr. Hernandez decided to talk to the salesperson for the Johnson Co. about the high number of returns. They also decided to decrease their Johnson Co. order.

Activity C Number your paper 1 to 5. If the statement is true, write *True* next to the number. If the statement is not true, write *False*.

1. The Grow It Co. had less than a 1% rate of return.

2. The Green Co. fertilizer had a 4% return rate.

3. The Johnson Co. had a 20% return rate.

4. The Grass Green Co. had the most merchandise returned.

5. The most a section on this graph could show in returns is 10%.

Index

A list of items in a book that gives page numbers where those items can be found; an index is usually at the back of a book

Can't find something in an index? Think of what it might be a part of and look for that major heading.

Jimmie found that in order to make good use of a technical manual or other instructional book, he had to know how to use an **index.** One evening when he was reading about snowblowers in a technical manual, he wanted more information. He turned to the index at the back of the book. This is what he found.

Snowblowers 7–27

    attachments 2, 10–12

    changing oil 2

    compact models 12

    safety gear 21

    seasonal care 24

    single-stage engine 18

    two-stage engines 19–22

Snow throwers 25–39

    electric 32

    manual 34

If he wanted information specifically about attachments, for example, he would look on page 2 and pages 10–12. He used the major headings that appear at the left margin to find the general topic. Then he used the subheadings that appear under the major headings to locate more specific information.

Activity A Number your paper 1 to 3. Then write short answers to the following questions about the sample index above.

1. What two kinds of snowblower engines can you find information about in the book?

2. Are snowblowers and snow throwers the same thing? How can you tell?

3. On what page would you find seasonal care tips?

Activity B Number your paper 1 to 5. Then write short answers to the following questions about this sample index.

> Applications, 326–366
>
> > credit, 345
> > educational, 328, 347
> > financial, 365
> > job, 333
> > permits, 357
> > work benefits, 360
>
> Area codes, 214–218
>
> Catalogs, 127–198
>
> > business, 134
> > mail order, 144–168

Writing Tip

When you make a pie chart, use a compass to draw the circle. Then divide the circle into sections.

1. How many major headings appear in this sample index? What are they?

2. If you want to find out what area codes are and how to use them, on which pages would you look?

3. If you want information about ordering from a mail order catalog, on what pages would you look?

4. Does this book appear to have information about using an atlas?

5. If you want to fill in an application for college, where in this book would you look?

Vocabulary Builder

Graphs

Three types of graphs are *bar graphs, line graphs,* and *pie charts.* A *bar graph* has parallel bars that show the amount of something or how often it occurs. A *line graph* shows how things change over a period of time. A *pie chart* is a circle divided into pieces, like a pie. Each piece is marked to tell what it represents and how much or what percent of the pie it includes.

Write the answers to these questions on your paper.

1. What kinds of information can you chart on a bar graph?

2. What kinds of information can you chart on a line graph?

3. What kinds of information can you chart on a pie chart?

Part of Jimmie's job included getting stock from the stockroom. At the training program, the instructors taught him how to read and interpret the **labels** on packages so he would know that he was getting exactly what he needed. Labels are words or abbreviations attached to objects to help people identify or describe them.

First, Jimmie had to learn the names of the stock items in the stockroom. Then he had to learn the abbreviations most commonly found on the labels on the items. These abbreviations dealt with size, number, material, and color. This list helped.

Label Abbreviations	
Size	**Number**
sm.—small	doz.—dozen
med.—medium	gr.—gross (12 dozen)
lg.—large	rm.—ream (500 sheets)
Material	**Color**
st.—steel	blk.—black
cop.—copper	wh.—white
plas.—plastic	yel.—yellow
pap.—paper	grn.—green

When Jimmie went to the stockroom to get a *gr. of lg. grn. plas. garden hoses,* he had to know he was to get a *gross of large, green, plastic garden hoses.* He also had to know that there are 12 dozen, or 144, in a gross. He used the above list as he was learning the most important abbreviations used in the stockroom.

***Activity* C** Number your paper 1 to 5. Then rewrite these labels, writing out the words for the abbreviations.

1. Plas. Tubing sm. 2 doz. lengths wh.
2. Pap. Wallboard 1 gr. yel.
3. St. Pipe med. 3 doz.
4. Cop. Wires sm. 1 doz. yel.
5. Lg. wh. Paper 3 rm.

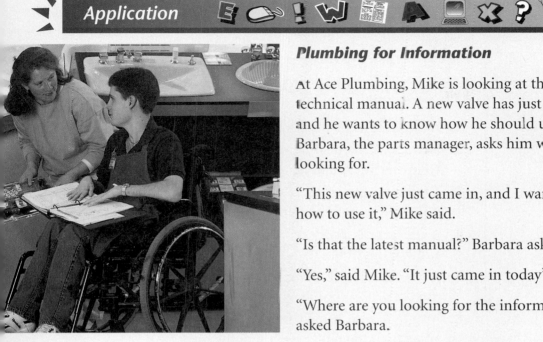

Plumbing for Information

At Ace Plumbing, Mike is looking at the latest technical manual. A new valve has just come in, and he wants to know how he should use it. Barbara, the parts manager, asks him what he's looking for.

"This new valve just came in, and I want to know how to use it," Mike said.

"Is that the latest manual?" Barbara asked.

"Yes," said Mike. "It just came in today's mail."

"Where are you looking for the information?" asked Barbara.

"I'm just looking through the manual," said Mike.

"You might want to look in the index," said Barbara. "You'd probably find the information faster."

"What would I look under?"

"You might start with *valves*. If you don't find it there, you might need to narrow your topic to a type of valve," said Barbara.

"Thanks," said Mike. "Ah, it's on page 179."

For Discussion

1. Where did Mike look for information about the valve?

2. What was the first thing Barbara asked Mike to check?

3. What did Mike look under in the index?

4. What did the listing tell him?

5. If Mike had not found what he needed under *valves*, where else might he have looked?

Chapter 9 R E V I E W

Part A Number your paper 1 to 10. Then write the correct answer from the Word Bank that completes each sentence. Use each answer only once.

1. A _____ explains how to do something.

2. A _____ on the Internet can be a main entrance to company information.

3. Type in a _____ on a search engine to search for information on the Internet.

4. A _____ is a connection you can click on to take you to another location.

5. A _____ is a computer software program commonly used to process numbers.

6. An _____ is usually found in the back of a book and is a guide to finding information in the book.

7. A _____ is a sheet of information arranged as a table.

8. A _____ uses lines and shaded areas to present and compare information.

9. A _____ is fastened to an object to tell what it is, who made it, or where it is going.

10. A _____ allows you to search the Internet by using key words.

Part B Write short answers to the following questions that are based on the index at right.

11. This index comes from a technical manual. What do you think the manual is teaching you?

12. What key words would you use to search for ways to measure a countertop?

Counters, 74–90

  building, 74–90

  installation, 80–85

  measurement, 74–78

  tops, 85–90

Drains, 214–218

  appliance, 72

  fixture, 72

  floor, 60

Part C Number your paper 13 to 17. Match the words in the left-hand column with their definitions.

13. row

14. cell

15. column

16. worksheet

17. formula

A box on a spreadsheet where a row and column meet

B a single spreadsheet page

C a line of cells going straight across a page

D a way to multiply, divide, add, or subtract numbers on a spreadsheet

E a line of cells going from top to bottom on a page

Part D Use the drawing on the left to answer these questions. On your paper, write the letter of the correct answer.

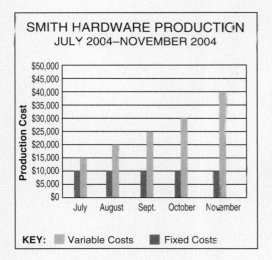

SMITH HARDWARE PRODUCTION
JULY 2004–NOVEMBER 2004

KEY: ▮ Variable Costs ▮ Fixed Costs

18. What were the fixed costs for Smith Hardware Production for September?

A $10,000   **C** $25,000

B $20,000   **D** $40,000

19. This drawing is a _____ .

A line graph   **C** spreadsheet

B pie chart   **D** bar graph

20. During what month are the variable costs the highest?

A September   **C** November

B October   **D** July

Test-Taking Tip When studying for a test, learn the most important points. Practice writing or saying the important points out loud. Have a partner listen to check whether you are right.

10

Filling Out Business Forms

Many jobs require that you know how to complete business forms. Whether you have to fill out sales slips, fax invoices, or go online to order, it is important to be accurate. This chapter will help you gain confidence in these areas.

In Chapter 10, you will review different kinds of forms that you will have to fill out in some companies. You will also learn how to use catalogs to write order letters, and you will learn how to write a follow-up letter when an order is wrong.

Goals for Learning

◆ To learn how to fill out sales slips and invoices

◆ To be able to use computer printouts to maintain a company's inventory and to know when to reorder items

◆ To know how to use catalogs to reorder supplies

◆ To learn how to place an order

◆ To be able to write a follow-up letter

Inventory

The amount of goods and materials on hand; stock

Sales slip

A form that a store uses to keep a record of a sale

Some stores have their inventory computerized. When they scan a product at the cash register, the inventory automatically changes to show the sale.

Manuel Baca is a sales clerk for Value Office Supplies, which has five stores in Memphis, Tennessee. In the main store on South Street, Manuel sells office supplies to walk-in customers, and he also takes phone orders.

Manuel's friend, Latasha Jackson, works for the same company in the stock department. She works with the **inventory** in all five stores and in the warehouse. She lists the amount of goods or materials on hand and makes sure that each store has enough of the right items. Each day, both Manuel and Latasha have to fill out several kinds of forms. Latasha also has to write letters to order stock items and follow up on orders.

Manuel has to fill out a **sales slip** every time a customer buys supplies. He keeps a copy of this form so that the company has a record of who bought what, how much they paid, and when they made the purchase. At some companies, employees enter this information into a computer. Here is a sample of the sales slip that Manuel completes for each sale.

Value Office Supplies
14 South Street
Memphis, Tennessee 38101

Date _March 17, 2004_

Sold to _John Murray_

Address _2736 Natchez Place_

City, State, ZIP _Memphis, TN 38113_

How Many	Item #	Description	Unit Price	Amount
5 pkgs.	9738	Legal pads	$5.60	$28.00
1 box	7638	Butterfly clips	4.00	4.00
1	1121	Name stamp	7.00	7.00
			Subtotal	$39.00
			Sales Tax	3.22
			Total	$42.22

Notice how neatly and carefully Manuel filled out the sales slip with the date, customer's name, address, city, state, and ZIP code. Below that information are five columns. The first column asks, "How many?" The second column asks for an **item number** that is a code for each separate item sold by the company. Manuel can find the item number on the label on the item or on a list printed by his company. Then, in the third column, he described what the item was.

He wrote the price for each item in the fourth column. That column contains the price for one unit of each item. Sometimes this **unit price** is not just for each single item but rather for each box, each dozen, or each gallon. Mr. Murray bought five packages of legal pads. Manuel had to multiply $5.60 (the unit price) by 5 (the number of packages) to get the **amount** in the last column. The cost for five packages, therefore, was $28.00. Because Mr. Murray bought only one box of butterfly clips and one name stamp, Manuel did not have to multiply to get those amounts. After Manuel listed everything Mr. Murray bought, he added the amounts in the last column to get the **subtotal** of $39.00.

In Memphis, customers have to pay an 8.25% **sales tax** on the things they buy. As a result, Manuel had to figure the amount for sales tax. He multiplied the subtotal of $39.00 by 8.25%. He found that the sales tax for this order came to $3.22. Finally, he added the subtotal and the tax to get a **total** of $42.22 for Mr. Murray's bill.

Manuel told Latasha that he always checks his math to make sure that every sales slip is correct. He also checks to make sure that he has copied the item numbers correctly. He added, "A sales slip is an important record for the store and for the customer. An incorrect sales slip can make customers angry and can cost the company money."

Activity A Number your paper 1 to 10. Then list 10 mistakes made in filling out this sales slip.

Value Office Supplies
14 South Street
Memphis, Tennessee 38101

Date _____

Sold to __Wolanski_____

Address __Calhoun Ave._____

City, State, ZIP __Memphis_____

How Many	Item #	Description	Unit Price	Amount
3	9711	Typing paper		$12.51
6		Correction fluid	1.00	6.00
2	8321			7.00
4	9101	Memo pads	1.25	6.00
3	4320	Liquid adhesive	3.00	9.15
			Subtotal	$50.76
			Sales Tax	3.93
			Total	$54.85

Manuel also has to fill out **invoices.** An invoice, which is similar to a sales slip, contains a list of goods sold. It gives the price of each item and the terms of sale. Manuel uses an invoice for customers who have accounts with Value Office Supplies. These customers pay a monthly bill rather than pay for each sale. On the next page is a sample of an invoice Manuel completed.

A space for the name and address of the person or company who bought the goods appears on the top left side of this invoice. There is also space for Manuel to write a delivery address if it is different from the billing address. The directions say, "Complete if delivery address is different from billing address."

Value Office Supplies
14 South Street
Memphis, Tennessee 38101

- Office Supplies
- Printing
- Office Furniture

DELIVER TO

Complete if delivery address is different from billing address.

BILL TO
Franklin N. Brussells
2345 Beech Street
Memphis, Tennessee 38024

Invoice Number	591006
Date	4 - 1 - 04
Customer Order Number	37 - 24
Ordered by	Smith
Sold by	Hill
Audit	

√	Quantity Ordered	Quantity Delivered	Unit of Sale	Description	Unit Price	Per	Amount
	2	2	dz.	948 Pads	$12.00	dz.	$24.00
					Subtotal		$24.00

Service Charge of 1½% per month, 18% per annum, will be applied to all 60 day old balances.

Received above items in good condition

Regular stock merchandise can be returned for exchange, credit, or refund if in perfect condition and if returned within 30 days of date of purchase.

Sales Tax	1.98
Total	$25.98

Proofread invoices to make sure that the company's name and address are correct. Misspelled words or incorrect addresses make you—and your company—look careless.

The invoice number, which always appears on the form, is on the right side. The date, customer order number, name of the person who ordered the goods, and name of the salesperson who made the sale appear below the invoice number. It is Manuel's job to list information on the correct lines.

One copy of the invoice goes to the customer for his or her personal or company's records. The salesperson keeps another copy. The third copy goes to the billing department, and the last copy goes to the inventory department.

Many companies today use computers. Instead of writing out invoices, an employee enters the information into a computer. Then the computer prints out the invoice.

Activity B Number your paper 1 to 5. Then answer the following questions about the invoice above.

   1. Where was the order delivered?

   2. What was the unit price for the order?

   3. What is the customer's invoice number?

   4. How much is sales tax on this order?

   5. What is the subtotal on this order?

Computer printout

A printed record produced by a computer; also called a spreadsheet

Latasha's department receives copies of the sales slips Manuel and the other salespeople fill out. She and her coworkers need to adjust the inventory. An inventory is a list of items a company such as Value Office Supplies has on hand. When sold items are subtracted from the inventory, the workers know which items are left in stock. The workers also know which inventory items may be running low.

The people in Latasha's office need to know when it is time to reorder an item. Latasha decides ahead of time the least number of items that the company should have in stock. Most companies reorder before the inventory runs out.

To decide this number, Latasha uses the history of the item's sales. This record tells how many of the item sells each month. It also shows the times of year that the item sells best.

But that's not the only deciding factor in knowing when to reorder. Latasha also has to keep in mind how long it will take to receive the order. Remember, companies do not want to run out of stock.

Value Office Supplies, like most other businesses, uses computers to keep its inventory. Keeping track of the inventory by computer is easy and exact. Every day copies of the sales slips arrive in Latasha's office. She enters the items that the salespeople have sold into the computer. If she needs to know which store is selling a certain item, a **computer printout,** or spreadsheet, can tell her. A computer printout is a printed record produced by a computer. A sample computer printout appears on the next page.

For example, on March 17, Manuel sold John Murray one box of butterfly clips. Latasha entered that item into the computer.

```
BOXES SOLD
BUTTERFLY CLIPS
    DATE         MAIN STORE       PLAZA       THIRD ST.       OPERA       FINE ST.
    3/15             92             5            12             8            7
    3/16             56             4            10            11            6
    3/17             71            10             5             9            3
```

This computer printout tells how many boxes of butterfly clips Value Office Supplies sold in each of its five stores for three days. Included in the 71 boxes sold at the main store on March 17 is the one box that Manuel sold to Mr. Murray.

When Latasha has these figures entered into the computer, she has the information she needs to determine whether the company's stock of butterfly clips is low enough to reorder.

```
ITEM:    BUTTERFLY CLIPS                          REORDER BELOW: 500 BOXES
3/10       IN STOCK - 1,050 BOXES
3/13       TO MAIN STORE - 510 BOXES
           REMAINDER - 540 BOXES
3/14       TO PLAZA STORE - 35 BOXES
           REMAINDER - 505 BOXES
3/14       TO THIRD ST. STORE - 10 BOXES
           REMAINDER - 495 BOXES                  REORDER
3/14       ORDERED 2,016
3/21       RECEIVED ORDER
           TOTAL - 2,511
```

Latasha can tell from the information on the computer printout that on March 10, the company had 1,050 boxes of butterfly clips in stock at the warehouse. Because the main store was getting low on butterfly clips, she sent 510 boxes there on March 13. The next day, she also sent the Plaza store 35 boxes and the Third Street store 10 boxes. That meant that only 495 boxes of butterfly clips were left in inventory in the warehouse.

To the right of figure 495 on the printout, the word *reorder* appears. Look at the last column at the top of the computer printout. It says to reorder butterfly clips when the number of boxes on hand falls below 500. Because Latasha's inventory of boxes fell below that number, she ordered 2,016 boxes of butterfly clips on March 14. The printout states that she received the order on March 21.

Activity A Number your paper 1 to 5. Then write short answers to the following questions about this computer printout. It shows the inventory of correction fluid.

```
ITEM: CORRECTION FLUID                    REORDER BELOW: 30 DOZ. BOT.
3/10      IN STOCK - 76 DOZEN BOT.
3/10      TO FINE ST. STORE - 10 DOZ. BOT.
          REMAINDER - 66 DOZ. BOT.
3/14      TO OPERA STORE - 12 DOZ. BOT.
          REMAINDER - 54 DOZ. BOT.
3/15      TO MAIN STORE - 20 DOZ. BOT.
          REMAINDER - 34 DOZ. BOT.
```

1. Did Latasha have to reorder correction fluid from March 10 through March 15? Why or why not?

2. How many bottles of correction fluid were in stock at the close of the day on March 10?

3. Why do you think there is no entry for March 13?

4. How many bottles of correction fluid did Latasha send to the main store? When were they sent?

5. How many bottles of correction fluid were in stock at the close of the day on March 15?

Where To Find It

Using an Atlas

When you order something from a company, part of the cost is for shipping the product. The distance from the supplier to the customer helps determine shipping costs. Distance also helps determine how long it takes for the order to arrive.

An atlas is a handy reference book that can help you find the distance from one place to another.

An atlas is a book of maps. Each map has a scale that tells how many miles each inch represents. Using that scale, you can find the distance from one city to another. You can look up a city in the index and find the page number of a map that includes the city.

Using an atlas, find a map of the United States. Then find the city you live in and measure how far your city or town is from Los Angeles; New York City; and Houston, Texas. Then answer the following questions.

1. How many miles does each inch on the map represent?

2. Approximately how many miles are you from each city?

3. Which city is closest to your city?

4. What is the difference in distance between the two closest cities?

5. Which city is farthest from your city?

When Latasha had to reorder butterfly clips, she used the **catalog** put out by the paper clip company. A catalog is a book that lists items in a certain order. Latasha read the catalog descriptions to tell which kind of clip she wanted. She was careful not to make a mistake. Mistakes cause delays that might result in not having enough butterfly clips to sell when their customers are ready to buy.

Here is the section of the catalog that Latasha used to make her order. In this order, the unit price is for each gross, not each box. There are 12 dozen boxes, or 144 boxes, in a gross.

Writing Tip

After you have typed an order letter, check the item numbers in the catalog to make sure that they are correct.

Clips

#5566 – paper	100 per box	**$5.78** per gross
#5567 – paper	500 per box	**$20.11** per gross
#5580 – butterfly	50 per box	**$4.90** per gross
#5581 – butterfly	100 per box	**$9.20** per gross

Latasha remembered that the clips she wanted came 100 per box, so she reordered item #5581.

If Latasha had ordered item #5566, she would have received regular paper clips—the ones shown in the top drawing on page 175. They would not have been what the stores needed. Instead, she ordered item #5581, the butterfly clips—shown in the bottom drawing on page 175. Apparently, most of Value Office Supplies' customers need clips that hold thick stacks of paper.

Vocabulary Builder

Lie/Lay; Sit/Set; Rise/Raise

Some common pairs of verbs that sound alike and are close in meaning can be confusing. Three of these pairs are *lie* and *lay*, *sit* and *set*, and *rise* and *raise*.

The first word in each pair of words does not take a direct object. This means that *lie, sit,* and *rise* do not do anything to another noun or pronoun in a sentence. Each of these words can make a correct sentence just by adding a subject. For example, *I lie, I sit,* and *I rise.*

The second word of each pair must pass their action on to a direct object. This means that they do something to a noun or pronoun in a sentence. For example, *I lay the invoice on the counter, I set my briefcase on the floor,* and *I raise my hand.* You can tell whether these words require a direct object if you ask what you *lay, set,* or *raise.*

Number your paper 1 to 5. Read the following sentences. If the italicized word is correct, write C. If it is incorrect, write the correct word.

1. *Lay* those invoices on my desk, please.
2. Please *set* down.
3. *Rise* the shade if you need more light.
4. The manager always *sets* at the head of the table.
5. The sales slips will *lie* on the counter until accounting picks them up.

Pens

Ballpoint, throwaway	$7.70 doz.
Ballpoint, refillable	$11.55 doz.
Ballpoint, retractable throwaway	$10.45 doz.
Ballpoint, retractable refillable	$14.33 doz.

Activity A Number your paper 1 to 5. If the following statements about this catalog entry are true, write *True* next to the number. If the statements are not true, write *False*.

1. This catalog entry lists four kinds of ballpoint pens.

2. The lowest price is for throwaway pens with retractable points.

3. You cannot buy refillable pens that do not have retractable points.

4. Refillable pens with retractable points are the most expensive pens.

5. Businesses that provide pens for their employees and/or customers probably would buy throwaway pens without retractable points because they are the least expensive.

Spelling Builder

Rules for Writing Numbers

When you write a letter or a business message, you often need to include numbers. When do you use numerals and when do you write out numbers with words?

These rules can help you:

- Usually we write whole numbers from one to ten as words.

- If a number begins a sentence, always write it as a word or words. If this looks awkward, or if there are other numbers in the sentence, rewrite the sentence to move the number.

- If many numbers appear in a sentence, such as 3 pencils, 42 boxes of paper clips, and 100 boxes of staples, use numerals even if some of the numbers are one to ten.

Write a sentence for each of the following numerals.

1. 21
2. 13
3. 6, 46, 33, 185
4. 5 (at the beginning of a sentence)
5. 1

Order letter

Written to order supplies from a company

Fax machine

Sends copies of printed pages over telephone lines

Part of Latasha's job is writing **order letters** to order supplies from a company. She does not order all items by mail. Sometimes she places a rush order over the telephone, online through the Internet, or by **fax machine.** A fax machine sends copies of printed pages over telephone lines.

Some businesses prefer to order by fax rather than by telephone. Faxed letters gives them a record of what they ordered and when. If companies receive the wrong items, they can refer to their copy of the letter to prove that they did not make the error. Other companies prefer to order online because it is easy and fast. Products ordered online often arrive the next day.

Some businesses use fax machines to send order letters.

Latasha is careful to include all the information the supplier will need to fill her order. When she ordered butterfly clips, for example, she followed these directions when she wrote the body of her order letter.

Information to Include in an Order Letter

1. Include the billing/shipping address of the company.
2. Write the item number from the catalog.
3. Include a description of the item along with each item number.
4. Write the unit, or individual, price of each item.
5. Include the number of units you are ordering.
6. Find the subtotal for the units, figure the amount of the sales tax, and add the subtotal of the units and the sales tax. Write the total cost for the order.
7. Tell how Value Office Supplies will pay for the items (cash, check, or charge).
8. Tell how you would like the order delivered.
9. Write the date when Value Office Supplies needs the delivery.

If Latasha leaves out any of this information in her order letter, the order may take longer to arrive. Worse yet, Latasha might not get the right order. For example, if Latasha included the item description but no item number, the company might send her something different from what she wanted. Latasha realizes that including all of the necessary information in an order letter can save time and money.

Instead of writing an order letter, Latasha could place an order by telephone. She also could place the order online by going to her supplier's home page on the Internet. However, she still needs to tell her supplier the same information.

Some companies allow their customers to set up a **company account.** The customer can charge the supplies they need and pay a bill at the end of the month. This benefits both companies. The supplier keeps a loyal customer. The customer can combine many smaller charges onto a larger bill. Most companies, however, will establish a **credit line**—or maximum amount that a customer can charge to the company account.

Activity A On your paper, list any information Latasha left out of this order letter. Use the list on page 179 to help you.

Value Office Supplies
14 South Street
Memphis, Tennessee 38101

March 14, 2004

Mr. Robert Michael
Arlington Clip Company
6500 Wright Avenue
Trenton, NJ 08608

Dear Mr. Michael:

Please ship to the above address 14 gross of butterfly clips, 100 per box, at a cost of $9.20 per gross.

Thank you for your cooperation.

Sincerely,

Latasha Jackson

Latasha Jackson
Stock Department

Activity B On your paper, write a letter ordering 10 dozen boxes of heavy-duty envelopes, measuring 9" × 12". Make up the name and address of the company from which you are ordering. Add any other information to your letter. At the end, request that the company charge the total cost of the envelopes to your company account. Use the list on page 179 to help you write your order.

No matter how carefully Latasha checks her order letters, sometimes a mistake occurs. Sometimes the order contains the wrong products or does not include the correct amount. Even worse, sometimes the order never arrives. If any of these mistakes occur, Latasha has to follow up on the order.

A **follow-up** is a phone call, a letter, a fax, or an e-mail that corrects a mistake. It should explain the problem clearly and politely. It also should tell what the company wants done to correct the mistake.

When Latasha writes a follow-up letter, she always includes some of the information from her first order letter. She also adds new information. She follows the directions listed below when she writes the body of her follow-up letter.

Information to Include in a Follow-Up Letter

1. An explanation of the problem
2. The item number from the catalog or Web site
3. A description of the item
4. The unit price, or individual price, of each item
5. The total number of items ordered
6. The subtotal (total of items purchased before sales tax)
7. Copies of bills, invoices, or other helpful information
8. Ideas on how to solve the problem

Latasha sends this information by fax or by e-mail, or she calls the supplier.

Latasha always carefully checks the information in her follow-up letter to make sure that it is correct. It is just as important for a follow-up letter to be correct as it is for an order letter to be correct.

Imagine that you need to find a supplier for extra-large binder paper clips made by the E-Z Fastener Company, 123 East Street, Kingston, ON K7L 3H1. Write a letter to the company asking for the name and address of a supplier close to you.

Activity A On your paper, list any information Latasha left out of this follow-up letter. Use the list on page 181 to help you.

Value Office Supplies
14 South Street
Memphis, Tennessee 38101

March 23, 2004

Mr. Robert Michael
Arlington Clip Company
6500 Wright Avenue
Trenton, NJ 08608

Dear Mr. Michael:

On March 14, I ordered from your company 14 gross of butterfly clips, 100 per box, at the cost of $9.20 per gross. The item number for those clips is #5581.

On March 21, I received from you 14 gross of butterfly clips, 50 per box, for which Value Office Supplies was charged $9.20 per gross. Attached is a copy of the invoice sent with this order.

Please send us the correct merchandise immediately. Credit our account for the orginal order that we shipped back to you today. We must have the correct order by March 31 to keep enough stock in our inventory.

I would appreciate your immediate attention to this matter.

Sincerely,

Latasha Jackson

Latasha Jackson
Stock Department

Registering New Equipment

Kristy is the technology director for Lake City Schools. Josh is her new assistant. His job is to fill out and file paperwork.

"Kristy, three new computers just came in. Do I need to keep all of this information that came with them?" asked Josh.

"Send the technical manuals to the people who will use the computer. However, keep the product registration forms," said Kristy. "Fill them out and send them back to the company."

"Why?" asked Josh.

"Those forms contain the product model and serial numbers for the equipment we bought. Registration forms also tell the company the names, addresses, and phone numbers of the people who bought their products. Company representatives will know who we are if we call them with a problem. Also, if the company has a problem with this line of computers, they can contact us," Kristy said.

"Does that happen often?" asked Josh.

"Not really, but last year one company had a problem with the wiring on one of their models. Because the wiring could start a fire, the company recalled the computers and replaced them," said Kristy.

"Then it really is important to return these cards," said Josh.

For Discussion

1. Why is it important to return a registration form?

2. What information do registration forms include?

3. When might the seller need the information on a registration form?

4. What uses might the registration card have for the purchaser?

5. What other uses might the registration card have for the seller?

Chapter 10 R E V I E W

Word Bank

amount

computer printout

credit line

fax machine

inventory

invoice

item number

order letter

sales tax

subtotal

total

unit price

Part A Number your paper 1 to 12. Then write the correct answer from the box that completes each sentence. Use each answer only once.

1. The _____ is the stock that a company keeps on hand.
2. The _____ is the number of items purchased multiplied by the unit price.
3. An _____ identifies each item sold by a company.
4. _____ is a tax figured as a percentage of the cost of the sale.
5. The _____ on a sales slip is the sum of the amounts of the items purchased before adding in the sales tax.
6. The _____ is the sum of the subtotal and the sales tax.
7. The cost for one item is the _____ .
8. An _____ includes the price of each item and the conditions of the sale.
9. A _____ is a printed record.
10. An _____ is written to order supplies from a company.
11. A _____ sends printed pages over telephone lines.
12. The maximum amount that a customer can charge to a company account is the customer's _____ .

Part B On your paper, write an e-mail message to Phillips Paper Company. Order 7 boxes of $8\frac{1}{2}"\times 11"$ ripple erasable bond paper that costs $18 per box. Phillips Paper Company is located on 115 Howard Street, Newark, DE 19711. The company's e-mail address is phillipspaper@personsname.net. Ask the paper company to bill your company account.

Part C The Phillips Paper Company sent you 7 boxes of $8\frac{1}{2}"\times 14"$ erasable bond paper instead of what you ordered in Part B. Write a follow-up letter explaining the company's mistake and explaining what you want Phillips Paper Company to do to correct it.

Part D Number your paper 13 to 15. Then write the letter of the correct answer on your paper. Use this entry from a supply catalog.

Paper—$8\frac{1}{2} \times 11$
Bond, erasable . . . . $15.00 per box
Bond, nonerasable . . . . $12.25 per box
Bond, ripple erasable . . . . $18.00 per box

13. How much does one box of $8\frac{1}{2}"$ × 11" ripple erasable bond paper cost?

    A $15.00   **B** $12.25   **C** $18.00   **D** $24.00

14. What is the price of least expensive kind of paper in this entry?

    A $15.00   **B** $12.25   **C** $18.00   **D** $24.00

15. What is the cost of 10 boxes of nonerasable bond paper?

    A $150.00   **B** $122.50   **C** $180.00   **D** $240.00

Part E Number your paper 16 to 20. If the statement is true, write *True* next to the number. If the statement is not true, write *False*.

16. Because you write the remaining inventory on a sales slip, sales slips help keep inventory records up to date.

17. A follow-up letter never repeats information from an order letter.

18. An incomplete sales slip may cause problems with keeping an accurate inventory count.

19. In a follow-up e-mail message, you should always state that the mistake caused your company serious problems.

20. A computer printout contains copies of all invoices.

Test-Taking Tip If you will have to define certain terms on a test, write the term on one side of a card. Write its definition on the other side. Use the cards to test yourself, or work with a partner.

11 Communicating with the Public

All jobs today require some form of communication. Employees may have to greet customers, answer the telephone, send e-mail messages, or answer customer letters. What you say and how you say it often will determine how successful you will be at your job.

In Chapter 11, you will become familiar with several work situations that require good communication skills. You will see how knowing what to say and what to write can help you handle yourself with confidence.

Goals for Learning

◆ To understand the correct way to answer a telephone call

◆ To learn how to take helpful telephone messages and transfer calls

◆ To learn to send e-mail messages

◆ To recognize the elements of a good business letter to customers and to be able to write one

Hector Rosario works as a clerk for Smith, Marchi, and Glassman, a small insurance company. One of his most important duties is talking and writing to the company's customers. He makes sure that customers get answers to their questions. He also answers all letters and e-mails that request information from the company.

Hector's job is important because he is often the first person to speak with new customers. In fact, whether or not Hector makes a good impression sometimes makes the difference between getting a new customer or not. As a result, the company's partners were very careful when they promoted him. They knew they needed someone who could do a good job talking and writing to customers.

Everyone at the company is very pleased with Hector's work. The company is growing fast, and Hector's job has become too big for one person. His supervisor has asked him to train Michiko Kono to help him.

Michiko works well with people and has done a good job as an administrative assistant. She has a pleasant personality and a good speaking voice. It's up to Hector to teach Michiko some customer service jobs.

The first thing that Hector believes Michiko should know is the correct way to answer the telephone. Her voice and manner will be the first impression many people have of the company. The company wants that impression to be a good one. "An unpleasant tone in your voice can make customers decide to buy insurance from someone else," explains Hector. "It's a good idea to make people feel comfortable and know that we want their business."

Remember to speak clearly and slowly enough that the customer can easily understand you.

Here are eight tips that Hector gives Michiko about using the telephone.

1. Pick up the telephone after the first or second ring. A long wait may make some customers feel that the service from the company will be slow, too.

2. Be pleasant and sincere.

3. After you give the name of the company, give your own name. For example, Michiko would say, "Smith, Marchi, and Glassman Insurance Company. Michiko Kono speaking."

4. Listen carefully. Nothing is more annoying to customers than being asked to repeat what they said because you were not listening.

5. Always be polite, friendly, and helpful. Even if a customer is unpleasant, remain friendly and cooperative.

6. Take accurate and complete messages. Also, make sure that the messages get to the right people as soon as possible.

7. End a call by making the customer feel that you care, that you will help with any problem, and that you were glad to help.

8. Allow the customers to hang up first. That way you can be sure that they have said everything they wanted to say.

Michiko knows that good telephone manners are important to her company. She sets a goal for herself. Every time she talks to a customer on the telephone, she will make a good impression.

Activity A Number your paper 1 to 5. Then write the word or words that complete each of these hints for good telephone manners.

1. Pick up the telephone on the _____ or _____ ring.

2. If you let the telephone ring too many times, it makes the customer feel that service from your company will be _____ too.

3. When you answer the telephone, first give the _____ of your company.

4. Don't make customers _____ what they have already said.

5. If the customer is angry or rude, remain _____ and _____ .

Activity B Number your paper 1 to 5. Then write what you would say in response to these remarks that customers might make on the telephone.

1. "What company did you say this was?"

2. "What do you mean Ms. Singer is not available? Stop trying to give me the runaround."

3. "Make sure that Mr. Guth gets my message."

4. "My name is Mr. Kzidklsl." (The name is unclear. You cannot understand what the person has said.)

5. "Ask Ms. Singer to call me at (216) 555-9846 before three o'clock."

Good telephone manners will help Michiko succeed in her new job.

Taking Care of a Customer

"These hints are not all there is to talking to people on the telephone, Michiko," warned Hector. "After customers tell you why they are calling, you have to know what to do."

"What do you mean?" asked Michiko.

"Well," said Hector, "suppose that a customer asks to speak to Mr. Smith. You can answer in several ways. For example, if Mr. Smith is in his office, you can say, 'One minute, please. I will connect you.' But what would you do if you buzz him, and Mr. Smith is not in his office?"

"I would call him on the office **intercom**," Michiko said. "If he doesn't answer, I would tell the caller that I cannot reach Mr. Smith. I would also offer to take a message."

"That's right," said Hector. "However, never keep a customer waiting on the line for more than 10 or 15 seconds without explaining why." Hector thought for a minute and then added, "Now, suppose that a caller doesn't give his or her name. How would you ask for it?"

"I would probably say, 'May I have your name, please?'" replied Michiko.

Hector said, "That's good. You also could ask, 'May I tell Mr. Smith who is calling?'" Then Hector added, "If Mr. Smith is out of the office or in a meeting, here are some other things you can do."

---

1. Ask whether anyone else could help the caller.
2. Offer to help the caller yourself.
3. Offer to take a message for Mr. Smith.
4. If the company has a **voice mail** system, ask the caller whether he or she wants to leave a message on Mr. Smith's voice mail.
5. Offer to have Mr. Smith return the call.
6. Give the caller Mr. Smith's e-mail address.

Activity C Number your paper 1 to 5. Then write short answers to these questions.

1. Why shouldn't you leave a caller waiting on the line for more than 10 to 15 seconds?

2. If the person the caller wants to talk to is not available, what are five things you can do?

3. Why is the person who answers the telephone so important to a company?

4. What should you say if you can't hear the caller?

5. Imagine that the caller gives you his or her name very quickly and you don't understand it. What would you do?

Activity D On your paper, write how you would handle each of these situations. Remember that you want to make the customer happy.

Situation 1   The caller asks to speak to Mrs. Marchi, but she is out of town.

Situation 2   The caller asks to speak to Mr. Smith, but he is out to lunch. He will be back in the office at 1:30 P.M.

Situation 3   The caller wants to increase her life insurance, but she wants to talk to someone who can give her some advice. Ms. Glassman is the company expert on life insurance.

Situation 4   The caller is angry because he believes his bill is too high. The accounting department at the company handles the bills.

Situation 5   John Acree, a very important customer, calls and wants to speak to anyone who is available.

Taking messages correctly is an important office skill. Hector gives Michiko these suggestions on taking accurate, clear, and complete messages.

Extension

An extra telephone connection to the main line; the number to connect to such a telephone line

Taking a Message

1. Keep a pad of message forms, a pen, and a pencil near the telephone at all times.

2. When customers tell you to whom they want to speak, write that person's name on the correct line of the message form.

3. Fill in the date and the time correctly. If you receive the call at 9:15 A.M., write 9:15 A.M., not 9:00 A.M.

4. Write the name of the caller, the company he or she is with, and the caller's telephone number and **extension**. Remember to include the area code if it is different from yours.

5. Check the right box or boxes on the message form—such as *telephoned, called to see you, wants to see you, please call, will call again, urgent,* or *returned your call.* See the sample message form on page 194.

6. Include any additional information the caller gives.

7. Finally, sign your name at the bottom of the message form. The person receiving the form will know who took the call, in case there are any questions about it.

Writing Tip

If your handwriting is difficult to read, print the messages you take. This will help make the messages clear to the reader.

The information on a message form should be correct. For example, if you are not sure how to spell the caller's name, ask the person to spell it. If you have trouble hearing some information the caller gives, ask the caller to repeat it. In fact, before you hang up the telephone, repeat the message to the caller so that you will be sure you wrote everything correctly. Finally, sign your name at the bottom of the form. This way the person who receives the message will know who took the message

When you take a message that includes a telephone number, read back the number slowly to the caller. This will help you make sure that you have written it correctly.

Activity A Number your paper 1 to 8. Then list the eight mistakes on this message form.

To: _Joe_

Date: _____ Time: _9:38_

WHILE YOU WERE OUT

M _Eagles_

of _____

Phone: _(216)_   _555-9876_

        Area Code   Number   Extension

TELEPHONED		PLEASE CALL	
CALLED TO SEE YOU		WILL CALL AGAIN	
WANTS TO SEE YOU		URGENT	
	RETURNED YOUR CALL		

Message: _wants an estimate on_
          homeowner's insurance

Call taken by: _____

Activity B Number your paper 1 to 5. If a statement is true, write *True* next to the number. If it is not true, write *False*.

1. A pencil is the only thing you need by your telephone to take messages.

2. It is not important to learn the name of the caller.

3. You should write all numbers carefully so that they are easy to read.

4. You don't have to bother checking any box on the message form because the person receiving the message will know what the caller wants.

5. The person getting the message does not have to know who took the message.

Transfer

To switch a business telephone call to another department or person

Disconnected

A telephone call that has been cut off

If Hector cannot help the person who is calling, he **transfers,** or switches, that call to another department, to another person in the company, or to the voice mail system. He pointed out to Michiko that transferring business calls correctly is as important as taking accurate messages.

"When you transfer a call," said Hector, "first explain to the caller what you are doing. Then make sure that you give the caller the name and extension number of the person who will receive the call. That's important," he said, "because if the caller accidentally gets **disconnected,** he or she can call back and ask for the right person."

Then Hector showed Michiko how to transfer a customer's call so that she wouldn't disconnect a caller. Finally, Hector told her to stay on the line until she is sure that she transferred the call successfully. Hector explained that more people hang up when someone transfers a call than at any other time. Make transfers quickly.

Transferring a call quickly is as important as taking an accurate message.

Activity A Number your paper 1 to 4. Then list in the right order these steps for transferring a call. Begin with the step that you should do first.

A Use the correct method for transferring a call.

B Explain why you have to transfer the call.

C Remain on the line until you know that your call transferred successfully.

D Give the caller the name and extension of the person to whom you are transferring the call.

Activity B What would you do in the following situations? Number your paper 1 to 5. Write *Transfer the call, Send the call to voice mail,* or *Answer the question.*

1. A caller wants to know how late your company is open.

2. A caller wants to talk to Bob Simmons in the sales department. You just saw Bob in the lunchroom.

3. A caller would like to speak to Mrs. Warren, the head of marketing. She is out of town.

4. Your voice mail system is down when Mr. Chen calls with a question for Mrs. Marcus.

5. A caller wants to know whether your company is open on Saturday.

Vocabulary Builder

Name or Number?

Often people use a number instead of the name of a month when they are recording a phone message. For example, instead of writing December 21, they write 12/21, meaning the twenty-first day of the twelfth month of the year.

Write down the twelve months of the year in order from January to December. Then, next to each month, write the number of the month.

On your paper, change the following dates to all numbers.

1. July 4   **4.** February 28

2. May 21   **5.** April 19

3. November 11

Smith, Marchi, and Glassman has some customers who live out of town or in another state. These customers sometimes call long distance, write letters, or send e-mail messages. Part of Hector and Michiko's job is to answer their questions.

Hector received a letter from a customer who lives in Philadelphia, Pennsylvania. The woman asked whether her homeowner's insurance covered the theft of lawn chairs from her patio. The chairs were missing when she came back from a trip. She wanted to know whether her insurance policy included coverage of items that were taken from outside of the house. If so, how much would the insurance company pay, and what should she do next?

Hector checked her insurance coverage and wrote her a letter. This is part of the body of that letter.

> You have our standard homeowner's policy. Since your policy has a $100 deductible clause, you must pay the first $100 of loss. Then we will pay any loss over $100. If the value of your lawn chairs comes to more than $100, send us the receipt for the cost of the replacements, and we will issue you a check for any amount over $100.

Hector's letter was well written. He explained the kind of policy the customer has and described the coverage. He told her how much she would have to pay to replace the lawn chairs. He also told her how much the insurance company would pay. He then told her exactly what to do next.

Activity A Number your paper 1 to 5. If a statement is true, write *True* next to the number. If it is not true, write *False*.

1. When responding to letters, give customers all the facts necessary to answer their questions completely.

2. A letter answering a question should be as short as possible.

3. Make customers believe that you take their questions seriously. Answer their questions carefully and completely.

4. Provide every bit of information you can when answering customers' questions.

5. Some customer letters don't need an answer. Throw them away.

Activity B Suppose that Mrs. Rose O'Connor has written you a letter for information on public transportation in your city. She wants to know whether there are buses or subways and whether the public transportation runs all night.

On a separate sheet of paper, write a letter to Mrs. O'Connor. Give as much information as you can about public transportation in your area. Make sure that your letter is clear, easy to understand, accurate, and complete.

Spelling Builder

Prefixes

A prefix is a syllable or part of a word that is added to the beginning of a word. Prefixes change the meaning of a word.

Two common prefixes are *re-* and *un-*. *Re-* means *again,* and *un-* means *not*. When *re-* is added to a word, it means *again* plus the meaning of the word. *Redone*, for example, means *completed again*. The same is true with *un-*; *unhealthy* means *not good for a person's well-being*.

Add the prefix *re-* to the following words. Write down the meaning of the new word; then use the new word in a sentence.

1. run
2. read
3. write
4. heat
5. think

Answering E-Mails

One form of communication is electronic mail, or e-mail. To send and receive e-mail messages, two or more computers communicate with one another. E-mails are faster than letters, less distracting than phone calls, and less complicated than faxing. E-mail allows you to have "live" written conversations with another person. That means that the tone of an e-mail is less formal than that of a letter. A word of warning, however: Your e-mail messages are not always private.

E-mail messages are different from letters or telephone calls. E-mail does not convey emotions as well as face-to-face conversations or even telephone conversations. The person who receives your e-mail can't hear your voice or see your gestures. Certain rules apply to e-mail messages just as they do to letters and telephone calls.

Hector reviewed the following e-mail rules with Michiko.

1. Always include a subject line. It tells the receiver the topic of your message.

2. Make sure that the subject line is meaningful. A message to Brown Moving Co. with the subject line *Tuesday* is not helpful. A better subject line would be *Schedule for the Lee Family*. A good subject line also will help you—and the person receiving your e-mail—file the e-mail later.

3. Don't type in all capital letters. They are hard to read and generally mean the same as shouting at another person.

4. Always include a greeting, such as *Hello* or *Dear*.

5. Keep your sentences short. Begin a new paragraph when you begin a new thought.

6. Use correct grammar and spelling.

7. Be careful about sending personal and private information such as credit card numbers. E-mail is not protected while it is going from one computer to another.

8. Always sign your e-mail messages with your name.

9. Many e-mail writers use abbreviations to say what they mean. For instance, ASAP means *As Soon As Possible*, FYI means *For Your Information*, and IMO means *In My Opinion*.

E-mail is a fast, easy way to send business messages, but don't misuse it. Do not send messages to your family and friends from your business computer. Also avoid game playing, personal use of the Internet, and other activities that interfere with your work and your coworkers' jobs.

Activity C Number your paper 1 to 5. If a statement is true, write *True* next to the number. If it is not true, write *False*. Then change the wording to make the false statements true.

1. Don't identify the subject of your e-mail message.

2. Type your message in capital letters. It looks more important.

3. Don't bother to use correct grammar and spelling in your e-mail message.

4. Include a credit card number on all your e-mails.

5. Always sign your e-mail messages with your name.

Where To Find It

Grammar Checker
When you write a letter to a customer, it is a good idea to use a grammar checker on your word processor. This feature will review your letter and highlight mistakes. Some grammar checkers automatically mark possible mistakes. You can find other mistakes if you check in the Edit heading of your word processing program. Also remember to proofread to catch errors the grammar checker does not highlight.

Smile into the Phone

Mika had a flat tire on the way to work and was an hour late. When she finally got to her workstation, she was angry and upset. She had just sat down when the telephone rang.

"Hello," she barked into the telephone.

"Is this the White Pine Agency?" asked the caller.

"Yes," grumbled Mika.

"This is Mr. Jacobs. May I speak with Miss Jones?" asked the caller.

"She doesn't work on Mondays," Mika snapped. "Call back tomorrow," she said as she hung up the telephone.

Mika's employer heard Mika's end of the conversation. She then told Mika that she should never speak to a caller like that, no matter how bad she feels or how angry and frustrated she is.

"People learn about our agency from your tone of voice. If you sound angry and unpleasant, they may never call again. Remember to keep a smile in your voice no matter what has gone wrong," said her employer.

"I'm sorry," said Mika. "That's good advice. It would be hard to be angry when there's a smile in your voice."

For Discussion

1. What upset Mika?

2. What impression do you think she made on the caller?

3. What would you think of a company that answered the telephone this way?

4. What would you do to be more pleasant when you are having a bad day?

5. What does Mika need to remember when she answers the telephone and she is in a bad mood?

Chapter 11 REVIEW

Word Bank

disconnected

extension

intercom

transfer

voice mail

Part A Number your paper 1 to 5. Then write the correct answer from the Word Bank that completes each sentence.

1. A two-way system called an _____ has a microphone and a speaker that allows people in nearby offices to talk to one another without leaving their desks.

2. _____ is an electronic system that records telephone messages that are played back later by the person receiving the calls.

3. An _____ is an extra telephone connection to the main line.

4. To switch a business telephone call to another department or another person, you _____ the call.

5. A _____ call is one in which a telephone connection has ended.

Part B Ms. Carol Dryer wrote to you, asking for the fares for the Spring Cruise from Miami to the Bahamas. Tell her the prices: $499 per person for the 3-day cruise and $599 per person for the 4-day cruise. Write the text of a letter to her. Ask her what city she will be leaving from and what day she would like to leave. Mention that the travel agency you work for has special prices on other cruises, too.

Part C Number your paper 6 to 12. If the statement about answering telephones is true, write *True* next to the number. If it is not true, write *False*.

6. An unpleasant voice answering the telephone can make customers take their business elsewhere.

7. Give the name of your company.

8. Don't give your name unless the caller asks for it.

9. Do not ask callers to repeat anything—even if you don't understand them.

10. If customers get nasty first, you can be rude back.

11. Make sure that messages you take are complete and accurate.

12. End all calls quickly. You don't want to waste time.

Part D On your paper, write the letter of the correct response.

13. Which of the following is a proper e-mail rule?

    A Don't include a greeting.

    B Forget capitalization and punctuation.

    C Close the letter with a signature.

    D Don't write on the "subject" line.

14. Mr. Ramirez calls for Dottie Green. Dottie is on another line. What do you say to Mr. Ramirez?

    A Ms. Green is on another line. Would you like to hold?

    B Please call back when she finishes this call.

    C I'm sure that Ms. Green doesn't want to talk to you.

    D I don't know nothing about Ms. Green's schedule.

15. A customer sends you an angry e-mail, complaining about poor service from your company. What should you do?

    A Delete the message from your computer.

    B Send an angry e-mail message back to the customer.

    C Ask how you can make the situation better.

    D Wait three days. Give the e-mail to your boss.

Part E On your paper, write the message you would give to your boss as a result of this telephone call.

You:	Carbone Company. This is Mr. Williams.
Caller:	Mr. Williams, this is John Denny. I would like to speak to Mr. Carbone.
You:	I'm sorry, Mr. Denny, but Mr. Carbone is in a meeting now. May I take a message?
Caller:	Tell him to call me as soon as possible at (216) 555–8746. The order he sent is missing several items. I want to know why.

Test-Taking Tip Read the directions twice. Sometimes they will give you a hint. For example, the directions may tell you to look for the most likely answer.

12 Conducting a Business Meeting

You have probably attended more meetings than you realize. You could have attended a casual gathering of your coworkers in the hall or the annual sales presentation of your company. You could have attended meetings of community groups or service clubs. Whether they are casual or formal, business meetings run more smoothly when there is a set of rules.

You'll learn the basics of those rules in Chapter 12, as well as ways to prepare an agenda and hints for taking minutes of a meeting. At the end of this chapter, you will feel more comfortable attending a meeting and will know how meetings are conducted.

Goals for Learning

◆ To understand the basic rules of attending and conducting a meeting

◆ To read and understand an agenda

◆ To prepare an agenda for a business meeting

◆ To take minutes of a meeting

Meeting

A gathering of people for a common purpose

Agenda

A list of things to do or to discuss at a meeting

Minutes

A written record of what happened at a meeting

For the past five years, Matthew Huang has worked as an office manager for ABC Plastics, a small plastics supplier for automotive companies. He makes sure that the office runs smoothly.

Recently, his company bought another small factory and combined the offices at the ABC location. Matthew would now need to spend more time training new employees. His immediate supervisor promoted Renea Jones to be Matthew's assistant.

Renea's job would be to schedule **meetings,** or gatherings of people to discuss a common purpose. She would prepare an **agenda,** or list of things to do or topics to discuss at those meetings. She would also take notes, or **minutes,** at the meetings she scheduled, creating a written record of what happened and what the people at the meeting said. Renea was eager to learn new things. She and Matthew sat down one Friday morning and reviewed the basic rules of the new job. He told her, "These meetings may be different from the ones you attended before."

"In what way?" asked Renea.

Matthew pointed out that many people share ideas during a business meeting, so there has to be an orderly way for everyone to take part. "Mr. Vega has called a meeting of the sales staff for next Monday," he said. "He wants you to attend. You will see for yourself."

Companies hold meetings for the following reasons:

- to create team spirit
- to make decisions
- to provide training
- to plan projects
- to introduce new ideas
- to report on company progress

In 1876, Henry M. Robert wrote a simple version of parliamentary procedure. His handbook, *Robert's Rules of Order,* is the main set of rules for conducting meetings.

"What is the purpose of Monday's meeting?" asked Renea.

"Mr. Vega and the sales department are launching a new product," Matthew said.

On Monday morning, Matthew explained that the company meetings followed **parliamentary procedure.** He said that parliamentary procedure is a widely accepted set of rules to help a group work together. These rules help groups of people work in an orderly way and make good decisions.

"Mr. Vega is the leader, or **chair,** of this meeting," Matthew continued. "He begins with the **call to order,** welcomes the members, and explains the purpose of the meeting. As a chair (or chairperson) he keeps the discussion on track and encourages people to take part in the meeting. He solves problems fairly and makes sure that the meeting stays within the scheduled time. He **adjourns,** or ends, the meeting and sets up a time for the next one."

"You and I will be the secretaries for today's meeting," Matthew continued. "That means that we will write an official record of what happens, check attendance, and read a report from the last meeting."

"Even if you are not taking notes of the meeting, it's important to pay attention. When you attend a meeting or conduct one, don't squirm. Don't talk when another person is speaking."

"So it's important to be polite and respectful at a meeting," Renea said.

"That's right," said Matthew.

Sometimes a meeting starts with a reading of the minutes of the last meeting. Members can correct or add to the minutes and then vote to approve them. After members have accepted the minutes, they become an official record.

Activity A At the ABC Plastics meeting, Renea saw some employees acting correctly and others acting incorrectly. Number your paper 1 to 10. Identify each statement as *Correct* behavior or *Incorrect* behavior.

1. Selene interrupted the speaker four times.

2. Matthew chewed bubble gum and blew bubbles during the meeting.

3. Josh took notes and paid attention during the presentation.

4. Joel clipped his nails while the group discussed one of the main topics.

5. Melanie politely introduced herself to the speaker during the coffee break and asked a question about the presentation.

6. Matthew got up and left the room every 10 minutes.

7. Norah tapped her pen every time the room was silent.

8. While others were speaking, Kim whispered to Jena about the company picnic.

9. Robert returned from coffee break a half an hour late.

10. Margo wanted everyone to notice her new perfume, so she used a lot of it that morning.

Following parliamentary procedure helps a meeting run smoothly.

Renea's new job also included preparing meeting agendas. An agenda is a list of things to discuss or to do at a meeting. People attending the meeting want to know what will happen and when. Matthew told Renea to give the agenda to members before the meeting. She also should give them any handouts or background material from people who would speak at the meeting. This allows people attending the meeting to read the materials and make notes on them. Matthew reminded Renea that she would need time to copy and hand out these materials before the meeting. He asked her to prepare the agenda for the next meeting at least a week in advance.

The first step in preparing an agenda is to ask the chairperson how many people will speak and how long the meeting will be. Matthew said, "You then can ask each speaker how much time he or she will need. Allow each speaker no more than an hour, and break the meeting schedule into parts. People get restless if a speaker talks too long."

"Okay," said Renea. She then organized the agenda, listing the times, the topics, and the speakers next to the scheduled times.

Agenda for Annual Sales Meeting

8:00 to 8:30	Registration
8:30	Call to Order
8:35	Company address by Ramon Vega, Chairman of the Board
9:00	Keynote address: Improving Sales in 2005 by Sharon Lutz, Vice President, Sales
10:00 to 10:15	Break
10:15	Production report, Tim O'Leary, Head of Manufacturing
11:00	New Ideas in Engineering, Dr. Jamal Warren
11:30	Discussion on Ideas from Marketing Department
12:00	Adjourn

Check the spelling of the speakers' names on the agendas you prepare.

Activity A On your paper, write the following agenda items in the proper order.

4:00	Adjourn
8:30	New Business
2:30	Break
12:00	Lunch
8:10	Old Business
10:00	Break
9:30	Full Group Discussion
8:00	Call to Order
8:45	Presentation on New Products, Roberta Manheim, Manufacturing
1:45	Marketing Strategies for New Products, Karen Hoffman, Sales
11:00	Discussion, Employee Concerns with New Strategies
1:00	Group Discussion on Using New Advertising Media
9:20	The Importance of New Products for the Company, Ed Simmons, Research and Development
3:00	What Every Employee Can Do, Sid James, Vice President
10:30	The New Marketplace, Ichiro Susuki, Finance
3:45	Final Comments

Spelling Builder

The Right Way with Titles

Have you ever wondered when to capitalize a person's title? When you are writing an agenda or minutes for a meeting, you may ask this question.

If you are using a title as part of the person's name, capitalize the title: *Chairperson McKinley* or *Karen McKinley, Chairperson.* If the title is not part of the person's name, don't capitalize it: *Ms. McKinley is the chairperson.*

The same rule applies to politicians and those holding public office.

Number your paper 1 to 5. Rewrite these sentences using correct capitalization.

1. We saw president Bush.
2. Mr. Johnson is the Chairman of our company.
3. Ms. Walker will be the new Company President.
4. If senator Smith had been elected, she would have been the first female president.
5. Will the Secretary or the Treasurer lead the meeting?

Motion

A formal suggestion made at a meeting

Resolution

A formal statement of opinion

Second

A statement that one supports a motion being discussed at a meeting

Objective

True to facts

The day of the meeting, Matthew reminded Renea that she would be taking minutes of the meeting. Minutes become an official record of what took place at the meeting. As a result, the person who takes the minutes needs to take careful, accurate notes of what actually happens.

Because Renea had never taken minutes before, she asked Matthew to help her. He gave her this list of tips on how to take minutes at a meeting.

1. Take notes on anything that happens that you think is important. You can just state the main points of a discussion, but you must write down word for word any **motions** or **resolutions** that are made. A motion is a formal suggestion or call for action made at a meeting. For example, someone might say, "I make a motion that we spend $10,000 for advertising." A resolution is a formal statement of a decision or an opinion a body or group votes on. Include the name of the person who made each motion or resolution and the name of the person who **seconded** it. To second a motion means to support what is under discussion.

2. If you do not understand something that is being discussed, ask someone at the meeting to explain it to you.

3. Type a final copy of the minutes as soon after the meeting as possible so that everything is fresh in your mind.

4. Remember that the minutes you write must be accurate and **objective** reports of the decisions made and the actions taken at a meeting. Include only the facts. Do not add your opinions or let your personal feelings affect the words you use. The minutes must be true to the facts.

If taking notes
will be part of
your job, practice
taking notes of
conversations or
other meetings
you may attend.

Note Taking

"Write down key words and phrases that will help you remember what people discussed at a meeting," Matthew advised Renea. "In most cases, don't write down every word. Instead, sum up general discussions and ideas." He added, "You also can abbreviate words. For example, suppose that a committee is talking about ways to get more customers, and Mr. Kingman suggests that the company advertise in the newspaper. You could write down something that looks like this."

> Ways to get cust.
> Kingman — adv. in paper.

"If Ms. Ives suggests advertising in books, magazines, and newspapers, your notes could look something like this."

> Ives — adv. in all media.

"Always write the final draft of your notes as soon as possible after the meeting. That way you will not forget the meaning of your abbreviated words and phrases."

Matthew cautioned, "Just remember to write down motions or resolutions word for word. You should even use quotation marks and write down complete names and figures. Let's say that Sharon Lutz makes a motion that the company budget $10,000 for advertising. Mrs. Chen seconds the motion. You would probably write down something that looks like this."

> Lutz – "I move that we budget $10,000 for advertising in all media."
> Chen – "Seconded."

"Remember," warned Matthew, "everybody takes notes differently. Write down what you need to remember about what happened at the meeting. Later, you will have to use those notes to write complete sentences and paragraphs that other people can read and understand."

"Writing minutes seems like a hard job," said Matthew, "but it gets easier the more you practice. The big secret is to listen carefully and to take accurate notes."

Vocabulary Builder

More Meeting Terms

Business meetings use special terms. Here are a few phrases with which you should become familiar.

old business
   topics discussed at previous meetings

to refer to committee
   to ask a small group to study an idea

to call for the question
   to ask for a vote on a motion

Imagine that you must explain the following sentences to someone who has never been to a meeting. Rewrite the sentences so that this person will understand them.

1. Mr. Hernandez called the meeting to order at 10 o'clock.

2. He asked whether there was any old business.

3. Ms. Lowe said that the people at the last meeting referred the employee attendance issue to committee.

4. The members discussed advertising, and Mr. Vega called for the question.

Activity A On your paper, write the notes you would take from this discussion during a meeting.

Ms. Ives: We have had it with trying to collect money from some of our customers. I make a motion that we hire a collection agency to manage accounts that are more than 90 days past due.

Mrs. Chen: I'll second that motion.

Mr. Kingman: How much will a collection agency cost us? Can our billing department take some action before we get outside help?

Mr. Rodrigez: Those are good questions. The billing department could call people who have overdue accounts and maybe send them a warning letter.

Ms. Ives: Let's ask Emily Raye from the billing department to come to our next meeting. She can report on what her department is doing and what more it can do. I'll withdraw my original motion.

Mrs. Chen: And I'll withdraw my second.

Ms. Ives: I move that we invite Emily Raye to our next meeting. She should report on what her department can do to collect on overdue accounts.

Mr. Rodrigez: I second that motion.

Mr. Kingman: All those in favor of the motion, say "Aye." [*pause during which all the people at the meeting say "Aye."*] Good. The motion passed. Joe, would you make sure that Emily receives that invitation?

Activity B On your paper, write minutes for the meeting in Activity A, using the notes you took. Do not refer to your textbook.

A Noteworthy Secretary

Shawna decided to join a new community organization. Two months later, the group elected her its secretary. Her friend Talisa is secretary of the employees' group at work.

"Congratulations, Shawna," said Talisa. "When does your term begin?"

"At the next meeting," said Shawna. "I am a little nervous. This is the first time I have ever been secretary of an organization."

"Haven't you taken notes for business meetings here?" asked Talisa.

"Of course," said Shawna, "but there are a lot more people at the organization's meetings, and I don't know some of their names."

"Just ask the president for a list of members. Then ask that speakers give their names before they talk. That way you can record the name of each speaker."

"But what if people speak too quickly?" asked Shawna.

"Don't be afraid to ask them to repeat what they said if you don't hear the motion or resolution. Remember that you are keeping the official record for the organization, just as you have kept official records of our meetings," said Talisa.

For Discussion

1. What is Shawna's new assignment in the organization, and what is she supposed to do?

2. Why is Shawna worried?

3. What suggestions does Talisa have?

4. Why does Talisa tell Shawna that she should have no problems?

5. Why is it important to keep correct minutes at an organization's meetings?

Chapter 12 REVIEW

Word Bank

adjourn

agenda

call to order

meeting

minutes

motion

objective

parliamentary
procedure

resolution

second

Part A Number your paper 1 to 10. Then write the correct answer from the Word Bank that completes each sentence. Use each answer only once.

1. A _____ is a formal suggestion made at a meeting.
2. When you take _____ of a meeting, you record the events and discussions at the meeting.
3. A _____ is a formal statement of opinion.
4. A statement that one agrees to a motion is a _____ .
5. _____ means true to facts.
6. An _____ is a list of things to discuss or to do at a meeting.
7. A _____ is a gathering of persons for a common purpose.
8. The call to begin a meeting is the _____ .
9. When you reach the end of the meeting, you _____ .
10. _____ is a set of rules for running a meeting.

Part B Write short answers to these questions.

11. Name one thing a chairperson does.
12. Why is it important to give people an agenda and handouts before a meeting?
13. What is the difference between a *motion* and a *resolution*?
14. List three things you have to remember when taking notes.
15. Write a brief paragraph describing acceptable behavior during a meeting.

Part C Read the situation below. Then write the notes you would take for this meeting.

Latisha Jackson made a motion to accept the council's proposal for a new park. David Hennessee seconded the motion. Danita Moore and Josh McIntyre disagreed. Danita Moore thought an area for parking was more important. The motion passed by a vote of nine for and two against.

Part D Write the letter of the correct answer on your paper.

16. When you take notes, you must write down any motions or resolutions _____ .

   A in summary form

   B word for word

   C without the names of the people involved

   D only if they relate to money

17. When you take notes, you should _____ .

   A sum up discussions

   B write down word for word discussions

   C write down only the motions

   D ignore discussions

18. Minutes of a meeting should include _____ .

   A the writer's feelings   **C** facts

   B prejudices   **D** outlines

19. At formal meetings the chair first _____ .

   A adjourns the meeting

   B makes a motion to accept old business

   C calls the meeting to order

   D introduces new people

20. The first step in preparing an agenda is _____ .

   A scheduling the breaks

   B taking minutes

   C getting the names of people who will speak

   D copying handouts for the people attending the meeting

Test-Taking Tip When you are reading a test question, pay attention to words that are emphasized in bold type or in capital letters. Those words will help you decide how best to answer the question.

Writing Business Reports

S ome jobs will require that you write a business report or present one orally. Although much of what you learned about writing reports in school will apply to writing a business report, you will need to know a few new steps.

In Chapter 13, you will learn the six steps for writing a business report. You also will learn how to give an effective oral presentation.

Goals for Learning

◆ To determine the purpose of a business report and to create an action plan for one

◆ To collect information from different sources and put the information in a logical order for a business report

◆ To make an outline of a business report

◆ To know how to write conclusions and suggestions

◆ To write a business report and present it orally

Business report

A spoken or written account of information

Conclusion

A decision or opinion reached by reasoning

Suggestion

Plan or idea for action based on the information gathered

Julia Michaels had worked for Linsey-Wolsey Company for six years. She was a good employee, and her supervisor had already promoted her several times. Then one day her boss, Mrs. Kowalski, took her aside and said, "Julia, I would like to recommend you for a job opening in the sales department. Mr. Shobe will be retiring at the end of the year. He travels all over the country, talking to our customers. You would have to learn some new skills, but I think you would do a good job."

"What kinds of skills would I need?" Julia asked.

Mrs. Kowalski explained, "For this job, you will have to learn how to speak in front of groups of people. You will need to know how to give reports. The company wants to find the right person to replace Mr. Shobe. I think you would do an excellent job. To be considered for the position, however, you will have to learn a lot very quickly."

Julia was excited. She knew immediately that she wanted the promotion. She asked Mr. Shobe to help her learn what she needed to know for the job. He agreed, and they decided to meet a half an hour before work every day.

Mr. Shobe first showed Julia how to write a **business report.** Like reports that Julia wrote in high school, a business report is a written account of facts. In a business report, however, Julia would have to draw **conclusions** from the facts and make **suggestions** about how to solve problems.

He explained that most business people write reports to share information with others. Julia needed to learn the kind of information to include in a business report. She also needed to know how to put the information together in a clear way. To help her, Mr. Shobe wrote the following steps for writing a business report on a sheet of paper. He explained that the order in which she might do these steps could change.

Steps for Writing a Business Report

1. Write answers to the following questions:
    - Why am I writing this report?
    - What is its purpose?
    - What questions should this report answer?

2. Make an **action plan** for completing the report. Set dates to complete each part of the plan. Develop a brief **outline** of the report.

3. Collect the information you need to answer your questions.

4. Make a final outline that arranges your information in a **logical order.**

5. Plan how you will explain or sum up any information your readers may not understand. At the end, draw conclusions from your information, and make suggestions on what to do next.

6. Then follow these steps:
    - Write a rough draft of your report.
    - Proofread it carefully.
    - Make any necessary changes and corrections.
    - Make sure that the final copy of your report is free from errors.

Julia and Mr. Shobe decided to discuss each of these six steps separately. They started by looking at how to determine the purpose of a report. Mr. Shobe told Julia always to consider these four questions.

Questions to Determine Purpose

1. Why is this report being written?
2. For whom is this report being written?
3. How will this report be used?
4. How much information should this report cover?

Mr. Shobe explained, "Suppose that at a sales meeting you mention that customers are complaining about one of our products. Ms. O'Hara is head of our quality control department. She would probably ask you to write a report about the complaints that you have heard." Then he added, "How would you answer the four questions in that situation?"

Julia thought carefully before she answered each question.

1. Why is this report being written?
   "To find out how many customers are complaining and tell what they are complaining about."

2. For whom is this report being written?
   "Ms. O'Hara, who may send the information to the production department."

3. How will this report be used?
   "To answer complaints and possibly correct something that is wrong with a product."

4. How much information should this report cover?
   "The number and nature of the customers' complaints about one product."

Activity A On a sheet of paper, answer the four questions that determine purpose, based on this situation:

You work for a clothing store. The men's clothing department has lost customers during the last three months. The sales director asks you to write a report that explains why.

Questions to Determine Purpose

1. Why is this report being written?
2. For whom is this report being written?
3. How will this report be used?
4. How much information should this report cover?

Vocabulary Builder

Know Your Audience

One of the most important steps in determining purpose is deciding who your audience is. *Audience* means the people who will read or listen to what you write or say.

Knowing your audience helps you decide what your listener or reader already knows. It helps you decide how much background and detail to give. It also helps you understand how the listener or reader may already feel about your subject.

Look for the word *audience* in a dictionary. Write the definition or definitions on your paper. Then list three reasons you should know your audience before you write or speak.

Next, Julia and Mr. Shobe talked about developing an action plan. An action plan tells the steps you need to complete to write a business report. An action plan usually includes a statement of purpose. It also lists major topics and suggests how to gather information. It includes a schedule of dates for completing the steps.

Then Mr. Shobe shared this list with Julia. It listed information she could include in the action plan for any report.

General Information for an Action Plan

1. An explanation of the problem or subject of the report
2. A statement on why the report is necessary
3. A list of the ideas to solve the problem or topics that relate to the subject of the report
4. The definitions of words that may be unfamiliar to people who read your report
5. A schedule of where and how you will gather information
6. Possible conclusions and suggestions

Mr. Shobe told Julia, "At this point, you will want to make a brief outline to add to your action plan." He added, "I always change the outline as I gather information, but an outline helps organize your ideas."

"Also, you might come up with some conclusions about the problem and ways to solve it as you develop your outline. If so, include those ideas as well," Mr. Shobe said. "Be sure to schedule your time to type, proofread, and copy the report. It's very stressful to leave all the work until the last minute."

Here is Julia's action plan for the report on complaints about a product.

An Action Plan for a Business Report

I. Purpose: To find the number of and reasons for complaints regarding men's walking shorts (#345-687). Are the complaints reasonable? If they are, how do we correct this mistake?

II. Data gathering: I will contact all members of the sales staff and give them a survey to determine the number and nature of the complaints.

III. Rough outline

    A. Statement of purpose

    B. Survey form

    C. Results of survey

    D. Conclusions based on research

    E. Suggestions

IV. Schedule

    A. Distribute survey 6/12

    B. Collect survey 6/18

    C. Finish gathering information 6/20

    D. Write rough draft of report 6/25

    E. Submit final draft of report 7/1

Activity A Number your paper 1 to 5. If the statement is true, write *True* next to the number. If the statement is not true, write *False*.

1. The only thing you have to think about when you plan a business report is its purpose.

2. It is important to know who will read your report so that you can direct your information to that person or group of people.

3. An action plan will help you organize your report.

4. An action plan has only three parts.

5. One part of an action plan is an explanation of what is being reported on.

Activity B On your paper, write an action plan to help you write a report. The report will explain why the men's clothing division has been steadily losing customers for the last three months. Use the following information to help you.

- The report is due on Monday, March 26. You were given the job of writing the report on February 2.

- Look back at the previous pages to follow the action plan that Mr. Shobe suggested to Julia.

Survey

Finding information by asking people questions

Getting the necessary information for a business report is probably the most important step in writing a report. "It doesn't matter how good your report looks. It doesn't matter how well you state your purpose. If the information you gather is not complete and correct, your report isn't worthwhile," Mr. Shobe emphasized.

There are many ways you can gather information. One way is to take a **survey,** or ask people what they think. You also can find information in books, magazines, newspapers and on the Internet.

You can conduct interviews with your customers. You also can look at how your company does something. For example, if a new product is taking longer to make than it should, watch the workers who are making the product. You might observe what is causing the delay.

The sources you use for your information often depend on the purpose of a report. Books and magazines, for example, probably will not help you find out why you are getting complaints about a product. However, they might help you understand why your company is losing customers. For instance, books and magazines could tell you whether businesses similar to yours are losing money. These sources also could help you decide whether there is a need for a particular product or service. They could tell you what other companies are doing to solve the problems that your company is having.

Newspapers can give you the same kind of information. Local newspapers are especially good sources of information about businesses in your city or town.

Activity A Number your paper 1 to 5. Each number stands for one of the five following topics. Next to each number, write the letters of the sources listed on the next page that you could use to find information on that topic. You probably will use more than one source for each topic, and you will use some sources more than once.

Topic 1   Your report looks at the latest trends in using machines to build cars. How effective are the machines? How much do they cost? What jobs can they do? What can't they do? How many workers get laid off when factories install machines to build cars?

Topic 2   Your company makes rowboats. Your report discusses whether to make certain changes in the design of the rowboat. Will an improved rowboat sell more boats? Will it appeal to a larger group of customers? How will these changes affect the cost of the rowboat?

Topic 3   Your report explains how your company can improve employee attendance. What have other companies done to improve attendance? What do workers in your company think would improve their attendance? What does your human resources department suggest?

Topic 4   Your company makes dining room chairs. Your report is about the use of a new fabric to cover the seats of these chairs. How sturdy is the new fabric? Will it increase the cost of the chairs? Does it stain easily? Is it available in different colors and patterns?

Topic 5   Your report examines the chances of building a successful restaurant in Daytona Beach, Florida. How many restaurants are already in the area? What kinds of restaurants are they? What is the economy like in Florida? What kinds of restaurants do people in Daytona Beach go to most often?

Sources of Information

A fabric journals

B restaurant journals

C surveys of the sales staff and of your customers

D books and magazines with articles about the use of machines to build cars

E personal interviews with customers

F letters to the Daytona Beach Chamber of Commerce asking for a list and descriptions of all the local restaurants

G surveys of heads of companies who are using machines to build cars

H magazines, booklets, and other publications on what companies do to improve attendance

I calls to chair makers who have used this fabric

J tests your company performs on this fabric

K calls and letters to companies that have improved worker attendance

L the production department of your company

M articles from magazines published in Florida

N newspaper articles

O magazines on making boats

P surveys given by human resources departments that asked workers what would improve their attendance

Spelling Builder

Titles

When you use information from a source such as a magazine or newspaper, it is a good idea to tell what it is, or cite it.

Enclose the title of an article from a newspaper or magazine in quotation marks. Also use quotation marks around the title of a book chapter. Underline or italicize titles of books, magazines, and newspapers.

Rewrite the following sentences, punctuating them correctly.

1. I read the book How to Create Business Reports.

2. It included the chapter Concluding the Report.

3. Did you see the article Business Outlooks in the Daily Post?

"After you gather all of your information," Mr. Shobe explained to Julia, "arrange it in a logical order. In a business report, use any order that makes sense."

He then explained that certain things that might determine the order in a report. "Sometimes it makes sense to give the information according to the order in which it happened, its importance, or the money involved," he said. "Think about your audience, or the people who will read your business report. They may want to read all of the facts first and consider the conclusions last. Or they may be just the opposite. They may want to see the conclusions first and then look at the information that led to those conclusions. Your audience determines how you arrange your information.

"The topic of a report itself may be a clue to deciding the best order to use," Mr. Shobe continued. "Imagine that you are reporting on the advantages of a certain fabric. Your audience might want to compare it with the fabric the company is now using. The way in which your company will use a report may help you decide on a logical order.

"Finally," he said, "remember to include charts and graphs. In some business reports, they appear at the end of the report. In others, the charts and graphs appear within the report because they are important to understanding it. The best advice is to consider your audience."

Activity A Number your paper 1 to 10. If the statement about business reports is true, write *True* next to the number. If the statement is not true, write *False*.

1. The order in which you arrange information in a report should depend only on who is going to read the report.

2. One correct way to arrange the information in a report is to give the conclusions first and the information that supports those conclusions later.

3. The topic of a report is important in deciding the order of information.

4. Graphs and charts can appear at the back of the report.

5. Include graphs and charts when they are well made and attractive.

6. Graphs and charts can appear at the front of the report.

7. Sometimes you may want to arrange a report so that the readers can compare two or more things.

8. Including charts and graphs as part of the report helps people see some information as they read about it.

9. If charts help the audience understand information, place the charts at the back of the report.

10. Learning to choose the correct order for information in a report can make the difference between a successful report and an unsuccessful one.

Mr. Shobe told Julia that the best way to decide on the final order of information is to make an outline. He gave her this format to refer to when she developed her outlines.

A Sample Outline

I. Introduction

    A. Purpose

    B. Survey of sales staff

        1. Number of complaints

        2. Nature of complaints

II. Explanation

    A. Explanation of survey data

    B. Problems with survey data

III. Conclusions

IV. Suggestions

    A. Stop making product

    B. Redesign garment

Julia noticed main headings, subtopics, and details. Roman numerals (I, II, III, etc.) identified the main headings. Capital letters (A, B, C, etc.) identified the subtopics, which were indented under the main heading. Regular (Arabic) numbers (1, 2, 3, etc.) identified additional details about the subtopic. Details were indented under the subtopic.

Julia saw that the first word of each topic, subtopic, and detail began with a capital letter. The Roman numerals, capital letters, and regular numbers all had periods after them. She also noticed that the main headings appeared in the same order as they would appear in the report.

Basically, an outline is a general plan of your report. It serves as a way to organize the ideas in your report. Using an outline will help you decide how to arrange main topics and details the best way. For example, on a rough draft of an outline, you can rearrange ideas until you are able to include all of the related information in a logical order. Sometimes working with an outline also will show you that a few pieces of information you have gathered do not belong with the rest of the information.

Activity B On your paper, write these parts of an outline in the correct order.

A. Grizzly	B. Polar
III. Fruit	2. Tiger sharks
A. Sharks	A. Lemons
I. Bears	C. Rockfish
1. Great white sharks	C. Oranges
II. Fish	B. Cherries
B. Tuna	D. Salmon

Activity C On your paper, write these parts of an outline in the correct order.

1. On-site studies	I. Introduction
B. Proposed renewal site	1. Survey of area for proposed new store
IV. Suggestions	B. Sources of information
A. Purpose of report	II. Explanation
2. Written survey of local merchants and customers	2. Projected sales
III. Conclusions	A. Survey data

Activity D On your paper, write the main topics in the correct order for an outline from this list.

1. Statement of purpose

2. Sources of information

3. Suggestions

4. Survey forms

5. Store records

6. Conclusions

7. Interview with clerks

8. Explanation

Where To Find It

Online Search

Many libraries have access to online magazine indexes. If you look up a topic in these indexes, you will find a list of magazine articles about your topic.

When you search a magazine (periodical) index, be sure to narrow your topic; otherwise you will find too many articles that do not tell you about your particular topic. For example, if you search for *insurance,* hundreds of articles will appear. Limit your topic to the particular information you need, such as *life insurance providers.*

Choose a topic and narrow it to a particular part of the topic. Then go to a computer with an online periodical index and search for a list of magazine articles on your topic. Print out the list.

The next step for writing a business report, Mr. Shobe said, was explaining what the information means. He explained that Julia would have to come to some conclusions about the information she presented in her report. Conclusions are decisions or opinions that you reach after you present all the facts. "Always base your conclusions on the information you gather," Mr. Shobe explained.

"Let's say, for example, that you gather facts about the advantages of plastic washers compared with rubber ones. You find that rubber washers are less likely to break. They provide a more drip-free seal. Unlike the plastic washers, rubber washers do not create much wear and tear on the fixtures. Your conclusion might be that rubber washers are better to use than plastic washers."

Making Suggestions

Based on the basis of the information she gathered and the conclusions she reached, Julia would have to make suggestions about what the company should do next. Let's imagine, for instance, that Julia has to give a business report on improving employee attendance. She found that many companies offer cash bonuses to employees who have perfect attendance. She found that attendance was better because of the bonuses. The bonuses encouraged workers to come to work. She could reach the conclusion that the bonuses didn't cost the company any money. Fewer workers called in sick, and the company made more products. In fact, she found that four of the companies she surveyed saved money by giving bonuses. Julia might make the suggestion that her company should give employees bonuses for perfect attendance.

**Writing
On Your
Own**

Suggest a change of policy for your school or workplace. Identify a problem, give reasons for the change, and suggest a new policy to replace the old one. Support your suggestions with research.

From these two examples, you can see that getting the facts, understanding those facts, arriving at sound conclusions, and making good suggestions are all very important. If you make a suggestion without having all the facts, or if your suggestion is not based on the facts, your company could spend a great amount of money with no positive results.

Activity A Number your paper 1 to 8. Then list the kinds of facts that you would need for each of these eight suggestions to be good ones.

1. Use machines on the production line on a trial basis.

2. Do not change the design of the rowboat.

3. Rate workers on their attendance as well as on other factors. Employees who don't show up for work should not qualify for pay increases.

4. Use the new fabric to cover all maple dining room chairs. The new fabric resists stains, wears well, and will increase the cost of each chair by only $5.

5. Think about opening a restaurant in Daytona Beach if the company finds a suitable site in the northwest section of the city.

6. Continue to ship products by train. It is the least expensive and most convenient method.

7. Get a toll-free telephone number for customers to use; then advertise that you have it. Most toll-free numbers increase business by 32%.

8. Stop making men's shirts with button-down collars. Only 6% of the men in this country wear them.

Writing a Rough Draft

Mr. Shobe told Julia that the next step is to write the rough draft of her business report. After she writes it, she should read through it carefully, making all needed changes and corrections so that the report is as good as it can possibly be. Then Mr. Shobe told her that she should read through the final version of the report one more time, proofreading the final copy and correcting any last errors.

Finally Mr. Shobe said to Julia, "Usually you should make enough copies of your report for everyone in your audience. It's also important to keep a copy for yourself."

Activity B Use the following 10 steps as a guide to write a business report of your own.

1. Write a business report on a job or a career that interests you.

2. Write a clear statement of purpose. Make sure that your purpose answers these four questions.
   • Why am I writing this report?
   • Who needs to see it?
   • How will the company use this report?
   • How much information should I include?

3. Prepare an action plan and collect information from several appropriate sources. For example, find out how many people work in that field, what the salaries are, what chances there are for promotion in that field, and what kind of training or education you would need to get a job.

4. Arrange your information in a logical order.

5. Prepare an outline for your report.

6. Write your report.

7. Within the report, explain all terms and information clearly.

8. Include any conclusions you can reach as a result of the information in your report.

9. Include suggestions based on the information that you gathered for your report.

10. Proofread the first draft of your report and correct any errors. Then make a final copy that is neat and accurate.

Oral business report

A report that is spoken out loud; a spoken account either based on outlined notes or read from a written report

Mr. Shobe told Julia, "Follow those same steps in preparing an **oral business report.** The only difference between a written report and an oral one is that you may not have to write out a final oral report. In some cases, you might give your oral report from your outline or notes. At other times, though, you may have to write out a report and give a copy to everyone in the meeting. You would give an oral summary of your written report."

Then he added, "When you give an oral report, remember that your eagerness, your use of language and voice, your self-confidence, and your appearance all play a part in how well other people receive your report."

"I have seen many oral business reports fail," Mr. Shobe told Julia. "Usually, it's not the information that makes the report fail but the way someone gives that information. For example, have you ever seen speakers give an oral report—and they look as though they aren't very interested in the information they are presenting?"

"Oh, yes," said Julia. "Those speakers usually put me to sleep."

"I agree with you," Mr. Shobe said. "Their lack of interest makes audience members wonder why they should care about the subject. However, when speakers are excited, their listeners usually get excited, too!" Mr. Shobe paused for a minute and then added, "Always act interested in what you are saying, Julia. Look at the people you are speaking to. If you are eager, your audience will believe that what you are saying is important!"

"Your audience will be distracted if you use incorrect grammar or if you do not pronounce words correctly," Mr. Shobe continued. "They will not pay attention to what you have to say. One way to eliminate errors is to record your report and then listen for your mistakes."

Then Mr. Shobe explained that it is important to speak loudly and clearly when giving an oral report. "Your oral report will be meaningless if the people listening to you can't hear or understand what you are saying," he said.

Mr. Shobe then told Julia that a nervous speaker can make an audience feel uncomfortable. "Sometimes people think that a nervous speaker isn't telling the truth. People also may think a nervous speaker does not know the subject well," said Mr. Shobe.

"What's the best way to be less nervous and be more sure of myself?" asked Julia.

"That's easy," said Mr. Shobe. "Be well prepared. The more times you practice and rehearse, the less nervous you will be."

Then Mr. Shobe talked about how to dress for an oral presentation. "The way you look is important," he said. "Wear business clothes, and be neat and clean. You don't want to distract your audience with the wrong kind of clothes or jewelry. They might not listen to what you have to say!"

Activity A Number your paper 1 to 5. Then write the correct word or words that complete each sentence.

1. If your oral report shows that you think what you are saying is important, the _____ will think so, too.

2. Avoid making mistakes in _____ and in the way you _____ words so that the audience can pay attention to the information in your report.

3. A good way to eliminate mistakes is to _____ your report and then listen for mistakes that you tend to repeat.

4. It is important that you speak loudly enough so that the _____ who are listening can _____ you.

5. The best way to avoid nervousness is to be well _____ .

Business meetings run smoothly when there's an action plan.

Playground Reporting

Jerry is the secretary of a local community club. The club has asked him to find information on the best park equipment for young children.

"Amy, I need to find information on children's park equipment and let the club know what is best," said Jerry.

"Do you remember the business report that we did last year for Ace Construction?" asked Amy.

"Do you mean the report on fencing for its parking lot?" Jerry asked. "We compared wood and steel to see which would hold up better."

"Yes. You need to do research and recommend the best playgroud equipment, just like we did for Ace," said Amy. "Keep in mind that the city of Springvale bought new equipment last month. It is made of wood. You might call Jennifer Cox at the Springvale Community Center. Ask her what she learned. Remember that the club will be spending a lot of money. We want to make sure that the children will be safe, but the equipment has to be fun."

"Okay," said Jerry. "Maybe I could also call the elementary school and see what the kids like about their playground."

"Good idea," said Amy.

For Discussion

1. What must Jerry research?

2. How should he report the information?

3. What should Jerry be checking for?

4. What sources could Jerry check?

5. Give two reasons Jerry might want to write his report.

Chapter 13 R E V I E W

Word Bank

action plan

business report

conclusions

logical order

oral business
report

outline

suggestions

survey

Part A On your paper, write the correct word or words from the Word Bank to complete each sentence.

1. A presentation of information about a business situation is a _____ .

2. _____ are final, logical opinions based on facts.

3. _____ are advice based on the information you gather.

4. The steps needed to complete a business report are outlined in an _____ .

5. An _____ is a list of points in a report.

6. _____ is the arrangement of information in a way that will make sense to a reader or listener.

7. In a _____ , you discover information by asking questions.

8. An _____ is spoken aloud.

Part B On your paper, write the letter of the correct answer.

9. Which of the following is NOT a good reason for writing a business report?

   A to share information with others

   B to compare one product with another product

   C to share results of a survey

   D to keep busy during the day

10. Which of the following is NOT included on an action plan?

   A an explanation of what is being reported

   B a statement on why the report is needed

   C an account of the number of times you practiced

   D conclusions and suggestions

11. Which of the following would NOT be a source of information on a new line of children's clothing?

   A a survey of children about their favorite clothing

   B magazine article on "Trends in Kids' Clothing"

   C personal interviews with customers at the mall

   D your taste in children's clothes

Part C Number your paper 12 to 15. The following paragraph describes a toy called a Quink. Read the paragraph and answer the questions.

> Your company produces a fast-selling children's toy called a Quink. Demand is brisk. The company is having trouble keeping Quinks on store shelves. The head of the sales department has asked you to write a report on ways to increase production of Quinks.

12. Why are you writing this report?

13. For whom are you writing this report?

14. How will the company use this report?

15. How much information should this report cover?

Part D On your paper, write an outline using the following information. Include main headings, subheadings, and minor details. Turn back to pages 232–233 if you need help.

Purpose *To decide whether to close the Piedmont Street store*

It is losing business	It is losing customers
Sources of information	Hire a new manager
Sales records	It is losing money
Researched information	Interviews with former customers
Conclusions	
Suggestions	Interviews with Piedmont Street employees
Remodel the store	
Introduction	Close the store

Test-Taking Tip Effective studying takes place over a period of time. Spend time studying new material for several days before a test. Don't wait until the night before a test to learn new material.

14 Advancing Your Career

Once you have a job, how do you get promoted to a better one? How do you get pay raises? How do you learn the skills to become a manager?

In Chapter 14, you will find some answers to these questions. This chapter has good advice for employees who want to improve themselves and advance in their careers.

Goals for Learning

◆ To recognize ways to advance your career, including company-sponsored training, night school classes, and additional education

◆ To understand the benefits of additional training and education

◆ To understand the importance of reading professional journals

◆ To become familiar with college forms

◆ To improve your test-taking skills

Nick Pappas has worked at Henson Mills for five years. During the first three years, he received several promotions. Since then, however, he has not received a promotion or an increase in pay. One day he talked with Maria Rivera. She has received many promotions in the 10 years that she has worked at Henson Mills.

"Maria, why don't I get promoted the way you do?" asked Nick.

"One reason is that you haven't received any additional training," she replied. "I try to take advantage of any training classes the company offers. The company pays for them, but I go to classes on my own time," she explained.

She continued, "What I would really like to do, though, is work in computer support. I know a few software programs, the wages are better, and the outlook for jobs is good. In January, I started a class in computer programming at the community college. Henson Mills is changing, and I want to change with it."

"How is Henson Mills changing?" Nick asked.

"More of the business will depend on computers," Maria said. "That could mean that the company will need fewer people on the looms, and more people working on computers," she said.

"What should I do?" Nick asked. "I don't like the idea of giving up my evenings to go back to school. I also don't like to think I could be out of a job in the next few years."

"Think about it over the weekend," Maria said. "Registration at the community college begins on Monday. We could go together if you are interested."

Nick went home and discussed the idea of additional training with his wife, Sara. She pointed how much he enjoyed designing Web pages for his friends. She thought Nick should take classes in graphic design. "Why don't you talk to Pete?" she asked.

Nick's friend Pete started out in the shipping department. He liked Henson Mills but wanted higher pay and better hours. Pete had good grades in math in high school and decided to take some accounting classes at the tech center.

"That was the best decision I ever made," he told Nick. "I've applied for an opening in accounting. Ms. Jackson, the head of human resources, was impressed with my résumé. Those classes will really help my career."

"Do employers want workers to learn new skills?" asked Nick.

"Some companies believe that it is so important that they will pay the fees if an employee completes the class and earns a good grade," said Pete.

Activity A Number your paper 1 to 3. Match the person in Column 1 with the class title in Column 2 that would advance his or her career.

Column 1

1. Joe is a receptionist at a small animal clinic. He would like to be a vet's assistant.

2. Shelby is a cashier at a supermarket. She wants to be a manager.

3. Jason is a dishwasher at a nursing home. He would like a job preparing food there.

Column 2

A Hiring and Keeping Employees

B Healthy Eating for Older Adults

C Dental Care for Dogs and Cats

Pete explained to Nick that employees who really want to get ahead should read as much as they can about business. He said, "The more you know about what is going on in the business world, the more valuable you are to your company."

He gave Nick a **professional journal** about e-mail. Here is part of an article from that magazine.

The number of e-mails that come through a company's servers has increased by 60 percent since 2002. Such large growth is causing important changes in the way businesses deal with e-mail. Some companies are setting policies that limit the size of attachments that their e-mail systems will accept. Sometimes attachments cause computer problems and take a long time to download.

The information that appears in an e-mail tells quite a bit about the company. When companies or their employees send e-mail, it is important for them to follow these guidelines.

- Time is money in business. Write messages that are short and clear to the reader.

- Do not attach files. Copy the information and paste it into the body of the message.

- Do not write anything in an e-mail that would embarrass you if someone else read it.

- Fill in the subject box to help the person receiving the message know why you are sending the e-mail.

Pete pointed out that the article talked about a problem that every business has. Nick began to see how knowing something about business might help him advance his career.

Activity B Number your paper 1 to 5. Reread the article Pete gave Nick. On your paper, write short answers to these questions about the article.

1. What does this article discuss?

2. Why isn't it a good idea to attach files?

3. Why should employees avoid e-mailing information that they do not want someone other than the planned reader to see?

4. Why is it important to fill in the subject box?

5. Why should messages be short and clear to the reader?

Many colleges now allow students to register online or by telephone.

Rolf Muller, another friend of Nick's, was taking an **adult education** course at a local high school. People sign up for adult education classes to learn special skills, such as keyboarding, or to learn more about a certain subject, such as a foreign language. Rolf was going to night school to earn a high school diploma. Nick helped Rolf decide which courses to take. Here is Rolf's application.

**Grand City Public Schools — Adult Education Division
Night School Application**

(Please print or type.)

Muller	Rolf	T.

Name   (Last)   (First)   (Initial)

27 Lynch Circle, Grand City, FL   33162
Address   (ZIP Code)

407-555-1112   407-555-2899
Telephone Number   Emergency Telephone

Flagler High School, 1700 Rise Drive, Grand City, FL 33162
Name and Address of Last School Attended

10 th   2001
Highest Grade Completed   Last Year Attended

How did you find out about this night-school center?
A neighbor told me.

What are your educational goals?
I would like to get my high school diploma.

List below the course or courses you wish to take.
English III, Algebra I

Activity C Number your paper 1 to 5. Then answer these questions about Rolf's application form.

1. Why do you think the instructions tell you to print or type?
2. If Rolf got sick at school or had an accident, what telephone number should the people at the school call?
3. Where did Rolf go to high school?
4. When did he leave high school?
5. What two courses does Rolf want to take now?

The following Tuesday Nick and Maria went to the community college to register for their courses. They found lots of other people signing up, too. Some, like Nick and Maria, were taking a few courses to improve their job skills or to learn more about a certain subject. Others were taking courses to earn a degree.

You can earn an **undergraduate degree** after completing a two-year or a four-year college program. By completing a college program with two years' worth of courses, you can get an associate's degree. Another kind of college degree, a bachelor's degree, usually takes four years of full-time attendance. After earning a bachelor's degree, you can continue your education to earn a master's degree and then a doctorate.

College forms use some words you may not understand.

Undergraduate degree

A degree offered for completing a two-year (Associate of Arts) or a four-year (Bachelor of Arts or Bachelor of Science) college program

Some colleges offer one-year certificate programs in technical fields. Many colleges also offer courses online. You can use your home computer to take the class and complete assignments.

College Form Vocabulary	
Course number	A number given to a course to show that it is different from all other courses. Course numbers are found in college catalogs and course listings.
Course title	The name of the course: for example, Computers 101
Section	One of several class offerings of a course
Credit	Points given by a school or college when a student has completed a course

Following is an example of the **registration form** that Nick and Maria completed to take their college courses.

**Strasburgh College
Registration Form**

(Please print or type)

Name _____ Pappas _____ Nick _____ F. _____
　　　　　Last　　　　　　　First　　　　　Middle Initial

Address _____ 10 Elm Street _____

_____ Miami _____ FL _____ 33153 _____
　　　　　City　　　　　　　State　　　　　　ZIP

Course No.	Section	Title	Days Offered	Credits
736- 0003	3	Computer 1	Tu	3
736-10041	1	Programming 1	W	3

Nick F. Pappas
Signature

Nick looked in the college guide to get the correct course number and title. Then he copied the section number, days offered, and credits from the master schedule of classes.

Activity A Number your paper 1 to 3. Then match each term in the first column with its description in the second column.

Terms	Descriptions
1. section	**A** the name of the course
	B one of several class offerings
2. credit	
	C the number of points earned for a course
3. course title	

Where To Find It

Online Course Guide

Colleges post course descriptions and offerings online. Search the Internet for the name of a college in your area. Go to its Web site. Click on the Course Guide or Master Schedule of Classes. After you have found the Course Guide, you can find the subjects that interest you and the course listings for the next semester.

Nick's friend, Peg O'Reilly, was also taking college courses. However, Peg was planning to get her degree from Central College. In addition to the forms that Nick and Maria had to fill out, she also had to complete a **college application** to ask for admission to take college courses. Peg wanted to be a **degree candidate,** someone who wants to complete a degree program. When Peg showed the five-page form to Nick, he laughed and said, "Filling out all that information would take me all night!"

"No, it wouldn't," smiled Peg. "It's not hard to complete these forms when you understand what information they're asking for."

Activity B Number your paper 1 to 5. Peg's college application is on page 253. Match the item from Peg's application form in Column 1 with the information you would need to complete that item.

Application Items	Information Needed
1. list colleges attended	**A** the date when you began to work for a company and the date when you stopped working for that company
2. years of attendance	
	B the kind of work you did for a company
3. type of work	**C** the amount you were paid
	D the year you started in a school and the year you left that school
4. dates of employment	
5. salary	**E** the names of colleges you have attended

Application for CENTRAL COLLEGE

1. Name in full: ~~Mr.~~ (Ms.) ~~Mrs.~~ O'Reilly   Peggy   Nora   2. Sex F

                Last   First   Middle

3. Permanent home address   211 5th St.   Miami   Dade   FL   33152

                              Number/Route Street   City   County State ZIP

    Mailing address (if different from #3)   N/A

                              Number/Route Street   City   County State ZIP

4. Soc. Sec. No. 318-58-0745   Phone No. 407-555-3122   Emergency phone no. 407-555-4873

5. (a) Date of birth   2 / 12 / 79   Age 24   (b) Place of birth Ocala, FL

                 Month / Day / Year

    (c) If not born in the United States, when and where were you naturalized? _____

6. Married Yes _____ No ✓

7. Name and   Father Samuel O'Reilly, Ocala, FL 32670   Phone No. 407-586-1621

    address of   Mother Elaine O'Reilly, Same   Phone No. _____

    Guardian   Guardian _____   Phone No. _____

8. (a) List all senior high schools attended:

Name of School	Location	Years of Attendance	Date of Graduation
Ocala Senior High	Ocala, FL	1993 - 1997	1997

    (b) Have you received a GED? Yes____ No ✓ Date you received your GED:_____

    (I have taken)/ I plan to take the Scholastic Aptitude Test (Date) 7/6/03 and will have the results forwarded.

9. (a) List all colleges and/or universities attended:

Name	City & State	Dates Attended	Reasons for Leaving	# of Credits Completed
N/A				

    (b) If ever suspended or dismissed, please explain in detail on separate attached sheet.

    (c) Have you ever attended Central College? No ✓ Full____ Part-Time ___ Evening___ Summer _____ Last Date _____

10. (a) In what extracurricular activities have you participated in high school? For example, athletics, dramatics, music, publications, etc. List offices held.

        1. Newspaper (editor)   2. Yearbook

        3. Glee Club   4. _____

    (b) Name any special honors you have received in school _____

11. Work experiences, including summer or part-time employment. If you are not a recent high school graduate, you must account for each year intervening between date of leaving high school and date of this application. (Use separate sheet if necessary.)

Type of Work	Name and Address of Employer	Phone Number	Dates of Employment	Part- or Full-Time	Salary
Administrative Assistant	S. Franz 2387 Flagler St. Miami, FL 33154	407-555-1175	1997 to Present	Full-time	$22,250 per year

The courses Nick took at night would advance his career.

Vocabulary Builder

Introductory, Intermediate, and Advanced Courses

College catalogs and course listings include words in course title names to help you match your skills to information you will learn in the class.

Introductory means beginning. These courses introduce students to a subject.

Intermediate means in the middle. These courses are more advanced than introductory courses but less difficult than advanced courses.

Advanced means that students should already have a good background in the subject. These are the most difficult courses.

Number your paper 1 to 5. Imagine that these students want to sign up for a college course. Write whether they should enroll in an *introductory, intermediate,* or *advanced* course.

1. Josh knows nothing about Spanish but wants to learn it for his job.

2. Julie is a senior in college and has studied computers for three years. She wants to take the next course.

3. Sam enjoyed the one night school class he took in writing. He wants to sign up for another one.

4. Selene finished her freshman class in accounting and wants to continue.

5. Peter doesn't know any of the technical terms in cooking, but he enjoys preparing meals at home. He wants to sign up for an adult education course.

After a few weeks, Nick and Maria's teacher announced that there would be a test during the next class. "I've been dreading that," moaned Nick. "I haven't taken a test in years. I never did very well on tests anyway. Sometimes I get so nervous that I can't even think straight."

"Have you understood everything the instructor has explained so far?" asked Maria.

"Yes, in fact, I feel very good about the material. I studied between classes, read all the chapters the teacher assigned, and completed all the homework," Nick said. Then he added, "Tests just make me so nervous."

"They used to bother me, too, but a while ago a teacher gave me some ideas for taking tests. I haven't had any trouble since then," Maria explained.

"Please tell me what those ideas are," Nick told Maria. "They sound like what I need to make a good grade!"

These are the ideas that Maria explained to Nick.

> As you read through a test, answer the easy questions first. Then go back and work on those questions that will take more time.

1. **Know the material the test will cover.**

    Do not wait until just before a test to study. Study each new piece of material as it is given to you. Keep up with reading assignments. Take careful notes as you read. Review your notes regularly. If some information is not clear to you, ask questions until you understand it completely.

2. **Concentrate on the parts of the test that are worth the most points.**

    The teacher may tell you whether some parts of the test are worth more points than other parts. Spend most of your time on the parts of the test that are worth the most points.

3. Plan the time that you have to take the test.

Before you begin a test, skim over it. Get an idea of the number and type of questions on the test. Then figure out how much time you have for the whole test and how much time you can spend on each question. True-false and multiple-choice questions usually require the least amount of time. Questions that require a two- or three-sentence response need more time, and questions that require an essay for an answer need the most time. If, for example, you have an hour to finish a test, try to be halfway through in 30 minutes. Pace yourself. Then, if you finish the test early, use the remaining time to look over your answers.

4. Read each question carefully.

Answer the questions that are asked, not the questions you hoped would be asked. If you don't read a question correctly, you will end up giving a wrong answer.

5. Save any questions you are not sure of for last.

If you are not sure of an answer, continue through to the end of the test. After you have finished, answer any questions that you skipped. If points are taken away for unanswered questions, then try to answer all the questions.

6. Mark your answers clearly and accurately.

Some teachers use **preprinted answer sheets,** which allow them to use a computer to grade the tests. If you use one of these preprinted sheets to mark your answers, check the numbering often. Also make sure that your marks are dark. If you skip a question, skip a space on the answer sheet. Finally, make sure that you know what to do if you want to change an answer.

7. Change answers only if you have a good reason for doing so.

Usually it's best not to change an answer based on a guess. However, if you believe you have good evidence that your first answer may be wrong, change your answer.

Activity A Number your paper 1 to 10. If the statement is true, write *True* next to the number. If it is not true, write *False*.

1. You will do better on a test if you wait to study the night before the test.

2. You should study each new piece of material as it is given.

3. It is better to do your reading assignments all at one time.

4. You shouldn't ask questions in class because asking questions will make the teacher think you didn't read the assignment.

5. If you read a question on a test incorrectly, your answer probably will be wrong also.

6. Before you begin to take a test, you should look it over to see how many and what kinds of questions you will have to answer.

7. If you are not sure of the answers to some questions, you should skip them and go on to finish the test. Then go back to those questions.

8. You should allow the most time for multiple-choice questions and the least time for questions that require an essay.

9. If you have been told how much each part of a test is worth, it is a good idea to concentrate on those parts that are worth the most points.

10. If you are using a preprinted answer sheet, you should check the numbering of your answers often.

Spelling Builder

To Capitalize or Not to Capitalize?
For college courses, that is the question.

Do not capitalize the name of the school subject, such as *biology* or *algebra*.

Capitalize a course name followed by a number. Also capitalize the names of language classes. *Mr. Owens teaches Biology 101. I took Spanish III and an English class.*

Write the following sentences on your paper, using correct capitalization.

1. I will take computer science 101 and a chemistry class.

2. On Tuesdays I have german and japanese 101.

3. When I study my algebra, it reminds me of algebra I took in high school.

Activity B Number your paper 1 to 4. Then write answers to these questions.

1. Your test has 20 multiple-choice questions. You have 50 minutes to take the test. How long should you allow for each question?

2. The true-false section of a test is worth 25 points. The essay section is worth 45 points. The short-answer section is worth 30 points. On which section should you spend the most time?

3. You have three hours to take a test. It has three parts. The first part of the test has 25 multiple-choice questions. Each question is fairly long. This section is worth 35 points. The second part of the test has 10 questions that require two-to three-sentence answers. This section is worth 20 points. The last part of the test has two essay questions. Each question requires an answer that is several paragraphs long. This section is worth 45 points. How will you budget the three hours you have to take this test?

4. You have been given a test that contains 100 multiple-choice questions. You have three hours to take this test. Write a short paragraph explaining how you would budget the three hours for each of the following requirements.

   • answering as many questions as possible.

   • allowing time to check the numbering of your preprinted answer sheet.

   • going back and answering any questions that you skipped.

   • rereading any answers you weren't sure about.

What's Cooking?

Corey works as a server in a family restaurant. He enjoys his job and wants to learn more about the restaurant business. He also enjoys cooking and would like additional training as a chef. He decides to talk to Jared, the evening chef.

"Jared, where did you learn to cook?" asked Corey.

"I did a lot of cooking at home, but then I took an adult education class on cooking and baking," Jared said. "The community college offers night classes on all sort of topics."

"Are the classes expensive?" asked Corey.

"No, and they last from a few weeks to a full semester. They are a good way to find out whether you really enjoy cooking," said Jared. "The community college offers all kinds of classes, including some on photography, music, woodworking, English, math, history, and science."

"Where can I find the schedule of classes going on now?" asked Corey.

"Call the community college, or look on its Web site," Jared explained.

For Discussion

1. Where did Jared learn to cook?

2. Why does Corey want to take a cooking class?

3. Who can take adult education classes?

4. What are some advantages of taking an adult education class?

5. What places besides a community college might offer these classes?

Chapter 14 R E V I E W

Word Bank

adult education

college application

degree candidate

preprinted answer sheet

professional journal

registration form

undergraduate degree

Part A Number your paper 1 to 7. Then write the correct answer from the Word Bank that completes each sentence. Use each answer only once.

1. A _____ is a form on which students mark answers to tests by filling in circles or circling letters.

2. The _____ is a degree offered for completing a two-year (such as an Associate of Arts) or a four-year (such as a Bachelor of Arts or Bachelor of Science) college program.

3. A form to ask for admission to take college courses to earn a degree is a _____ .

4. A form used to sign up for college courses is a _____ .

5. A magazine related to business in general or to specific areas of business is called a _____ .

6. _____ is classes for adults.

7. A _____ wants to complete a degree program.

Part B Number your paper 8 to 24. Then write the information you would provide for each item on a college application.

8. age

9. date of birth

10. place of birth

11. name of father

12. high school attended

13. years attended

14. date of graduation

15. special honors

16. colleges attended

17. extracurricular activities

18. emergency phone number

19. sex

20. Social Security number

21. telephone number

22. name of mother

23. community activities

24. mailing address

Part C Write the letter of the correct answer on your paper.

25. By completing a college program that contains two years' worth of courses, you can receive an _____ .

    A bachelor of arts degree   **C** associate's degree

    B bachelor of science degree   **D** master's degree

26. By completing a college program that contains four years' worth of courses, you can receive a _____ .

    A bachelor's degree   **C** associate's degree

    B doctorate   **D** master's degree

27. Which of the following is NOT a good way to advance your career?

    A reading professional journals

    B taking a course offered by your company

    C registering for additional training at a community college

    D playing video games

Part D Number your paper 28 to 35. Then write the word needed to complete each of these sentences about taking a test.

Word Bank
ask
begin
carefully
entire
least
section
understand
type

28. Make sure that you _____ the directions for a test.

29. If you don't, _____ the teacher to explain the directions.

30. Read the questions _____ .

31. Before you _____ a test, look it over.

32. Also notice the _____ of questions.

33. Figure out how much time you have for the _____ test.

34. Figure out how much time you can devote to each _____ .

35. Allow the _____ time for true/false questions.

Test-Taking Tip If you have to read a paragraph before answering some questions, look over the paragraph quickly, and then read the questions. Reread the paragraph, and answer each question correctly.

15 Health Insurance for Employees

One of the advantages of full-time employment is the ability to get health insurance at a lower, group rate. To receive any kind of health benefits, you will have to fill out some forms. However, the time and work the forms take to complete certainly will be worthwhile if you or any of your dependents ever need health care.

In Chapter 15, you will learn how to fill out health insurance forms accurately and completely. Each lesson will cover a different kind of form.

Goals for Learning

◆ To understand the value of health insurance

◆ To be able to fill out a health insurance form correctly

◆ To learn how to apply for health benefits

◆ To understand workers' compensation

◆ To be able to fill out an accident report completely

Health insurance

Insurance that pays certain medical bills; also known as medical insurance

Premium

Payment for insurance

Group insurance

Insurance bought by many people, such as employees of a company

When Nadia Connor began working for Beacon Industries, she applied for **health insurance.** Health insurance, or medical insurance, helps people pay bills caused by illness, injury, or accident. Beacon Industries deducted the **premium,** or payment for insurance, from Nadia's weekly paycheck.

One of the reasons Nadia took the job three years ago was the benefit of health insurance. The rates she paid at Beacon Industries were lower than those she would have to pay if she bought the insurance on her own. Health insurance is less expensive when many people buy it together as **group insurance.** Some companies offer life insurance in a group plan, too.

For three years, Nadia paid the premiums but never needed to use her health insurance. Then she learned she needed a minor operation that would involve an overnight stay in the hospital. Her health insurance would cover most of the hospital and doctor bills. Although she had to pay a small amount, the insurance was a real benefit. She was thankful she had seen Ms. Jackson, head of the human resources department at her company, on her first day of work. Ms. Jackson gave Nadia an application to complete and patiently answered all her questions about health insurance.

Nadia filled out this form three years ago.

Medical Insurance Application

Name: Connor (Last) Nadia (First) _____ (Middle)   Employer: Beacon Industries

Home Address (include ZIP Code): 1223 Long Blvd.   Salem, OR   97302

Date of Birth: 3/12/76   Spouse's Date of Birth: 7/21/76

✓ Female
Male
0 No. of dependents

Single
✓ Married
Widowed
Divorced

No Does your spouse have group health insurance with another employer, union, etc.?

Signature: *Nadia Connor*   Date: 3/18/01

Some companies offer health insurance as part of a benefit plan. Benefit plans may include vacation time, health insurance, life insurance, and retirement programs. Employers offer these in addition to wages or a salary.

Nadia had followed all the directions, giving her birth date and the birth date of her husband. She also put a zero beside *No. of dependents* because she didn't have children or other people who depended on her for food, shelter, and clothing.

Nadia included her husband in her health insurance plan. The health plan his company offered was more expensive. He decided to be covered under her policy. She paid additional money to include him, but they felt they saved money overall. Being covered under a group insurance plan really helped Nadia and her husband. They had coverage at an affordable price. However, if Nadia had not filled the form out correctly, her husband might not have been covered under her policy.

Activity A Number your paper 1 to 11. Then write the information you would put on each line if you were filling out this application for health insurance.

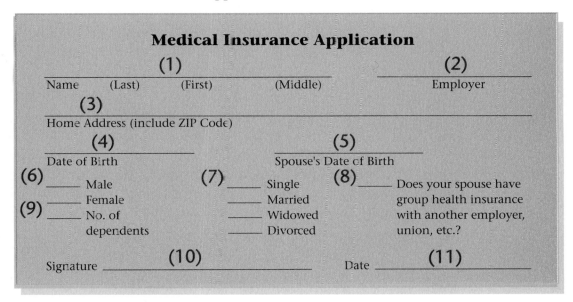

Medical Insurance Application

(1) _____   (2) _____

Name   (Last)   (First)   (Middle)   Employer

(3) _____

Home Address (include ZIP Code)

(4) _____   (5) _____

Date of Birth   Spouse's Date of Birth

(6) ____ Male   (7) ____ Single   (8) ____ Does your spouse have
____ Female   ____ Married   group health insurance
(9) ____ No. of   ____ Widowed   with another employer,
dependents   ____ Divorced   union, etc.?

Signature _____(10)_____   Date _____(11)_____

Before Nadia went to the hospital for her operation, she completed another insurance form. It allowed her health insurance company to pay the doctor and hospital bills directly. Some health insurance companies send their payments directly to the patient, who then pays the hospital and the doctor.

Nadia was not familiar with some of the terms on the form, however. She called the insurance company to get an explanation of those terms. She found a **toll-free** number on the application, so the call did not cost her anything.

1. The **patient** is the person being treated for an illness or an injury. In Nadia's case, she wrote her own name on the form. If her husband were the one having the operation, she would write his name on the form.

2. The employee or **insured** is the person who has the insurance. Nadia wrote her own name on the form. Even if her husband were being treated, Nadia would write her name here because the insurance is in her name. Some forms use the term *insured's name,* which is the same as *employee's name.*

3. *Do you have other health insurance coverage?* This question asks whether you have any other health insurance. If you do, write down the name of the other insurance company. In Nadia's case, she wrote *No.* It's important that you complete this item carefully. If you say you have other coverage and you do not, your health insurance company may not pay all the benefits owed to you.

4. *Is the condition related to the patient's employment?* This question asks whether the illness or injury has anything to do with the patient's job. In Nadia's case, she wrote *No* because her job did not cause her illness. This answer also affects the amount of money an insurance company will pay.

Nadia was wise to call her insurance company for an explanation of the unfamiliar terms. She was sure that she had filled out the form correctly.

When Nadia completed her part of the form, she took it to her doctor's office. The doctor's assistant would fill out the rest of the form and send it to the insurance company.

Activity B Number your paper 1 to 4. Then fill in the words that complete the definitions of these four terms.

1. patient's name
   the name of the _____ who is being _____

2. employee's name
   the name of the _____ who has the _____

3. Do you have other insurance coverage?
   the name of any other _____ with which you have

   _____

4. Is the condition related to the patient's employment?
   Does your _____ have anything to do with your

   _____ ?

Spelling Builder

Words Ending in -o
When you add -s to a word ending in -o, you must remember some rules.

Usually when you add -s to a noun that ends in -o, you just add -s. *We watched the videos on Friday.*

Usually when you add -s to a noun that ends in -o with a consonant before the -o, you add -es. *We heard echoes in the canyon.*

However, there are exceptions to the rules, especially with musical terms. When spelling musical terms, just add -s. Also, some words are correct spelled either way. Unless you are sure of the correct spelling, use a dictionary.

Add -s to the following nouns. Check a dictionary if you are unsure of the spelling.

1. potato   3. peso   5. shampoo

2. piano   4. hero

Here is a sample of the health benefit form that Nadia completed so that the insurance company would pay her doctor and hospital bills. Notice that she was supposed to fill out only the top part of the form. The doctor or the company providing the health service completed the rest of the form.

MAJOR MEDICAL CLAIM

PATIENT & EMPLOYEE INFORMATION

1 PATIENT'S NAME (First name, middle initial, last name) 2 PATIENT'S DATE OF BIRTH 3 EMPLOYEE'S NAME (First name, middle initial, last name)

4 PATIENT'S ADDRESS (Street, city, state, ZIP code) 5 PATIENT'S SEX MALE FEMALE 6 EMPLOYEE'S DATE OF BIRTH

7 PATIENT'S RELATIONSHIP TO EMPLOYEE SELF SPOUSE CHILD OTHER 8 EMPLOYEE'S GROUP NO. (Or group name)

9 OTHER HEALTH INSURANCE COVERAGE – Enter name of Policyholder and Plan Name and Address and Policy or Medical Assistance Number 10 WAS CONDITION RELATED TO A PATIENT'S EMPLOYMENT YES NO B AN AUTO ACCIDENT YES NO 11 EMPLOYEE'S ADDRESS (Street, city, state, ZIP code)

12 PATIENT'S OR AUTHORIZED PERSON'S SIGNATURE I Authorize the Release of any Medical Information Necessary to Process this Claim and Request Payment of MEDICARE/CHAMPUS Benefits either to Myself or to the Party Who Accepts Assignment Below. SIGNED DATE 13 I AUTHORIZE PAYMENT OF MEDICAL BENEFITS TO UNDERSIGNED PHYSICIAN OR SUPPLIER FOR SERVICE DESCRIBED BELOW SIGNED (Employee or Authorized Person)

PHYSICIAN OR SUPPLIER INFORMATION

14 DATE OF ILLNESS (FIRST SYMPTOM) OR INJURY (ACCIDENT) OR PREGNANCY (LMP) 15 DATE FIRST CONSULTED YOU FOR THIS CONDITION 16 HAS PATIENT EVER HAD SAME OR SIMILAR SYMPTOMS? YES NO

17 DATE PATIENT ABLE TO RETURN TO WORK 18 DATES OF TOTAL DISABILITY FROM THROUGH DATES OF PARTIAL DISABILITY FROM THROUGH

19 NAME OF REFERRING PHYSICIAN 20 FOR SERVICE RELATED TO HOSPITALIZATION GIVE HOSPITALIZATION DATES ADMITTED DISCHARGED

21 NAME & ADDRESS OF FACILITY WHERE SERVICES RENDERED (if other than home or office) 22 WAS LABORATORY WORK PERFORMED OUTSIDE YOUR OFFICE? YES NO CHARGES

23 DIAGNOSIS OR NATURE OF ILLNESS OR INJURY RELATE DIAGNOSIS TO PROCEDURE IN COLUMN BY REFERENCE TO NUMBERS 1,2,3, ETC. OR DX CODE
1
2
3
4

24 A DATE OF SERVICE	B PLACE OF SERVICE	C FULLY DESCRIBE PROCEDURES, MEDICAL SERVICES OR SUPPLIES FURNISHED FOR EACH DATE GIVEN PROCEDURE CODE (IDENTIFY) (EXPLAIN UNUSUAL SERVICES OR CIRCUMSTANCES)	D DIAGNOSIS CODE	E CHARGES	F

25 SIGNATURE OF PHYSICIAN OR SUPPLIER SIGNED DATE 26 ACCEPT ASSIGNMENT (GOVERNMENT CLAIMS ONLY) YES NO 30 YOUR SOCIAL SECURITY NO. 27 TOTAL CHARGE 28 AMOUNT PAID 29 BALANCE DUE 31 PHYSICIAN'S OR SUPPLIER'S NAME, ADDRESS, ZIP CODE & TELEPHONE NO.

32 YOUR PATIENT'S ACCOUNT NO. 33 YOUR EMPLOYER I.D. NO. I.D. NO.

* PLACE OF SERVICE CODES
1 - (IH) - INPATIENT HOSPITAL
2 - (OH) - OUTPATIENT HOSPITAL
3 - (O) - DOCTOR'S OFFICE
4 - (H) - PATIENT'S OFFICE
5 - - DAY CARE FACILITY (PSY)
6 - - NIGHT CARE FACILITY (PSY)
7 - (NH) - NURSING HOME
8 - (SNF) - SKILLED NURSING FACILITY
9 - - AMBULANCE
0 - (OL) - OTHER LOCATIONS
A - (IL) - INDEPENDENT LABORATORY
B - - OTHER MEDICAL/SURGICAL FACILITY

Activity C Number your paper 1 to 5. Then write short answers to these questions about the health benefits form.

1. Suppose that your mother lives with you and is dependent on you. If she is the person receiving treatment, where would you write her name, address, date of birth, and her relationship to you?

2. If your mother is the patient, what other information would you include about yourself?

3. If you are the patient, in which two places would you write your name?

4. Who must sign this form?

5. Why does the doctor need to supply so much information on this form?

Workers' compensation

Insurance coverage that pays money to employees who cannot work because of job-related injuries

If Nadia had an injury on the job or an illness related to her job, she could have applied for a different kind of insurance called **workers' compensation.** Employers must have this kind of insurance to help workers injured on the job. The insurance helps pay the worker's medical bills. In some states, workers who have to miss work because of job-related injuries or illnesses also receive a part of their regular paychecks.

After employees apply for workers' compensation, a board studies their applications and medical records. The board then decides whether the employee can receive benefits. On the next page is an application form for workers' compensation that Mike Jupo, Nadia's friend, completed. Mike works in the Oregon office of Beacon Industries. Notice that this application has extra space for a description of how the accident happened.

Vocabulary Builder

Insurance Terms

When you read a health insurance policy, you need to understand the words *co-pay* and *deductible*.

Co-pay is a set amount you must pay for an office visit or for a prescription, or medicine, that your doctor orders.

A *deductible* is the amount you must pay before your insurance company pays your medical expenses. For example, if you have a $100 deductible, you will pay the first $100 of your medical expenses and then your insurance company will pay the rest of your expenses.

Look at a health insurance policy, and answer the following questions. You may want to find a policy on the Internet.

1. What is the amount of the co-pay for prescriptions?
2. Who can be covered as a dependent?
3. How much is the deductible?

State Worker's Compensation Board

(Type or print.)

Jupo	Michael	J	718-32-0735
Name (Last)	(First)	(Middle)	Soc. Sec. No.

766 Strand	Salem	OR	97302
Address	City	State	ZIP

M	27	Mechanic
Sex	Age	Occupation

Beacon Industries 1550 Desalle, Salem, OR 97302
Employer's Name and Address

$450.00	11/17/04
Wages per Week	Date of Injury

How did the accident occur?
While I was changing a tire on a company truck, the jack slipped. My hand was hit by the bumper as the truck fell.

What kind of injury did you receive? I broke four fingers.

Have you been treated by a doctor for this injury? Yes

Dr. M. Santos 1417 Long Street, Salem, OR 97302
Name and Address of Doctor

Signature *Michael J. Jupo*   Date 11/20/04

Activity A Number your paper 1 to 10. Then write short answers to these questions about the workers' compensation application shown above.

1. What are Mike's weekly earnings?

2. When did the accident happen?

3. Describe how the accident happened in your own words.

4. What kind of injury did Mike have?

5. What is the address of the company for which Mike works?

6. What is his doctor's name?

7. Where is his doctor's office?

8. Why do you think the workers' compensation board has to know Mike's salary?

9. Why do you think the board has to know how the accident happened and the name of Mike's doctor?

10. If Mike is unable to work for four weeks, how much will he lose in wages?

Report any on-the-job injuries or illnesses to your supervisor immediately.

Accident report

Provides a description of how an employee was injured on the job

Safety equipment

Items such as goggles or a hard hat that employees wear to protect themselves on the job

Witness

A person who has seen or knows something about an accident and could tell what happened

---

Writing Tip

Write a description of an accident as soon after the injury as possible. If you wait to write it, you may forget important details.

Employees who have an injury on the job fill out an **accident report.** An accident report describes how an employee was injured on the job. Many of these accident reports are similar to the application for workers' compensation. Still, Mike was not familiar with some of the terms on the company's accident report form.

Mike understood the meaning of the words *shift,* **safety equipment,** and *supervisor,* but he was unsure of how they were used on the form. He wanted to use the word **witnesses** in his description of the accident, but he was not sure of the correct spelling. Someone in human resources helped him complete the form correctly.

Activity A Number your paper 1 to 4. Then match each term in the first column with its definition or example in the second column.

Terms	Descriptions
1. safety equipment	**A** 7:00 A.M.–3:00 P.M., 3:00 P.M.–11:00 P.M., 11:00 P.M.–7:00 A.M.
2. supervisor	**B** people who saw what happened
3. witnesses	**C** your direct boss
4. shifts	**D** heavy work gloves

Where To Find It

Finding a Doctor

Imagine that you have moved to a new area or to a different state. How do you find a new doctor?

Most hospitals have a doctor referral service. If you call an area hospital and explain what type of doctor you need, they can give you the names of local doctors who might fit your needs. You also can ask co-workers which doctors they recommend.

Activity B On your paper, list the numbers of five items on this accident report that contain mistakes. Then briefly describe each mistake.

Accident Report Form

1. Date this report _____9/13/04_____

2. Date incident occurred

MONTH/DAY/YEAR	TIME	SHIFT	SUPERVISOR
9/13/04	9:10 A.M.	8:30 A.M. — 4:30 P.M.	M.Lee

3. Social Security No. ___356-00-7611___

4. Employee's name (Last, First, Middle Init.) _Race, Franklin R._

5. Job title _Plumber_

6. Home address _1971 Fine Ave._

7. Phone   H _(309) 555-1111_   W _(309) 555-0723_

8. Date of Birth _2/12/63_

9. Age _41_

10. Sex ☑ male ☐ female

11. Date of employment _____

     Date assigned to present job _6/01_

12. Gross rate of pay _$9.50_ per _hour_ (hour, day, week)

13. Specify exact address where incident occurred.

     Also specify exact location at this address.

     1000 Blair Road

14. Describe fully how incident occurred. (Use additional signed sheets if necessary.)

     The thing blew up.

     Witnesses saw smoke coming from the machine.

15. Was safety equipment provided? ☑ yes ☐ no

     Was it in use at the time? ☑ yes ☐ no

16. According to employee, what part(s) of his/her body were injured?

     _____

17. Employee's signature _Franklin Race_ ☐ check here if unable to sign

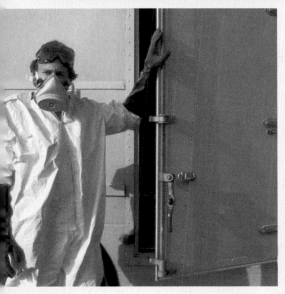

Toxic Tim

Tim often uses weed killers and liquid fertilizers at work. His employer offers frequent safety lessons for the workers and provides them with safety equipment.

"Terry, I think I'll leave my mask and coveralls here," said Tim. "It's too hot today to wear them."

"What?" said Terry. "You can't go out and use these chemicals without your safety equipment."

"Why?" asked Tim. "I don't like wearing all this gear when it is so warm."

"That doesn't matter," said Terry. "We must follow the safety rules. If you breathe in these chemicals you may injure your lungs. If you get them on your skin, your body may absorb them. Also, if you don't use your safety equipment, you will be fired."

"Why does my boss care?" asked Terry. "I am the one who will get sick."

"OSHA—the Occupational Safety and Health Administration—will care, too. It is a federal agency that sets rules to protect workers. The company is required by law to follow those rules," said Terry.

"I guess I'd better wear them then," said Tim.

For Discussion

1. What does Tim want to leave behind?

2. Why is the safety equipment important to Tim?

3. What will happen if he doesn't wear his equipment?

4. What is OSHA, and what kinds of rules does it have?

5. Why do you think that the federal government sets rules for worker safety?

Chapter 15 R E V I E W

Word Bank

accident report

group insurance

health insurance

insured

patient

premium

safety equipment

toll-free

witness

workers' compensation

Part A On a sheet of paper, write the correct word or words from the Word Bank to complete each sentence.

1. Employees of a company often buy _____.
2. _____ pays certain medical bills for those who are covered.
3. Money paid for insurance protection is a _____ .
4. A person can call a _____ number without cost.
5. A person being treated for an illness or an injury is a _____ .
6. A person who has insurance is _____ .
7. _____ is insurance coverage that pays money to employees who cannot work because of job-related injuries.
8. An _____ provides a description of how an employee was injured on the job.
9. Goggles and a hard hat are examples of _____ .
10. A person who has seen or knows something about an accident and could tell what happened is a _____ .

Part B Number your paper 11 to 13. If the statement is true, write *True* next to the number. If the statement is not true, write *False*.

11. Do not worry about completing a health insurance form correctly. You can complete another one when you have an emergency.
12. Applications for workers' compensation may be either approved or rejected by a special board of people.
13. Group insurance usually costs less than individual insurance.

Part C Write short answers to these questions.

14. In what space on the health insurance application would you put the name of the person who has the insurance?

15. What information would you put in a blank space on the application that says *other health insurance coverage?*

16. What information would you put in a blank space that says *was condition related to the patient's employment?*

17. Why does the insurance company need to know the patient's name and the insured's name?

Part D Write the letter of the correct answer on your paper.

18. The first thing to do if you are injured at work is to
  A call your supervisor.
  B drive yourself to the hospital.
  C take the day off without telling your supervisor.
  D call your health insurance company.

19. To receive money from a workers' compensation claim, you
  A do not do anything. It comes automatically.
  B fill out a worker's compensation application form from the human resources department.
  C call the workers' compensation board.
  D call your doctor.

20. Why is it important for the workers' compensation board to know the name and the address of the doctor or hospital who treated the person?
  A so the board knows whom to blame
  B to send the bill
  C to ask questions about the person's injuries or illness
  D to send a thank-you note

Test-Taking Tip When studying for a test, it may be helpful to make a time line to help you remember the order of events.

16 Business Travel and Expenses

I f a new job involves traveling, you might need to learn a few new related skills. You might have to book a hotel room, for instance, or an airline flight.

In Chapter 15, you will learn skills needed in responsible positions in a company—skills such as understanding transportation schedules and filling out expense account forms.

Goals for Learning

◆ To understand hotel rates and transportation schedules

◆ To know how to fill out an expense account form correctly

Hotel rate

The charge for renting a hotel room

Single room

A hotel room for one person

Double room

A hotel room for two people

Marc Goldman became assistant sales manager for the Linsey-Wolsey Company last month. Ms. Rosita Mendez is his new supervisor and will be training him. Marc was excited about his promotion. He was especially looking forward to meeting new customers and traveling on business trips.

Ms. Mendez told Marc that she would show him what he needed to know on a business trip. She gave him a list of hotels in the cities he would visit. The list helped him understand hotel rates and transportation schedules.

After each hotel name on the list was the **hotel rate** for a **single room.** Ms. Mendez explained that the company's policy was to book a room in the hotel with the most reasonable rates. Here is part of the list that Ms. Mendez gave to Marc.

Hotel Rates

In New York City:

The Newton	$125.00
The Howard	$158.00
The Sherwood	$132.00

What hotel should Marc contact first? What is the last hotel he should try?

A **double room** is designed for two people. Most hotels charge more if two or more people stay in a room.

Activity A Number your paper 1 to 5. Then write short answers to the following questions about this list of rates for the Hotel Crown.

The Hotel Crown
1128 Strand Avenue
Chicago, IL 60611

Rates	
*Single room, double bed	$97.00 per day
*Single room, queen-size bed	$112.00 per day
*Double room, queen-size bed	$120.00 per day
*Double room, two queen-size beds	$145.00 per day

*For extra person in room, add $10.00.

1. What is the charge for an extra person in a room?

2. What is the additional charge for a queen-size bed in a single room?

3. What is the least that a single person can pay to stay at the hotel for one night?

4. What is the charge for a double room with two queen-size beds for two nights?

5. What is the charge for a double room with a queen-size bed?

Transportation Schedule Abbreviations

Marc also would have to know how to read **transportation schedules.** These schedules list the departure and arrival times for trains, buses, and planes. Schedules use abbreviations and sometimes can be confusing. Ms. Mendez gave Marc this list of transportation abbreviations as a guide.

Transportation Abbreviations

ar. or arr.	— arrives at	MT	— Mountain Time
dp. or dep.	— departs at	PT	— Pacific Time
E.T.A.	— estimated time of arrival	M	— Monday
a	— A.M.	T	— Tuesday
p	— P.M.	W	— Wednesday
m	— midnight	TH	— Thursday
n	— noon	F	— Friday
ET	— Eastern Time	SA	— Saturday
CT	— Central Time	SU	— Sunday

Notice that some words have two possible abbreviations. A transportation company would use only one of these abbreviations on its schedules. For example, Travcon Airlines might use *arr.* to mean arrival, while Mountain Airlines might use *ar.*

Vocabulary Builder

Arrival vs. Departure

To plan a trip, you must know the difference between the word *arrival* and the word *departure.*

Arrival refers to the time you reach your destination. *We will meet you if you tell us your arrival time.*

Departure refers to the time you leave. *The plane's departure is set for 7:00 A.M.*

Write the answers to the following questions.

1. What is your departure time for school?
2. What is your arrival time at school?
3. What is your departure time from school?
4. What is your arrival time at home or at work?
5. Explain the difference between arrival and departure.

Ms. Mendez also showed Marc this transportation schedule.

Chicago to
New York City

Nonstop Flight #	Dep.			E.T.A.			Notes
176	5:32	a	CT	7:49	a	ET	M–F
184	6:18	a	CT	8:35	a	ET	SA only
246	7:23	a	CT	9:40	a	ET	M–F
273	9:43	a	CT	12:00	n	ET	SA,SU
350	1:17	p	CT	3:34	p	ET	M–F
381	7:43	p	CT	10:00	p	ET	SU only
397	9:43	p	CT	12:00	m	ET	M–F

Activity B Number your paper 1 to 5. Then write short answers to these questions about the transportation schedule shown above.

1. What time does the 9:43 P.M. flight from Chicago arrive in New York?

2. On what days does Flight 273 not operate?

3. If the *Notes* column had a *T*, a *W*, and a *Th* next to a flight number, what days could you take that flight?

4. The time in New York City is an hour later than it is in Chicago. How long is Flight 397?

5. What time does Flight 350 depart?

Where To Find It

Flight Schedules

You can find public transportation schedules on the Internet. Using a computer with an Internet connection, go to a commercial airline company's or a travel Web site. Select a departure city and a destination city. Request schedule information for a particular date and time of day, such as morning or afternoon.

Look at the schedule, and compare the length of the flights. Why do some flights take longer than others?

Print the schedule, and then select the flight that is most practical for a business trip. Write a brief paragraph explaining why it is the best choice.

Expense account form

A form an employee uses to list costs from a business trip; a company pays an employee back using this form

Receipt

Proof of purchase

In your briefcase, keep an empty envelope to save business expense receipts.

The Linsey-Wolsey Company does not provide a cash advance, or expense money before a trip. However, after Marc returned from a trip, he would have to fill out an **expense account form.** This form showed how Marc spent money on his trip. The accounting department would use the form to repay Marc's business expenses. Ms. Mendez said that he would have to include **receipts** from the trip along with the form.

She stressed, for example, that Marc would have to get receipts for his transportation costs. If Marc used his car, he would need receipts for gasoline, tolls, parking, and any other related expenses. If he took a cab or a bus or if he booked an airline flight, he would have to supply receipts for his fares as well.

"Do I need receipts for my meals?" Marc asked.

"Yes," Ms. Mendez said, "and expenses such as your hotel room and any business telephone calls." She added, "The company does not pay you for personal expenses such as personal phone calls, entertainment, or clothing."

When you're traveling on business, remember to save your receipts.

Writing Tip

During your trip, keep notes of the customers you meet and what happens at your meetings. If your employer asks for a written report, you will be able to write it accurately.

Activity A Number your paper 1 to 10. Then write *Yes* after each item that you could include on an expense account form—if you kept your receipts. Write *No* if you could not include the expense.

1. breakfast
2. cab fare to the airport
3. a new briefcase
4. taxi fare
5. 50¢ toll
6. parking
7. a long-distance call to a friend
8. gasoline used for a trip to see your customers
9. a cup of coffee you bought at the airport
10. dinner for your aunt and uncle

Activity B Number your paper 1 to 5. Then write short answers to these questions.

1. Why do some companies give employees money before they take a business trip?
2. Why would a company repay only those items for which an employee has a receipt?
3. Why would a company pay for taking a customer to dinner but not pay for taking a friend?
4. Why is an honest account of travel expenses good for both the company and the employee?
5. Why do you think the amount companies reimburse for mileage changes?

Ms. Mendez took out a copy of the expense account form that Linsey-Wolsey uses. She explained to Marc how to complete it. He took notes in each section. He included the meaning for the word **destination** (where he went). Other words on the form were **mileage** (how many miles he drove) and **lodging** (the cost of the place he stayed). Then he could fill out the form so that the company would **reimburse** him, or pay him back, for the money he spent on the trip. Here is the form Ms. Mendez gave to Marc.

Linsey-Wolsey Company
Expense Account Form

Name of Employee ___ *my name* _____

Social Security # ___ *my Social Security number* _____

Dates of Business Travel ___ *from   to* _____

Destination ___ *where I went* _____

Purpose ___ *why I went* _____

Use of Personal Car If I use my own car, I get 36¢ per mile.		Transportation	Meals	Telephone Calls
Mileage # of miles traveled	$@36¢/mile 36¢ × number of miles	total of fares	total cost of meals	total cost of business calls
Lodging	Miscellaneous		TOTAL Reimbursement Request	
total of hotel or motel cost	anything else I spent on business		total of mileage or fares, meals, business calls, hotels, and miscellaneous	

NO REIMBURSEMENT WILL BE MADE WITHOUT RECEIPTS

Ms. Mendez reminded Marc to fill in the proper sections of the expense form. There were spaces on the form for his name, Social Security number, dates of his business travel, destination, and purpose of the trip. She explained that the Linsey-Wolsey Company would need that information for its taxes. Marc's Social Security number would help the company keep track of the amount it paid Marc in wages and the amount it paid him for business expenses.

You are planning a business trip to a neighboring state. If you fly, you will go and return on the same day. If you drive, you will need to find lodging, and you will be gone for two days.

Write a paragraph to your supervisor. Compare the cost of flying with the costs of driving.

Activity C Number your paper 1 to 14. Then match the terms in the first column with their descriptions in the second column.

Terms	Descriptions
1. Name of employee	**A** total cost of meals
2. Social Security #	**B** where you went
3. Dates of business travel	**C** your name
4. Destination	**D** a total of the expense for mileage or fares, meals, business telephone calls, lodging, and miscellaneous
5. Purpose	**E** the use of your car for business travel
6. Use of personal car	**F** dates you were on the business trip
7. Mileage	**G** number of miles traveled in your own car
8. $ @ 36¢ per mile	**H** anything else spent on business that does not belong in another section on the form
9. Transportation	**I** total cost of business calls
10. Meals	**J** total hotel or motel cost
11. Telephone calls	**K** reason for taking the trip
12. Lodging	**L** 36¢ multiplied by the number of miles traveled
13. Miscellaneous	**M** your Social Security number
14. Total reimbursement request	**N** fares for taxi, train, bus, subway, or plane

Activity D Number your paper 1 to 10. Then write short answers to these questions about business travel and expenses.

1. Suppose that you used your own car for a business trip and your company reimburses you at the rate of 35¢ per mile. How much would you get back if you drove 110 miles?

2. Why do you think some employers want to know the dates you were away on a business trip?

3. Look on page 284 at the expense account form that the Linsey-Wolsey Company uses. Explain what to write in the section marked *Transportation*.

4. How can you figure the total you spent for meals?

5. How would a business diary or a telephone log help you figure out the business calls you made?

6. What is *lodging*? What do you put in that column?

7. List at least three miscellaneous expenses.

8. The expense account form that the Linsey-Wolsey Company uses asks for *destination*. What does that term mean?

9. If you were asked for the purpose of your trip, do you think it would be enough to write "business"? Explain your answer.

10. Why do you need to include your Social Security number on an expense account form?

Spelling Builder

Have, Of, and Off

Three frequently misspelled words are *have, of,* and *off.*

Have is often a helping verb used with a participle of another verb. *I should have known the answer.*

Of is a preposition. It introduces a prepositional phrase and may often show possession. *The cover of the book is colorful.*

Off is an adverb and is the opposite of *on. Jake turned off the light when he left the room.*

Fill in the blanks below with *have, of,* or *off.*

1. Turn _____ the computer before you leave the office.

2. The top _____ the building was painted black.

3. Sue should _____ finished the report by noon.

Noteworthy Notes

Nadine has just returned from her first business trip to New York for her employer, Associated Sportswear. Her supervisor, Ms. Lee, greeted her in her office.

"Did you have a good trip?" asked Ms. Lee.

"I really enjoyed it, and I met with several suppliers," said Nadine.

"What were their newest items?" asked Ms. Lee.

"I have a notebook with some sketches and notes about colors, sizes, and prices. I also have information about delivery and payment terms," said Nadine. "I would like to organize my notes. Could I meet with you later today to give you my report?" asked Nadine.

"Certainly," said Ms. Lee. "I am eager to see what you brought back. Don't forget to turn in your expense account form by Friday."

"I have an envelope with all of my receipts," said Nadine. "I'll get an expense account form from accounting."

"Great," said Ms. Lee. "We can talk about your next trip to Chicago when we meet later today."

For Discussion

1. What did Ms. Lee want when Nadine returned from her trip?

2. What had Nadine done on her trip to be ready to give her report?

3. What information did Nadine include in her notes?

4. Why can Nadine fill out her expense account form so quickly?

5. What do you think Ms. Lee will tell Nadine after they meet?

Chapter 16 **R E V I E W**

Word Bank

destination

double room

expense account form

hotel rate

lodging

mileage

receipts

reimbursement

single room

transportation schedule

Part A Number your paper 1 to 10. Then write the correct answer from the box that completes each sentence. Use each answer only once.

1. A hotel room for one person is a _____ .

2. An _____ is a form an employee uses to list expenses from a business trip.

3. Employees turn in _____ , or proofs of purchase, with expense account forms.

4. A _____ shows the arrival and departure times of trains, buses, planes, etc.

5. The place to which a person is traveling is his or her _____ .

6. A hotel room for two people is a _____ .

7. _____ is a place to stay while traveling.

8. _____ is the number of miles a person travels.

9. _____ is the money paid back to an employee for business expenses.

10. The _____ is the charge for renting a hotel room.

Part B Number your paper 11 to 15. If the statement is true, write *True* next to the number. If it is not true, write *False*.

11. If you use your car for business travel, you need to keep track of the miles you travel.

12. Many companies will repay you if you have to take a taxi.

13. A company will repay you for all telephone calls you make.

14. Most expense account forms ask for the dates and destination of your travel.

15. Presenting a report and getting an order from a customer are good reasons for a business trip.

Part C Number your paper 16 to 20. Then write the correct answers for the following questions about this transportation schedule.

Louisville to						
Los Angeles	**Nonstop**					
Flight #	Dp.			Ar.		Notes
32	8:15	a	ET	9:35	a PT	M–F only
57	11:33	a	ET	12:53	p PT	SA, SU only
144	3:15	p	ET	4:35	p PT	M–F only
76	4:10	p	ET	5:30	p PT	Th, F, SA only
117	7:22	p	ET	8:42	p PT	T, W only

16. On what days can you take Flight 57?

  A Monday through Friday only

  B Saturday and Sunday only

  C Tuesday and Wednesday only

  D Thursday, Friday, and Saturday only

17. Which flight operates only on Tuesday and Wednesday?

  A 32   **C** 76

  B 144   **D** 117

18. What time does Flight 144 leave Louisville?

  A 3:15 P.M.   **C** 4:35 P.M.

  B 12:53 P.M.   **D** 11:33 P.M.

19. What does the abbreviation *ET* mean?

  A estimated time   **C** Eastern time

  B exact time   **D** established time

20. You are attending a meeting in Los Angeles that begins at noon on Tuesday. Which flight should you take?

  A 32   **C** 76

  B 144   **D** 117

Test-Taking Tip When you are reading a test question, look for words such as *mainly, most likely, generally, major,* and *best*. Decide which answer choice fits with the meaning of that word.

Glossary

A

Abbreviation (ə brē´ vē ā´ shən) the shortened form of written words; for example *req.* for *required* (p. 2)

Accident report (ak´ sə dənt ri pôrt´) provides a description of how an employee was injured on the job (p. 271)

Action plan (ak´ shən plan) steps needed to complete a business report (p. 221)

Adjourn (ə jėrn´) to end a meeting (p. 207)

Adult education (ə dult´ ej ə kā´ shən) classes for adults (p. 249)

Agenda (ə jen´ də) list of things to do or discuss at a meeting (p. 206)

Allowances (ə lou´ ən sez) items that determine the amount of money to be withheld for a person's income tax (p. 112)

Alphabetical order (al´ fə bet´ ə kəl ôr´ dər) arranged in the order of the letters of the alphabet (A, B, C, etc.) (p. 5)

Amount (ə mount´) on a sales slip, the number of items purchased multiplied by the unit price (p. 169)

Apprenticeship program (ə pren´ tis ship prō´ gram) a work-training program (p. 13)

B

Bar graph (bär graf) a drawing that uses lines and shaded areas to present and compare information (p. 158)

Benefits (ben´ ə fits) services that companies pay for or provide for their workers; for example, vacations, pensions, and health insurance (p. 10)

Body (bod´ ē) the part of a letter that tells why the person wrote the letter (p. 23)

Business machines (biz´ nis mə shēnz´) office equipment including a telephone, a computer, a fax machine, and a copier (p. 45)

Business report (biz´ nis ri pôrt´) a spoken or written account of information (p. 220)

C

Call to order (kȯl tü ȯr´ dər) to begin a meeting (p. 207)

Career goal (kə rir´ gōl) what you hope to become or to achieve in your job (p. 48)

Catalog (kat´ l ȯg) a book listing items in a certain order; includes descriptions of the items (p. 175)

Cell (sel) a box on a spreadsheet where a row and a column meet; cells have addresses, consisting of their column letter and their row number (p. 155)

Chair (châr) the leader of a meeting or committee; also known as *chairperson* or *chairman* (p. 207)

Chart (chärt) a sheet of information using lists, pictures, or tables (p. 158)

Classified ads (klas´ ə fīd adz) advertisements (also known as want ads) that appear in the newspaper in different groups; for example, ads for cars are listed together, ads for pets are in another section, and job openings are in another (p. 2)

College application (kol´ ij ap´ lə kā´ shən) a form to ask for admission to take college courses (p. 252)

Column (kol´ əm) a line of cells going from top to bottom on a spreadsheet page (p. 156)

Communicate (kə myü´ nə kāt) to let others know how you feel about something (p. 100)

Company account (kum´ pə nē ə kount´) an agreement between a supplier and a customer; the supplier allows the customer to charge items rather than pay for them at the time of the sale (p. 179)

Complimentary close (kom´ plə men´ tər ē klōz) the polite ending to a letter; for example, *Sincerely,* or *Respectfully yours* (p. 24)

Computer printout (kəm pyü′ tər print out) a printed record produced by a computer; also called a spreadsheet (p. 172)

Conclusion (kən klü′ zhən) a decision or opinion reached by reasoning (p. 220)

Counselor (koun′ sə lər) a person at an employment agency or job placement office who helps another person find a job; a person who gives advice to someone else (p. 13)

Credit line (kred′ it līn) maximum amount that a customer can charge to a company account (p. 179)

D

Date (dāt) the month, day, and year on a letter that tells when the person wrote it (p. 23)

Deductions (di duk′ shənz) expenses considered when determining taxable income; you do not have to pay income taxes on such expenses (p. 113)

Degree candidate (di grē′ kan′ də dāt) a person who wants to complete a degree program (p. 252)

Dependents (di pen′ dənts) children or other people who may not work and who count on you for over half of their needs (p. 113)

Destination (des′ tə nā′ shən) the place to which a person is traveling (p. 284)

Disconnected (dis′ kə nek′ tid) describing a telephone call that has been cut off (p. 195)

Double room (dub′ əl rüm) a hotel room for two people (p. 278)

E

E-mail (ē′ māl) electronic mail, or messages sent between computers (p. 48)

Employment agency (em ploi′ mənt ā′ jən sē) a company that is in business to help people find jobs (p. 12)

Evaluation (i val′ yü ā′ shən) a rating of how well a worker does a job; many companies use a form to tell employees on a regular basis how they are doing (p. 124)

Exempt (eg zempt′) to free from a duty or rule; means money does not have to be withheld (p. 113)

Expense account form (ek spens′ ə kount′ fôrm) a form an employee uses to list costs from a business trip; a company pays the employee back using this form (p. 282)

Experience (ek spir′ ē əns) a job you have had or a skill you developed (p. 48)

Extension (ek sten′ shən) an extra telephone connection to the main line; the number to connect to such a telephone line (p. 193)

Extracurricular (ek′ strə kə rik′ yə lər) activities in school other than course work, including sports, band, chorus, and clubs (p. 46)

F

Fact sheet (fakt shēt) information about you; it should include personal, career, and educational information—plus references (p. 65)

Fax machine (faks mə shēn′) sends copies of printed pages over telephone lines (p. 178)

Follow-up (fol′ ō up′) a second telephone call, letter, fax, or e-mail written to correct a mistake, to give or ask for additional information, or to suggest solutions to a problem (p. 181)

Formula (for′ myə lə) a way to multiply, divide, add, or subtract numbers on a spreadsheet (p. 156)

Full block style (ful blok stīl) a form of business writing in which all the parts of a letter appear against the left margin; no paragraphs are indented (p. 26)

Pronunciation Key									
a	hat	e	let	ī	ice	ô	order	ù	put	sh	she		a	in about
ā	age	ē	equal	o	hot	oi	oil	ü	rule	th	thin		e	in taken
ä	far	ėr	term	ō	open	ou	out	ch	child	ᴛʜ	then	ə	i	in pencil
â	care	i	it	ó	saw	u	cup	ng	long	zh	measure		o	in lemon
													u	in circus

G

Good impression (gủd im presh´ ən) thinking well of someone because the person is polite and uses proper behavior, language, and so on (p. 84)

Group insurance (grüp in shủr´ əns) insurance bought by many people, such as employees of a company (p. 264)

H

Health insurance (helth in shủr´ əns) insurance that pays certain medical bills; also known as medical insurance (p. 264)

Help-wanted ads (help wäntəd adz) advertisements for employment or job openings (p. 2)

Home page (hōm pāj) a single page on the World Wide Web made by a person or company; it can serve as a main entrance to other information (p. 153)

Hotel rate (hō tel´ rāt) the charge for renting a hotel room (p. 278)

Human resources department (hyü´ mən rē´ sorsz di pärt´ mənt) the part of a company (also known as a personnel department) that deals with employees; a human resources department might hire people and keep records about how well they do their jobs (p. 64)

I

Indented (in dent´ id) set in from the left margin on the page (p. 29)

Index (in´ deks) a list of items in a book that gives page numbers where those items can be found; an index is usually in the back of a book (p. 160)

Inside address (in´ sīd´ ad´ res) the complete name and address of the person and/or company receiving the letter (p. 23)

Insured (in shủrd´) a person who has insurance (p. 266)

Intercom (in´ tər kom´) a two-way system that has a microphone and a speaker that allows people in nearby office areas to talk to one another without leaving their desks (p. 191)

Internal Revenue Service (IRS) (in tẻr´ nl rev´ ə nü sẻr´ vis) the government agency charged with collecting taxes (p. 112)

Internet (in´ tər net´) a computer network linked by telephone lines (p. 14)

Interviewer (in´ tər vyü´ ər) the person doing the hiring (p. 85)

Inventory (in´ vən tôr´ ē) the amount of goods and materials on hand; stock (p. 168)

Invoice (in´ vois) a form listing the items sold; some invoices include the price of each item and the conditions of the sale (p. 170)

Item number (ī´ təm num´ bər) a number for each item sold by a company; used in inventory lists, in catalogs, on sales slips, and so on (p. 169)

J

Job application (job ap´ lə kā´ shən) a form used in making a request to be hired (p. 64)

Job interview (job in´ tər vyü) a meeting during which the person doing the hiring asks questions and rates the answers of the person applying for a job (p. 13)

Job placement office (job plās´ mənt ȯ´ fis) a city or state office where a person can get help finding a job (p. 12)

Job sharing (job shâr´ ing) a situation in which two people divide one job; each person works part-time (p. 135)

K

Key word (kē´ wẻrd) an important word or words that give the main idea; clues to help people remember information (p. 142); a word or words that you can use to search on the Internet (p. 152)

L

Label (lā´ bəl) word or abbreviation attached to an object to identify or describe it (p. 162)

Letter of application (let´ ər ov ap´ lə kā´ shən) a letter that a person sends to ask for a job (p. 22)

Link (lingk) a connection you can click on to take you to another location on the Internet (p. 153)

Lodging (loj´ ing) place to stay while traveling (p. 284)

Logical order (loj´ ə kəl ôr´ dər) the arrangement of information so that it makes sense to a reader or listener (p. 221)

M

Margin (mär´ jən) the outside edge of a page (p. 27)

Meeting (mē´ ting) a gathering of people for a common purpose (p. 206)

Mileage (mī´ lij) the number of miles driven (p. 284)

Minutes (min´ its) a written record of what happened at a meeting (p. 206)

Modified block style (mod´ ə fīd blok stīl) in this form of business letter, the person sending the letter lines up the return address, date, complimentary close, and signature near the center of the page; paragraphs are indented (p. 28)

Motion (mō´ shən) a formal suggestion made at a meeting (p. 211)

N

N/A (ən ā) not applicable; used on job applications when a section does not apply to the person looking for a job (p. 74)

Nonverbal communication (non vėr´ bel kə myü´ nə kā´ shən) what people say with their body language; it includes how people sit or stand and how they look at others (p. 104)

O

Objective (əb jek´ tiv) true to facts (p. 211)

Oral business report (ôr´ əl biz´ nis ri pôrt´) a report that is spoken out loud; a spoken account either based on outlined notes or read from a written report (p. 238)

Oral directions (ôr´ əl də rek´ shənz) instructions given by talking; spoken rather than written orders (p. 142)

Order letter (ôr´ dər let´ ər) written to order supplies from a company (p. 178)

Organizational chart (ôr´ gə nə zā´ shən əl chärt) a list of company employees and their job titles (p. 122)

Outline (out´ līn´) a written plan of the most important points of a report or a story (p. 221)

P

Parliamentary procedure (pär´ lə men´ tər ē prə sē´ jer) a set of rules to help a group work together in a meeting (p. 207)

Patient (pā´ shənt) a person being treated for an illness or an injury (p. 266)

Pay week (pā wēk) one pay period of seven days (p. 132)

Performance (pər fôr´ məns) the act of doing your job (p. 124)

Personal information (pėr´ sə nəl in´ fər mā´ shən) your name, address, phone number, and e-mail address (p. 48)

Personal qualifications (pėr´ sə nəl kwäl´ ə fə kā´ shənz) qualities about a person that will be valuable on the job, including honesty and courtesy, as well as education and experience (p. 89)

Place of birth (plās ov bėrth) city and state or country where a person was born (p. 71)

Position (pə zish´ ən) a job or job title; the name of the job or the work that an employee does (p. 133)

Post office abbreviations (pōst ô´ fis ə brē´ ve ā´ shənz) two-letter state and province abbreviations that do not include periods (p. 37)

Premium (prē´ mē əm) payment for insurance (p. 264)

Pronunciation Key												
a	hat	e	let	ī	ice	ė	order	u̇	put	sh	she	a in about
ā	age	ē	equal	o	hot	oi	oil	ü	rule	th	thin	e in taken
ä	far	ėr	term	ō	open	ou	out	ch	child	ᴛ͟ʜ	then	ə { i in pencil
â	care	i	it	ȯ	saw	u	cup	ng	long	zh	measure	o in lemon
												u in circus

Preprinted answer sheet (prē prin´ təd an´ sər shēt) a form on which students mark answers to tests by filling in circles, circling letters, and so on (p. 256)

Probation (prō bā´ shən) a period of time during which workers prove that they can do a job (p. 116)

Professional journal (prə fesh´ ə nəl jer´ nl) magazine related to business (p. 247)

Promotion (prə mō´ shən) a raise in rank or position; it may include a pay raise (p. 124)

R

Receipt (ri sēt´) proof of purchase (p. 282)

Receptionist (ri sep´ shə nist) a person whose job it is to greet the public, answer questions, direct people to offices, etc.; the receptionist is often the first contact people have with a company (p. 103)

Reference books (ref´ ər əns bùks) books containing useful facts or information—such as a dictionary, an encyclopedia, or an atlas (p. 7)

References (ref´ ər ən səz) people who can tell what you are like and what kind of a worker you would be (p. 31)

Registration form (rej´ ə strā´ shən fôrm) a form used to sign up for college courses (p. 251)

Regulations (reg´ yə lā´ shənz) rules of behavior (p. 116)

Reimburse (rē´ im bėrs´) payment to an employee for business costs (p. 284)

Resolution (rez´ ə lü´ shən) a formal statement of opinion (p. 211)

Résumé (rez´ ə mā´) a summary of a person's skills, achievements, training, and jobs (p. 44)

Return address (ri tėrn´ ad´ res) the street address, city, state, and ZIP code of the person writing the letter (p. 22)

Rough draft (ruf draft) the first copy of a piece of writing; often contains errors that the writer corrects (p. 51)

Row (rō) a line of cells going straight across a spreadsheet page (p. 155)

S

Safety equipment (sāf´ tē i kwip´ mənt) items such as goggles or a hard hat that employees wear to protect themselves on the job (p. 271)

Salary (sal´ ər ē) payment of a fixed amount at regular intervals for work done (p. 10)

Sales slip (sālz´ slip) a form that a store uses to keep a record of a sale (p. 168)

Sales tax (sālz´ taks) a tax figured as a percentage of the cost of the sale and collected by the company that sells the goods (p. 169)

Salutation (sal yə tā´ shən) the greeting to the person receiving the letter; for example, *Dear Ms. Evans:* or *Dear Sir:* (p. 23)

Schedule (skej´ ül *or* skej´ əl) a plan that shows the time and order of each job (p. 139)

Search engine (sėrch en´ jən) a location on the World Wide Web that allows you to search the Internet by using key words (p. 152)

Second (sek´ ənd) a statement that one supports a motion being discussed at a meeting (p. 211)

Sexual harassment (sek´ shü əl hə ras´ mənt) doing or saying something sexual to someone who does not welcome it (p. 118)

Shift (shift) a scheduled period of work or duty; for example, a shift could be from 9 A.M. to 5 P.M. or from 7 P.M. to 3 A.M. (p. 134)

Signature (sig´ nə chər) a handwritten (rather than typed or printed) name following the close in a letter; business letters often include a handwritten signature above the typed full name (p. 24)

Single room (sing´ gəl rüm) a hotel room for one person (p. 278)

Slang (slang) language that is not formal or proper; for example, *ain't* or *yeah* are slang words (p. 89)

Social Security number (sō´ shəl si kyùr´ ə tē num´ bər) a nine-digit number used to identify Americans for government purposes relating to taxes, unemployment payments, old-age and survivor benefits, and so on (p. 65)

Spouse (spous) your husband or wife (p. 113)

Spreadsheet (spred´ shēt´) a computer program used for finance-related tasks (p. 155)

Status (stā´ təs) the condition or rank of an employee (p. 116)

Subtotal (sub tō´ tl) on a sales slip, the sum of the amounts of the items purchased before adding the sales tax (p. 169)

Suggestion (səg jes´ chən) plan or idea for action based on the information gathered (p. 220)

Supervisor (sü´ pər vī´ zər) someone who is in charge of others; a boss (p. 64)

Survey (sər vā´) finding information by asking people questions (p. 227)

T

Technical manual (tek´ nə kel man´ yü əl) a book that helps its readers understand or do something (p. 150)

Telephone directory (tel´ ə fōn dī rek´ tər ē) a book or collection of names, addresses, and telephone numbers (p. 7)

Time card (tīm kärd) a card used with a time clock to record an employee's starting and quitting times during each day on the job (p. 116)

Toll-free (tōl frē) without cost to the caller (p. 266)

Tone (tōn) a way of speaking or writing that expresses a certain mood, style, or feeling (p. 93)

Total (tō´ tl) on a sales slip, the sum of the subtotal and the sales tax; also known as the *total cost* (p. 169)

Transfer (tran´ sfèr´) to switch a business telephone call to another department or person (p. 195)

Transportation schedule (tran´ spər tā´ shən skej´ ül) a chart or table that shows the arrival and departure times of trains, buses, or planes (p. 280)

U

Undergraduate degree (un´ dər graj´ ü it di grē´) a degree offered for completing a two-year (Associate of Arts) or a four-year (Bachelor of Arts or Bachelor of Science) college program (p. 250)

Unit price (yü´ nit prīs) the cost for one item, box, dozen, gallon, pound, and so on (p. 169)

V

Voice mail (vois māl) an electronic system that records telephone messages that are played back later by the person receiving the phone calls (p. 191)

W

Wage (wāj) money paid for hourly work (p. 10)

W-4 form (dub´ əl yü fôr fôrm) an IRS form that decides the amount of money taken out of your paycheck for income tax (p. 112)

Withholding (with hōld´ ing) an amount of money subtracted from your paycheck and given to the IRS as part or all of your income tax (p. 112)

Witness (wit´ nis) a person who has seen or knows something about an accident and could tell what happened (p. 271)

Workers' compensation (wèr´ kərz kom´ pən sā´ shən) insurance coverage that pays money to employees who cannot work because of job-related injuries (p. 269)

Work schedule (wèrk skej´ ül) a plan that shows the exact hours or shifts each employee will work during a given pay period (p. 134)

Worksheet (wèrk´ shēt) a single spreadsheet page (p. 155)

Workstation (wèrk´ stā´ shən) the place where employees work or do a certain part of their job (p. 118)

Pronunciation Key									
a	hat	e	let	ī	ice	ȯ	order	ú	put	sh	she	ǝ	a in about
ā	age	ē	equal	o	hot	oi	oil	ü	rule	th	thin		e in taken
ä	far	ėr	term	ō	open	ou	out	ch	child	ŦH	then		i in pencil
â	care	i	it	ȯ	saw	u	cup	ng	long	zh	measure		o in lemon
													u in circus

Y

Yellow Pages (yel´ ō pāj´ əz) the section of a telephone book (or a separate book in large cities) that lists businesses in alphabetical order by kind of business; for example, you would find the names and telephone numbers of all places to eat under the heading *Restaurants* (p. 7)

Z

ZIP code (zip kōd) the postal delivery area number that is written after the name of a state in an address; in Canada, it is called the Postal Code and is written after the name of the province (p. 22)

Index

Photo Credits

Cover: background-© Chandra Clarke/CORBIS; inset-© Royalty-free/CORBIS; p. xiv, Jack Holtel/ Photographik Company; p. 14, Jack Holtel/ Photographik Company; p. 17, © David Young/Wolff/ PhotoEdit; p. 20, James L. Shaffer; p. 25, © Dana White/ PhotoEdit; p. 39, © Rex Heptagon Instock/ Stock Connection/PictureQuest; p. 42, James L. Shaffer; p. 47, James L. Shaffer; p. 59, © Patti McConville/ Unicorn Stock Photos; p. 62, Jack Holtel/ Photographik Company; p. 75, Jack Holtel/ Photographik Company; p. 77, © David Young/ Wolff/PhotoEdit Inc.; p. 80, © Bill Bachmann/Photo Network/PictureQuest; p. 89, James L. Shaffer; p. 95, © Tom McCarthy/Photo Network/PictureQuest; p. 98, Jack Holtel/Photographik Company; p. 100, James L. Shaffer; p. 107, © David Young/Wolff/ PhotoEdit; p. 110, James L. Shaffer; p. 126, © Ed Lallo/Index Stock Imagery; p. 127, © IFA BilderTeam/eStock Photography/PictureQuest; p. 130, James L. Shaffer; p. 138, James L. Shaffer; p. 145, Jack Holtel/Photographik Company; p. 148, © Jon Riley/Index Stock Imagery/PictureQuest; p. 156, © David Young/Wolff/PhotoEdit; p. 163, © Will and Deni McIntyre/Photo Researchers, Inc.; p. 166, © Harry Sieplinga/HMS Images/Image Bank/ Getty Images; p. 178, James L. Shaffer; p. 183, © L. Druskis/Photo Researchers; p. 186, James L. Shaffer; p. 190, James L. Shaffer; p. 195, © Lynne Siler/Focus Group/PictureQuest; p. 201, Jack Holtel/ Photographik Company; p. 204, © Charles Gupton/ Stock Boston Inc./PictureQuest; p. 208, James L. Shaffer; p. 215, © Arni Katz/Dreamtime Systems/ Unicorn Stock Photos; p. 218, Jack Holtel/ Photographik Company; p. 223, © Jef Greenberg/ Unicorn Stock Photo; p. 240, Jack Holtel/ Photographik Company; p. 241, © Elena Rooraid/ PhotoEdit; p. 244, James L. Shaffer; p. 254, James L. Shaffer; p. 259, © Rene Sheret/Stone/Getty Images; p. 262, James L. Shaffer; p. 273, © Jonathan Nourok/ PhotoEdit; p. 276, © Stuart McClymont/Stone/Getty Images; p. 282, James L. Shaffer; p. 287, © Michael Newman/PhotoEdit.

#North Side ^

#HCe ^

#YLIFE ^

10-12-13 ^